Praise for *Monica*

'Eye-opening . . . In this accc   *1es*

'Who would have thought t   ıb-
lished and under-promoted lecturer in the ~~English~~   at
University College, Leicester, would prove to be such a page-turner?
. . . It is a story as full of surprises as many a novel, and a story that
only he could tell'   Margaret Drabble, *New Statesman*

'One of the most brilliant biographies I have read – an extraordinary
achievement – brings Monica to life as she deserves, and not only for
what she did for Larkin and his work, but also her teaching skills. It
makes me wish I could have heard her lecture'   Claire Tomalin

'John Sutherland's memoir-cum-biography hinges on a profound
question: how well do we *truly* know a person? . . . Written with the
intimacy of an insider – Sutherland, Boswell-like, portrays her in all
her convivial wit and striking personality . . . Often moving, with
some wonderfully-expressed insights'
                               Tomiwa Owolade, *Evening Standard*

'Beautifully written, you can almost taste the beery, tweedy, smoke-
filled atmosphere of university life in the 1950s and 1960s. It's a
gripping love story too'   Roger Alton, *Daily Mail*

'Reading this book, it is hard to avoid the conclusion that Larkin
slowly destroyed Jones's life . . . But [it] is also an essay in the banality
of despair. Sutherland shows how a life can be ruined amid quite
ordinary things like *The Archers* and cricket matches and outings to
cathedral cities and English summer days'
                                        James Marriott, *The Times*

'[*Monica Jones, Philip Larkin and Me*] has a compelling flow of strong feeling and a touching sense of intimate connection . . . But Sutherland and Jones were never intimate or confiding – which means that the darkest revelations of her correspondence seem all the more shocking, to him first, and now to us'   Andrew Motion, *The Spectator*

'[Sutherland's] book pays generous tribute to the woman who kick-started his prolific academic career . . . The relationship was sad and sometimes toxic, as Sutherland's excellent biography shows . . . In thrall to his genius, her love for Larkin endured – and so did the misery that went with it'   Blake Morrison, *Guardian*

'I couldn't put it down. Vivid and penetrating, it's a brilliant portrait of a confounding, complex woman which will be indispensable to anyone interested in Philip Larkin. The fact that John Sutherland knew Monica Jones enables him to bring not only his scholarship but his uniquely wry observation to his subject. It's a tremendous book'
Cressida Connolly

'Monica Jones emerges as a woman at once wonderful and complicated. This is her life, not as accessory or afterthought, but as a full person, interesting in her own right and on her own terms. A warm and generous book which is a vital addition to the realm of Larkin biography'   Jessie Greengrass

JOHN SUTHERLAND is Lord Northcliffe Professor Emeritus at UCL and one of the best-known scholars, writers and critics at work in the UK today. He is the author of many critically acclaimed books, including *Stephen Spender: The Authorised Biography* and *Last Drink to LA*.

Monica Jones, Philip Larkin and Me

Her Life and Long Loves

JOHN SUTHERLAND

WEIDENFELD & NICOLSON

First published in Great Britain in 2021 by Weidenfeld & Nicolson
This paperback edition first published in Great Britain in 2022
by Weidenfeld & Nicolson,
an imprint of The Orion Publishing Group Ltd
Carmelite House, 50 Victoria Embankment
London EC4Y 0DZ

An Hachette UK Company

1 3 5 7 9 10 8 6 4 2

ISBN (Mass Market Paperback) 978 1 4746 2020 8
ISBN (eBook) 978 1 4746 2021 5
ISBN (Audio) 978 1 4746 2022 2

Typeset by Input Data Services Ltd, Somerset

Printed in Great Britain by Clays Ltd, Elcograf S.p.A.

MIX
Paper from
responsible sources
FSC
www.fsc.org   FSC® C104740

www.weidenfeldandnicolson.co.uk
www.orionbooks.co.uk

For Judith Priestman

'No doubt Larkin would still have become "a real poet" if he had never met Monica, though we can never know that for sure. What is certain is that he wouldn't have become the same poet, so profoundly was he influenced by the relationship.'

Peter Keating

Monica on Sark, mid-1960s

CONTENTS

PERSONAL FOREWORD, 2021

'I don't want to be and I won't be an object of pity like a beggar's sore'

Monica Jones to Philip, 1957

At the heart of this book, and my reason for writing it, is an acquaintance with Monica Jones over a decade in which my life was changed by her. I am in two minds: which is the more real? The Monica I knew as a young man in the 1960s? Or the Monica I now know from thousands of pages of manuscript documentation, sixty years on? The book turns on that pivot. I am fortunate to be the first scholar to have had full access to relevant (for my personal purpose) sections of the vast archive of Monica Jones's letters to Philip Larkin in the Bodleian Library. First but, in one respect, last. I am the last living, breathing, still actively writing, witness to what Miss Monica Jones actually was in her prime and in the flesh.

In crucial ways Monica made me. It's a grand assertion, but she asserted it herself to Philip Larkin:

I've got the boys, John and Bill,* that I've *produced* & I stood up for, & they're *my* boys, aren't they, they *know* they are, no matter who else taught them.

---

* For Bill Ruddick see below, passim.

Monica's 'producing' went beyond tutorials. In one aspect this book is debt repayment. I was moved, and disconcerted, to see her describe me to Philip as: 'heavenly Sutherland', 'smashing Sutherland' and 'that sweet creature Sutherland'. Reading her letters has made me think again about myself and our relationship.*

My larger aim in this book has been to salvage Monica Jones from the versions of Monica Jones which circulated in her life and still circulate. They are contradicted and complicated by her own words. Her 'Letters to Philip' being the only words she chose to leave un-destroyed, in their vast manuscript entirety, to posterity.† From the unplumbed depths of the fifty-four boxes in Bodley one can exhume a Monica Jones to stand alongside Philip Larkin, not behind him as his dim correspondent shadow.

Or worse: the slandered Monica: 'grim old bag' (Kingsley Amis); 'an *urka* [Russian: thug] . . . Real butch . . . a *beast*' (Martin Amis); 'insufferable . . . frigid, drab, and hysterical' (Christopher Hitchens); 'the biggest criminal in literary history' (Roger Lewis); 'Built like a scary Brünnhilde . . . blowsy-looking blonde with black horn-rimmed glasses and a sumptuously upholstered figure' (Maureen Paton).

Her teeth are particularly laughed at ('ogreish' Martin Amis calls them). Monica would admit they were not her best physical feature. She was especially proud of her head of hair and her legs. Philip Larkin, in the earlier years of their relationship, was similarly admiring. 'Your legs,' he said, 'are the only legs I ever see the point of, except for walking about on, of course.' Her hair, he told her, when caught by the twilight sun, was 'gold'. There was another quality Philip, a connoisseur photographer, particularly admired: the chiselled features of her face and high cheekbones – in a poetic draft he called it 'angled beauty'. It is evident in the frontispiece of this book.

---

* I reproduce in this book, which began as a memoir, relatively little of what she writes, at length, about me, not wishing to jog the spotlight off her, where it belongs.

† This needs qualification. There are about a thousand letters from her mother (none to her mother) that she kept. They are deposited, uncatalogued, in the Larkin collection at the Hull History Centre.

Her teeth, as I observed (this, I realise, is an odd way to start a book about Monica Jones) were not perfectly aligned, perhaps a bit stained by Gold Flake cigarettes. Warned by her vanity mirror, she was wary about smiling, which students often misread as disapproval. Philip took many pictures of Monica – in none I have seen is her mouth smilingly open. Nor any without her trademark horn-rim spectacles.

Monica, mid-1960s, in the college library

Less *ad feminam* among her many critics is the relegation of Monica as cumbersome life-luggage Larkin never left behind to let his poetry fly. It is because of Monica, the argument goes, that his reputation depends, meagrely, on five slim volumes. There was more poetry in him but she shrivelled it – left him, in Martin Amis's *j'accuse*, 'life starved'* and his admirers Larkin-starved. Was she Medusa Jones who turned Larkin's genius to fifteen years of lifeless stone, denying him and us a late phase? Keats had the tubercular bacillus as his excuse. Was Monica Jones Larkin's?

---

* Amis makes the point forcibly in his introduction to *Philip Larkin Poems Selected by Martin Amis*, 2011, pp. xxii–xxii, in his article, 'Philip Larkin's Women', in the *Guardian*, 23 October 2010 and in his auto-fiction *Inside Story*, 2020.

There is, I insist, another Monica. The one I knew, who should be lifted from the slough into which posterity has plunged her. Even her failings – some of which shock – merit thoughtful consideration. The case I make in the following pages is not partisan vindication, nor *nil nisi* memorial, nor the fond recollections of an undergraduate in the presence of a woman of cultivated mind and life-changing kindness to him.

But did I truly know her? I am shaken by some of the things I have now seen in her letters.* In her for-your-eyes-only intercourse with Philip there is a veritable basket of snakes: racism, spite, foul-mouthed lapses, shared misogyny and acidic streams of downright nastiness. She never opened that basket to me, close as I thought I was to her. But, then, she never displayed her Christian faith: something which has struck me reading her letters.† I have written this book in a shaken spirit. Was the Monica I knew, intimately as I thought until a year or two ago, illusory? 'I wish I'd never read the things,' I told the archive's curator, Dr Priestman, in a moment of gloom.

Reviewers of Anthony Thwaite's collection, *Letters to Monica* (2010), agreed that she brought out the best in Larkin as a letter writer. I expected to find the same qualities in her letters as in his: wit, irony, high literary sensibility founded on a stern belief in tradition, not novelty or modernism. Those qualities are certainly present in her correspondence – particularly that before the mid-1960s. But overwhelming all is one thing: pain, typically an enduring ache, too often agony.

Despite what has recently passed under my eyes, I hold on, stubbornly, to the image of what Monica was to me in the 1960s and what I believe Philip Larkin fell in love with in the 1940s and recalled at the end of his life in the 1980s. He did not, he said on his hospital bed, want to see anyone else: he 'wanted to see Monica to tell her I love her'. The acknowledgement was deathbed real. An act of confession

---

* See below, pp. 245–250.

† See, as confirmation of her religious belief, the appendix on Monica and Philip's respective wills.

and, conscious of the hardship that loving Philip Larkin meant, an act of contrition.

Her letters confirm Andrew Motion's judgement that Monica was the most important relationship of Philip's life. Larkin was, the evidence suggests, the only man Monica slept with in her seventy-eight years. Larkin slept with several women, but Monica most of all. And, one would like to think, with her most honestly; in his fashion. His honesty had its odd aspects. In his will he left virtually everything of value to Monica – but 20 per cent of 'residue' he left to his last, secret (at the time he was drawing up his will) mistress, with whom he betrayed both an unknowing Monica and his equally unknowing previous mistress, Maeve Brennan. His bequest was bountiful. In 1995 Monica was receiving £70,000 a year from Philip's booming literary estate and Betty Mackereth (the last mistress) £11,000. Maeve got nothing. Like the wasp, he could sting after death.

Monica deserves, after all these years, clear-sighted judgement. And, from me, overwhelming gratitude. Her two-thousand-odd letters to Philip are the last unclimbed peak in the Larkin range. Only one person, other than Philip, has scaled and assessed the full range: the collection's curator, Dr Judith Priestman. Conceivably Dr Priestman did so more scrupulously than the letters' addressee. Larkin, a librarian by primary profession (as he perversely insisted in his *Who's Who* entry and Monica contradicted on his gravestone) kept the letters of Kingsley Amis in a ring-binder for ease of multiple re-reading. Monica's letters were bundled and taped en masse. They mattered – as 'literary' letters – less to him. But Monica's letters escaped the wastepaper bin. Philip thought too much of their writer for that. There is, internal evidence suggests, barely a single Monica-to-Philip letter lost to posterity. The archive is her monument to the only relationship that, at the end, mattered.

I am most of all grateful to Dr Priestman as scholarly provider and counsellor. She was the book's first critical reader in typescript. I would have foundered in the Sargasso of the Jones letters but for her navigation. I dedicate this book to her. What follows is a personal memoir of Monica Jones in a refreshed biographical frame. My aim is to supply what I believe I can supply usefully, livingly and uniquely.

Which, to return to my original question, is truer: the felt impressions of the time – still vivid in my mind – or recollection enlarged and complicated by recently encountered archive evidence? Did I know a real Monica in the 1960s, both of us alive? Or do I know her better now in the 2020s – she long dead, Philip longer dead, and me not as long from it as I then was?

And which was – at the time I knew her – the real Monica? The woman who was cool as a cucumber, a calm and collected friend and teacher? The witty woman I ate, drank, conversed and on occasion holidayed with? Or the private Monica, in her one-woman *huis clos*, writing desperate, often drunken, letters to the only man she could love, who was so painfully seldom with her to receive her love? She was prepared to give him her life's blood; all she could give him was her life's ink. There are, in Bodley's vaults, boxes of lonely misery. And every piece of writing contained in them is addressed to one man.

The letters I now see as Monica's Cleopatra pyramid (his 'rabbit of old Nile', as Philip called Monica after her favourite Shakespeare female character). The statement her letters make, in their totality, echoes Jane Carlyle's: 'I too am here'. Monica struggled, but hers was a life that never got better. She would never escape Leicester, and would remain till the end, like Rapunzel, locked in her tower – red-brick, alas, not ivory – with no release until retirement. And then pensioned suffering.

What follows is an avowedly sympathetic treatment of Monica Jones. Given what I owe her, it could not be otherwise. But I withhold judgement on Philip Larkin. There are too many Philip Larkins to choose from. He is one of his nation's greatest poets; he was a good (if consistently belly-aching to others) son to his mother. He could be despised as an utter cad or apologised for as a kind man who did unkind things; a weak man entrapped by obsessive women; a coercive controller; a predator; a love-rat; a *littérateur* always more interested in the letter in hand than his addressee; a 'misogamist' who quarantined himself to perfect his poetry; an egotist who 'cared a tenth as much about what happened around him as he did about what was happening inside him'; an incorrigible racist; a marriage-averse polyamorist; a profoundly unhappy man whose unhappiness was catching. I subscribe to the first and last of those descriptions. Final judgements I leave to the reader.

I personally believe that the relationship of Philip Larkin and Monica Jones was a genuine, if epically bumpy, love relationship. I believe too, as Peter Keating says in the epigraph at the head of this book, that Monica was a significant force on Larkin's writing. I agree that his poetry would not be what it is without her in its mix. But there again I will leave it to readers to make their own judgements after they have reviewed the evidence.

I

Origins, 1850–1922

'I am a Northerner; what am I doing in this place?'
Monica to me, 1964; 'this place' is Leicester

Margaret Monica Beale Jones was born on 7 May 1922 in Llanelli, Carmarthenshire, Wales, destined to be her parents' only child.[*] She would, throughout life, be more her mother's child than her father's although she loved, lifelong, both parents. Her mother, Margaret Lily Jones, née Peart, always called 'Lily', was the daughter of a man whose life was a Victorian self-help parable. The males of Robert Peart's family had worked for generations in Weardale, rural Durham, as manual labourers in the lead mines and stone quarries which fed the Industrial Revolution. The base metal they dug up had veins of gold and copper running through it which the miners could extract and sell. Most used the bonus to treat themselves with comforts their hard work wouldn't otherwise stretch to. Robert Peart, a thrifty, god-loving, abstinent man, hoarded his treasure trove.

In 1898, the now fifty-year-old Robert, with a sleeping partner, set up his own quarrying business in whinstone – hard black rock used in construction, roadworks and drystone walls. The Peart firm,

---

* Some accounts have her date of birth 8 May 1922. She herself seems not to have been sure whether her middle name was 'Beale' or 'Beal'. Both spellings are on record.

its workforce fifty-strong, made money. Thrifty Robert bought up houses and farms around Weardale. The Peart family was able to move, at the turn of the century, from a cramped worker's cottage to a seven-room house in the upmarket village of St John's Chapel.

Monica loved the stories her mother, born in 1888, told about her early childhood life, before the family's prosperity. One survives. The Peart cottage was at the top of Copt Hill in Upper Weardale, beyond the reach of any main road. During winter they always kept a sledge and a month's supply of food in store for the inevitable snowing in. The Pearts' cottage was hard work year-round for the village postman. One blustery day, fighting his way up, the wind blew the single postcard needing delivery out of the postman's hands. 'Your guests aren't coming,' he serenely told Mrs Peart. Nor the postcard.

Although his firm was wound up in 1928, Robert's estate was still yielding profit as late as the 1960s from the sale of property and farmland he had acquired. Unspoiled by wealth, Robert retained his strict Wesleyan Methodist beliefs. He had married a local woman, Jane Rowell, who lived until 1937. Monica knew and loved her. Though she would never know her Peart grandfather, Monica would have good reason for loving him as much as she did her grandmother. Philoprogenitive Robert had eleven children – seven girls, four boys – all of them born in the small Copt Hill cottage, and all surviving into adulthood. Lily was the youngest girl; she was particularly close, through life, to the youngest boy, Wilfred. Monica knew him as a long-term family lodger when she was growing up. He, like her mother, had stories about Weardale which he told to his young niece, forming her into the Northerner she believed herself to be for the rest of her life.

Robert was determined his girls should get a good education, respectable husbands, and that the sons should take over the family business from him in due time. Unluckily the oldest son, Joseph, was killed by the dynamite he was handling in 1906. The three other sons survived the explosions of WW1, though two were severely wounded. A surviving photograph of the Pearts shows a troop of daughters uniformly dressed, standing to attention. The boys are in their Sunday best; Joseph, the heir apparent, bearded.*

The Peart family

The patriarch, in the centre, is wizened. Lead does cruel things to human brains and bodies. 'Senile decay' is given as Robert's cause of death in 1911, aged sixty-three. While his mind was still intact, Robert set up trusts for his wife, and for his children. The latter could live on the income of the firm (which enjoyed boom war years) until they made their own way in the world. The substantial Peart capital would in due course be divided equally among them. As a precaution, this would not be on Robert's death but when the youngest boy, Wilfred, reached twenty-one. This delay was to keep the estate

---

* The presence of Joseph (front right) indicates that the picture was taken before 1906, when he was killed in a work-related accident. The daughter at the extreme right at the back has a striking resemblance to Monica and is, I hazard, Margaret Lily. Wilfred, her favourite brother, whom she looked after as a child, is front centre with a lace bib.

intact. Robert was a careful father and for Monica, who could never thank him, a benevolent grandfather. Over the intervening years the value of the firm appreciated. The Peart girls had 'expectations' and attracted hopeful suitors.

Monica's grandmother, Jane Peart, survived until Monica was fifteen. She knew her through visits with her mother to Weardale and wrote a touching elegy in her school magazine after her death.* The family's daughters were, all but one, trained to earn their keep. The brightest evidently became a schoolteacher, another a dressmaker. Others are described as 'stocking knitters'. The young Peart women, all with financial 'prospects' from the family firm, married. The exception was the youngest, Monica's future mother. The census for 1911 (the year Robert died) describes Lily, now twenty-three years old, as employed in 'domestic work at home' – a housekeeper. Her role had been laid out for her. She was appointed to be her widowed mother's carer. With that role came, in all probability, voluntary spinsterhood. Miss Peart would be thirty-something years old when she became, in her modest way, an heiress. Not quite on the shelf, but edging towards it. This, then, was the situation of Monica's mother before she married Monica's father.

Monica's father, Frederick James Jones (hereafter 'Fred'), was cut from the same cloth as Monica's mother. He was brought up in a respectable, Methodist, working-class family. But Fred's father, Frederick John Jones (hereafter 'Frederick'), did not rise in the world as had Monica's Peart grandfather. Frederick was born in the village of Cookley, a few miles from Kidderminster, in 1864. On leaving school, aged fifteen, he went to work in the nearby Tilden Iron Works, a massive factory complex, owned by the Baldwin family. The future prime minister, Stanley Baldwin, was one of the junior managers.

Frederick was apprenticed as a tinplate polisher, along with his sister, and by his mid-twenties is listed as a skilled tinsmith. It was a thriving line of work. Victorian kitchens rattled with tinware and enamelled utensils. Frederick earned a good wage and moved house

* See below, pp. 21–22.

to upmarket Stourport-on-Severn, making a home for his mother and sister and an aged relative. The home could afford a thirteen-year-old live-in servant girl.

On 15 May 1894 Frederick married Alice Ann Busson. Family deaths, and his sister's marriage, had left Frederick and Alice free agents and he decided to acquire a better-paying job in Llanelli. The proverbially Welsh surname 'Jones' suggests there were relatives in the town. It was a shrewd decision by Frederick. The Welsh Tinplate and Metal Stamping Company was Llanelli's largest firm, employing a thousand workers, mainly women. It was famed countrywide for its 'Goat' brand of enamelled saucepans. Llanelli was duly nicknamed 'Sospan' and 'Tinopolis'. You would have had to dig deep to extract from Monica, when I knew her, that she was a Tinopolitan by birth. Or by upbringing Welsh.

Once settled in Llanelli, Frederick and Alice had two children: a boy, Fred (Monica's father), and a girl, Mary Jane. The factory wages were good and worldwide demand for 'Goat' produce ensured job security. The four Joneses lived a decent, working-class, devoutly Methodist life in a five-room, better than working-class house at 18 Glanmor Terrace. Frederick obviously earned well and spent wisely. The Joneses' happiness, however, did not last. Alice died in 1900 and Frederick found himself a widower with two children under five. He called on his unmarried sister-in-law, Florence, to leave her position as a domestic servant in Brighton and move in as his housekeeper. Two years later, Frederick married Florence. It was a quiet, register-office ceremony and details on the certificate were fudged. The reason is clear. Under 1902 law the marriage was illegal, Florence being a deceased wife's sister. If discovered, the union would be null and void. (Fred, born in 1896 of the previous marriage, was legitimate, as was his sister.) In 1907 the Deceased Wife's Sister's Marriage Act was passed, removing the prohibition and the fact Florence had been Frederick's sister-in-law ceased to matter. The 1911 census records that fifteen-year-old Fred had joined his father as an apprentice in the Welsh Tinplate and Metal Stamping Company. He did well over the next three years, coming to specialise as a fitter and tool-maker. Monica's father was good with his hands. She inherited some of that.

In the war excitement of 1914 Fred was among the first to join up. Now eighteen, he wanted more than factory life in Llanelli offered. Despite his engineering skills, Fred was recruited into the Royal Army Medical Corps. In April 1915 Private Jones was posted to the vast rear-echelon army encampment Étaples, near Boulogne. He would spend all his wartime service there. Étaples, the size of a small town, had diverse medical facilities. Fred was assigned to the infectious disease hospital. He was promoted to sergeant, which meant the comforts of mess life. There was little else comfortable at Étaples. It was a hellhole so awful that many of those passing through it were glad to go up the line and take their chances with death. Étaples' awfulness is recorded, graphically, by the war's most famous poets, Wilfred Owen, Robert Graves and Siegfried Sassoon.

Logistically the camp held 10 per cent of reserves for front-line infantry regiments. At its peak, this meant up to 100,000 men. While garrisoned there, soldiers were toughened up by brutal training. Because of its size and function, Étaples was a target for German aerial bombing and artillery. There was all-out mutiny in 1917. The camp police lost control. Men were shot among chaotic violence. Hospital staff, such as Fred, were armed to assist in restoring discipline. He shot no Germans, but he might have had to think about shooting his own countrymen. Fred it seems never talked about Étaples, although, as an adult, Monica was sentimental about 'the War called Great' and as late as the sixties tears would come to her eyes on Armistice Day if she heard a brass band, or the radio, playing 'Keep the Home Fires Burning'.

It was not, other than the fact he survived it, a good war for Fred. His time at Étaples, however, would ultimately lead to a happy, life-changing event. The oldest surviving Peart son, Thomas, having come down with dysentery and TB while serving on the Western Front, was treated at Étaples before being discharged with a war pension. The younger brother, John Robert Peart (known, now his father was dead, as 'Robert') was also wounded and sent to Étaples, around 1917. He and Fred became pals. Monica told Andrew Motion what happened next:

On leave shortly before the Armistice [Fred] met Margaret Lily Peart while visiting a friend in the village of St John's Chapel, near Stanhope in Northumberland, fell in love with her and was soon married.

The facts are more or less right. The timing is off. The 'friend' was Robert Peart, sent home for a spell of leave while recovering from his wounds late in the war. He was visited by his chum, Fred, himself on leave. Fred stayed in the house in St John's Chapel and met the last unmarried daughter: Margaret Lily.

Lily and Fred fell in love. He was twenty-one, she thirty. They did not, as Monica misinformed Andrew Motion, marry 'soon after' but considerably later, following Fred's demob (1919) and resettlement into civilian life. The ceremony took place on 7 November 1921, some three years after the lovers first met. The wedding was a small affair at the Wesleyan Methodist Church, St John's Chapel. John Robert Peart was the first witness.

The delay between the sweethearts meeting and marrying was to allow Fred to find work. In 1919 non-commissioned officers did not leave the army well off. It is also likely that with the young Wilfred's coming of age in 1921, the Peart legacy was a factor for the couple: they prudently waited until Lily came into her family bequest and they could buy a good house. It is clear that after marriage Lily regarded the Peart inheritance as hers. When she died, in 1959, she left £26,000 to her husband and daughter. While sharing, she must have retained her own bank account and solicitor over the thirty-seven years of her marriage.

2

Llanelli and Kidderminster,

1922–1940

'Where her childhood was unspent'
  adapted from Larkin's poem, 'I Remember, I Remember'

Finding no work in the North-East, Fred returned to Llanelli in 1920 and got his old job back at the Welsh Tinplate factory. It had been a good war for them – a metallic war. Once settled, the couple married. Lily accepted a future uprooted from her home to a town where she knew no one and where her northern accent marked her as an outsider. But, thanks to her nest-egg, the Joneses bought a substantial four-bedroom terraced house at 73 New Road.

A subsidiary reason for the Joneses' premarital delay had been finding someone to take Lily's place as her mother's carer. There was no delay when it came to starting a family. Monica was born in Llanelli on 7 May 1922, exactly six months after her parents' wedding in Northumberland. Monica knew about her parents' jumping the gun, hence her white lie to Motion about them having married two years earlier than they did. Dates were, fifty years on, still a sore point when talking to a biographer.

The child was christened Margaret Monica Beale Jones. Her mother's first name was Margaret but Monica's 'Margaret' went unused, just as Lily's had. 'Beale' was the maiden name of Fred's grandmother, of whom he had been very fond, and who, presumably, was the aged relative in the family's pre-Llanelli Stourport years. The Joneses were Methodists, though Lily would later move to Anglicanism and Monica would follow her into the same congregation. She chose to be high church but subscribed to a thoroughly latitudinarian theology. Did she believe in God, Monica was asked at the end of her life. 'Halfway,' she replied. But she loved *Hymns Ancient and Modern* all the way.

Because Lily was, modestly, an heiress, she and Fred could afford a better life, and more aspiration for their daughter, than a fitter's wages alone could support. Lily had been brought up in a household where education for girls mattered. She was well read. Monica recalls her mother knew the Brontës' work well – not just the two big novels. That Monica was, at the age of thirteen, reading the 'great baggy monster' Victorian novel *Pendennis* was not at the encouragement of her father. Fred was intelligent, smart with his hands, but not bookish.

In their early days in Llanelli the Joneses lived above a manual factory worker's level, buoyed up by Lily's inheritance and helped by there being only the one child. Why just the one? The Llanelli house had four bedrooms. Lily, one assumes, could not – having experienced it – face the wear and tear of a large family. Her health may not have been up to child-bearing. Monica told me her mother's hands were crippled with arthritis by her forties – not that long after marriage. Anticipating the same fate, Monica resolved to master the typewriter so she could tap when she could no longer drive her fountain pen. She never did: Philip, a good typist when drafting his poems or in the office, good-naturedly mocked her efforts. 'Rabbits don't type,' he told her. His other love at the time, Maeve Brennan (Potter-nicknamed 'Mouse'), did: 100 wpm at least.

Monica had her earliest education at Llanelli primary school and would have acquired a Welsh accent, perhaps even a smattering of the language. She saw a lot of her Jones grandparents, who lived a few streets away and had no other nearby grandchildren to spoil. She had a decent working-class early childhood and was a much-loved little girl.

The Joneses did not stay in Wales. Fred's firm's post-war boom didn't last. It was a good thing for Monica that it didn't; Llanelli would have stifled her. The 'Slump' of 1929 and the ten-year Depression which followed was awful for Welsh industry. There were thousands of lay-offs across the principality. The Welsh tinplate factory survived – saucepans were always needed – but Fred's days there were numbered. Monica was seven years old when the Joneses upped and left for Stourport-on-Severn, near Kidderminster. Fred had childhood roots and relatives there, although his father and stepmother stayed on in Llanelli. They had done well. Their house at 25 Coronation Road had a live-in maid. When he died in 1947 the widowed Frederick left Fred £1,200 (£42,000 in current value) – a working man's fortune. Monica's family, on both sides, were models of Victorian hard work and thrift.

It was a factor for Lily, one can be sure, that Kidderminster had better schools than industrial Llanelli. And her money again helped buy a comfortable house at 44 Summerfield Road, Stourport, where the Joneses would live until Fred and Lily died in 1959. Fred got a job as a works engineer (a word of which he was proud) in the kitchenware unit at the Wilden Iron Works. It was the firm his father had left thirty years before; it was still thriving, as were its owners, the Baldwins.

During Monica's childhood there was another resident in the Joneses' house: Lily's favourite brother, Wilfred. He was, Monica ruefully observed on his death in 1961, the only living relative who had known and loved her from childhood. Wilfred married in 1940 and left Summerfield Road at the same time Monica took off for Oxford.

3

Monica Rises, 1930–1940

'I've often felt like a child having to be brought along sitting outside the bright free-masonry of grown-ups'
Monica to Philip, 1952

Early in life Monica felt that what she wanted was 'a life chosen by one's self and not imposed on one'. She would – by her native wits and the investment her mother would make in her education – rise. Her parents, admirable though both manifestly were, had not risen above the station they were born in. But her mother was a main influence on the life Monica chose for herself. It was in the Peart part of the world, Haydon Bridge, that Monica bought the only house she would ever own. She hiked the Pennines in her twenties and acquainted herself with the house her mother was brought up in. She became lovingly close to her Peart grandmother and other Pearts, notably Uncle Wilfred. That she was a Northerner was a theme with her.

She rarely mentions her family in letters to Philip in the first thirteen years of his relationship with her. While her parents were still alive, he met her mother only twice, in Leicester, and never met her father. Philip is not recorded as ever visiting Stourport where, until her late twenties, Monica stayed up to half the year during vacations and teaching breaks. She, meanwhile, got to know Philip's mother and sister only too well.

One can wonder how aware Monica was of the skeletons in her family closet – her Jones grandfather's illegal second marriage and her own premarital conception. But she must have been aware how her life, from birth on, was eased, and the wings of higher education put on her heels, by her mother's Peart bequest. She must have been aware too of her mother's ambition that her daughter should have a better life, and better education, than she, Lily, had shared with her sisters.

Fred left a different bequest. Why did she speak so loudly? Philip once asked complainingly. Hers had been a noisy house, she told him: despite there only being three Joneses to bawl in it. Her father, from his early teenage years, was in a shouty trade. Try banging on a saucepan for half an hour. Philip's, she pointed out, had been a quiet house. His father was a local government manager, rising to the honour of an OBE, who spent his working life in offices where the loudest noise was the woodpecker tap of the secretary's typewriter. Anthony Thwaite, who knew both Philip and Monica personally in later life, says: 'They [were] born in the same year, 1922, and came from rather similar provincial middle-class backgrounds.' There is, however, a fine distinction. Philip was what Orwell called middle-middle-class and English to the bone. He spoke like his parents. He had a nice, rolling voice, pleasant on the ear, variable in pitch, lingering on open vowels, with an overlay of Oxford. Monica had streaks of Welsh and working class beneath her later higher-class carapace. Her spoken accent always denied it, sometimes too aggressively.

One of the things that Monica resented about her colleague Richard Hoggart, when he was the Leicester department's bright-gleaming star, was that he romanticised his working-class origins. He made a profession out of them. He was honest about where he started life. Hoggart spoke with a defiantly Yorkshire accent. Monica, in stark contrast, believed that you had to accept deracination if you accepted the gift of more book learning than the couple who gave you life. And you had to accept class and regional inauthenticity as a cost paid.

Monica's 'making of herself' began, aged thirteen, with a scholarship to the Kidderminster High School for Girls. She entered as a third-former. The evidence is scanty but fellow pupils at Kidderminster

High recall her as liked – although 'respected' may have been the more appropriate word. She described herself to Andrew Motion as a 'dull and dim' schoolgirl. He, rightly, did not believe her. Monica's chronic short sight was evidently detected early. Myopia as severe as Monica's meant no jolly hockey sticks. But she was in the school choir and got a prize for art. It was one of many prizes.

She was the school swot and, with her specs, flaunted it. One wisecrack survives. On the school bus another girl, overhearing a polysyllable, shouted out, 'Oh, she's swallowed a dictionary!' Monica smartly chipped in: 'I swallowed one years ago, and now I'm slowly digesting it.' Another schoolmate, who travelled daily from Stourport with her, recalls: 'She was brilliantly clever, always top of the class.' Monica was a day girl. Whether her success at school made her father proud, we don't know. Neither did she. Monica once told me, wistfully, that she wished she could have got closer to Fred. But did they, as she entered her teens, speak the same class dialect, did they have the same range of mind, that would enable them to be close?

Monica remembered a game she played with her schoolmates – giving her teachers marks out of ten for the seven cardinal 'deadlies'; i.e. the ugliest, most boring, most pathetic, dimmest, etc. They kept score in exercise books. She carried the game forward into her academic life, she told Philip. It was, she said, the only fun she had at 'poisonous' staff meetings. She was not, entirely, a nice little girl; or, come to that, a nice colleague.

Monica did not publish in her academic life but she was the queen of her school magazine. She wrote a sad tale, as a fourth former, about a young girl discovering there is no 'real' Santa and spending Christmas in tears. A year later she contributed a sceptical piece about the 'real' Guy Fawkes and his November 'night'. There are several poems. All her juvenile publications testify to her being a very clever pupil. One poem, 'Requiescat', written when she was sixteen and in the Upper Fifth, merits quoting. It is an elegy, commemorating the death of her beloved grandmother, Jane Peart, in March 1937:

She is all quiet now, only the sea
Booms sadly, sighing, surging over the hill,
And a bird in the trees is singing, singing – but she
Who was herself once like a bird, is still.

Nothing will break her quiet, here where she sleeps
Only the wild birds circle over her.
She will not know the dawn, or when night creeps
Cold-fingered, lays sleep on the flowers that cover her.

She is gone from us now, she is sleeping
Here, where there is no weariness, only repose;
For her there is no more anger, or sorrow, or weeping;
If she is forgot or remembered, she cares not, nor knows.

Rest she has found; and she has been very tired,
And now she has done with the world's turmoil and care;
Doubtless one might find a peace here, and peace she desired,
Now the quiet old earth is over her eyes and her hair.

The loss for Lily Jones was grievous and she would have found consolation in her daughter's verse at the funeral which they attended. What poetry had Monica been reading? Clearly Wordsworth's 'Lucy' poems ('no motion has she now, no force'). There is, in an unvisited box in Hull History Centre, a whole sheaf of Monica's poetry from school onwards into her twenties. That vein was stopped after she became close to Philip in her twenties. She could not compete; but she preserved her poems, even her juvenilia.

In adulthood, Monica thought about her schooldays from time to time. She might not have been sporty but she discovered early on she liked the stage. She recalled her precocious stardom for Philip, dwelling on something they both admired; her legs:

Even when I was thin [she was, at the time of writing, aged forty-four, ten stone, 5ft 4in] my legs were big enough to be sexy . . .

> When I performed in the pantomime which I wrote, at school, as a scholarly patriotic girl to make money for Spitfires I 'took Dick' because I considered that I had principal boy legs & I couldn't see any others.

The saucy impropriety is intended. The Spitfire remark means she was a sixth-former; and the pantomime she wrote was her version of *Dick Whittington*.

On a home visit in 1949, in the bedroom she had grown up in, she turned up a pile of her fourth-form Silverine exercise books (the ones, those of a certain age will recall, with wholly dispensable information on the back cover about how many pecks in a bushel, etc). She was hunting for blank sheets on which to write her daily screed to Philip. Riffling through the books, she had the experience of meeting young Monica.

Aged sixteen she had developed a mad 'pash' for Shelley, and bought with her pocket money a copy of André Maurois' *Ariel*, an ultra-romantic biography of Percy Bysshe Shelley. It had mouldered on her bedroom bookshelf since she first read it. She thought it 'all right' then, but 'when you are young and foolish you get pleasure from reading because you don't understand any of it'. Now, closing in on thirty, she found 'that fool Frenchman' full of guff and guilty of 'whitewashing the *silly* Shelley . . . why even at 16 I was prepared to read a Frenchman on the subject . . . I can't think'. As for Mary Godwin Shelley – she was 'an intolerable woman in every way that can be imagined . . . calculating and conceited'. And her mother, Mary Wollstonecraft? – an 'irritatingly wrong-headed woman'. As for Shelley himself – his poetry was 'a sort of literary Turkish delight'.

But falling in love with a poet struck a chord. Monica put back her English exercise books, replaced *Ariel* on its shelf and returned to her letter. The needed blank pages she tore out of 'geography'. She was rather impressed. Teenage Monica Jones would go far. Perhaps she might even find her Shelley. But first there was Oxford.

Monica in the sixth form (to the left of the teacher)

4

Oxford, 1940–1943

'The city we shared without knowing . . . Dull Bodley, draught beer and dark blue'

Philip, a private poem for Monica, 1975

Monica won a state scholarship and open exhibition at St Hugh's College Oxford in 1939. She went up in October 1940 as part of the same English Literature intake as Philip. Hers was an unhappy landing – so much so that her father wrote a 'Cheer up Monica' letter. 'Daddy' did not often write. He had school-taught copperplate handwriting and occasionally imperfect grammar (e.g. 'lots of love from we two'). But his surviving letters are fond and sensible.

The Chiltern 'rounded' hillocks made Monica yearn for her real northern hills and dales. And there were mice everywhere in the college. But her main distress was that – in an Oxford crowded to bursting – she was obliged to share digs with another student. As an only child, Monica Jones was not good at sharing. The college bursar was immovable. 'The old cow,' wrote an indignant Lily. Her motherly advice in such frustrations of life was 'just say "bugger".' Monica stuck at it and buggered her way into putting up with Oxford. Cigarettes helped. Her chain-smoking began at Oxford, as did Philip's.

Lily wrote two or three times a week in term about how the garden grew, the necessity for warm clothes and darning them, Stourport news and, most important, instructions to her daughter to eat well. Monica went home every vacation and during term sent clothes back –

via 'postal laundry' – for her mother to wash. It is clear (although few of Monica's letters to her mother survive) that her return letters were in the same vein as Lily's: talking about the little things of life during the great fact of war. She was, in the age of her majority, the loving daughter of loving parents. Her closeness to her mother and father rendered her a home-girl among Oxford sophisticates. If they looked down on her, that would change when her degree result arrived.

Oxford in the early 1940s was as much a wartime city as it had been when the Royalist capital was established there three hundred years earlier. There were ack-ack barrels among Matthew Arnold's dreaming spires.

Her Oxford, Monica wrote in one of her poems (she wrote many), was 'born in September 1939' when 'we heard the bomber in the bee's hum'. Her college, St Hugh's, was requisitioned by the wartime medical corps and Oxford was populous with blue-uniformed walking wounded. They made the male undergraduates, including Philip Larkin (graded 'unfit to serve'), feel puny. And guilty for being spared the Blitz. Oxford's historic centre was regarded as the safest bomb shelter in the country. Legend had it this was because Hitler wanted Oxford as a trophy when he conquered England.

Government offices moved wholesale to Oxford. St John's, Larkin's college, was taken over by the Department of Fish Supplies – something yet to be added to its heraldic emblem. St Hugh's women students moved to St Hilda's, where Monica came to the notice of the formidable (later Dame) Helen Gardner. Oddly, Gardner's women's college had been founded in 1893 by Dorothea Beale, who may have been a very distant relative of Margaret Monica Beale Jones.

War wholly occupied the Oxford mind when Philip and Monica were there. One didn't think into the future, Philip remembered,* beyond the day's headlines, or into the past beyond yesterday's. The suspense, as to defeat or victory, was grinding. During the war, Monica told me, she took regular two-week 'holidays from the news', reading no papers, turning off even Alvar Lidell and John Snagge – those rich voices which, like Churchill's, and later John Arlott's, dispelled, for

---

* Larkin makes this point in the 1963 preface to *Jill*, which Monica helped with.

the hour at least, alarm or despondency. Monica had an emotional relationship, which lasted lifelong, with the 'wireless' (she hated the word 'radio').

Larkin's novel *Jill*, set in 1943 Oxford, was the first thing of his he asked Monica to read. It captures the atmosphere of the city they both, 'unknowingly', inhabited within a few hundred yards of each other for three years. Wartime university, as *Jill* records, was Oxford minus Oxford – no tincture of *Brideshead*, plover's eggs, fine wines, or genteel Bullingdon riot. But the eternal 'tone', as Larkin called it, remained. There was still homoeroticism. Even Hitler couldn't stamp on that – at least until the Gauleiters arrived. Philip, as Andrew Motion records, tried man-on-man with as little success as his early heterosexual floundering. And, in the women's colleges, as Dorothy L. Sayers describes in her Oxford novel, *Gaudy Night* (1935) there was sapphism. What Monica made of it – other than that it was habitually ill-dressed – one can surmise. She liked men, particularly young men, from Oxford days to the end of her life.

Wartime degree courses were curtailed. Monica had the option of doing an accelerated two-year course (five finals papers) or a three-year full course (nine finals papers) if she undertook to teach school for two years after graduation in 1943. With so many male teachers in the forces there was a national need for womanpower in the classroom as much as in the factories. Monica chose the longer course with the postgraduate spell of chalk and blackboard. It would turn out to be a mistake for her later career to have the word 'schoolteacher' on her CV.

She was obliged to register for war service while an undergraduate but her eyes, as did Philip's, disqualified her. She had, nonetheless, to undertake specified 'war tasks'. In her case, it was initially first aid then fire-watching. Dick Watson, a close friend in later life, recalls her saying she was affected by the sight of the badly wounded being stretchered in daily to the requisitioned colleges. They needed more than first aid. The raids Monica watched for never came to Oxford.

None of the famous dons of the time – C. S. Lewis, Tolkien and his congenial Inklings – left any visible mark on Monica. The university's star lecturer, Lord David Cecil, may have given her some podium tips.

She sometimes mentioned his books, but usually with a slight sneer at the belletristic banality of milord's criticism. Who then influenced her? Her big-gun referee when it came to university job interviews was Helen Gardner. Her St Hugh's tutor was Mary Ethel Seaton. Neither was in a field of main interest to Monica. Seaton actually forbade Monica to spend too much time on Victorian literature, considering it too 'modern' by far for Oxford, AD 1943. Monica spent the rest of her life flouting Miss Seaton's ordinance.

The careers of Gardner and Seaton made it crystal clear that to succeed – or even to keep their job against the rivalry of men – a woman don (sexist word) or woman fellow (ditto) had best stay single and childless. And not wear feminine clothes. Leave them to the Cowley workers on their Friday-night-out razzle. If they were called battleaxes or shrews, ignore it.

The English Studies class, in war years, was minuscule. Its female 1940 intake was half a dozen. Monica was a fellow student at shared lectures (not tutorials) with Kingsley Amis and Philip Larkin. The young men had an eye for the ladies. Philip liked girls with glasses – all his long-term lovers wore them, as did he. Monica's eyes were strikingly horn-rimmed.

Philip may have noted the name Jones when the finals results lists were posted at the Sheldonian and wondered who this contemporary of his was. For three years he never saw her. She was evidently too mousey to arrest the male gaze, even one as hungry as his. When she read Philip's novel (at his invitation), Monica's eye would have been caught by the sexist description in *Jill* of her kind in 1943:

> The lecture room was full of young women in short gowns, carrying bulky handbags and enormous bundles of notes; they smelt inimitably of face powder and (vaguely) Irish stew, and they were dressed in woollen clothes.

Somewhere in that woolly gaggle is Miss Jones incognita. Somewhere else in Oxford was another undergraduate, Margaret Roberts (later Thatcher).

The war meant, as Monica put it, fifteen years of 'sacking'. The nation's women, were they not cunning with their scissors, needle and thread, might as well have been wearing mailbags made by HM's prisoners. Irish stew? In the era of meat rationing, mutton made its reappearance on the British menu. Unlike lamb, it smells. The British, unlike the French, do not like their noses to be reminded of the animal whose corpse they are devouring. Monica hated ration-book victuals. I once made the mistake of offering her canned Carnation milk. I like its creaminess in coffee. Her face contorted. She would not touch it. It recalled the loathed coupons and the ration book. She would have probably hurled an offered tin of spam at my head.

The one good thing about rations was that it made the nation whippet slim. Whoever got fat on Lord Woolton pie? In later years Monica, feeling like a 'fat pig', would fall back on bulimia, misery and 'tomato sandwich fever'. She could never eat food happily alone. But she loved cooking for others on whom it was worth bestowing her culinary art. After a particularly successful meal she would congratulate herself on having created something 'proper pre-war quality'. Post-war cuisine was a long time catching up.

5

First Love, 1941–1943

'you will not look my way'
                    Monica in a poem to her first lover, 1942

Despite conscription, there were eligible men in wartime Oxford; too many. Thirteen thousand recovering wounded servicemen – 'heroes' – were billeted at spacious St Hugh's over the war years, recklessly hungry for love before being posted back to service or discharged. There was also an explosive quantity of pent-up sex among Oxford students. Larkin was a virgin until two years beyond voting age, then twenty-one.

About Monica's love life at Oxford no hard evidence survives. But there was a love life. She recalled later to Larkin:

> The very first man that I was in love with – I really was in a terribly romantic 18-year-old-thing – was called Arnold; I didn't like him even at the time.

The last clause is pure Monica – I loved him: but didn't like him. As Larkin later tartly put it, she regarded warm emotion as like the lavatory – but less necessary.

All that we know of Arnold and Monica's affair is derived from a fascinating, oblique, narrative of its bumpy course. Monica had been a star poet in her school magazine. She exploded into verse in her three years in Oxford. In one of her poems she declares, neatly, what poetry did for her. It served: 'to fix the thought in the safety of the word'. Monica was proud of her Oxford poetry and kept it, among earlier efforts, clamped between the boards of a hardback school exercise book. She stopped writing poetry after meeting Philip in 1946. With *The North Ship* (1945) he was already a published author. Her neo-Georgian efforts looked too dated alongside his then Auden-influenced verse.

Monica, undergraduate

Many of Monica's Oxford poems are dedicated 'To AJS' – namely (but tantalisingly so) 'Arnold'. Who was Arnold? An AJS poem, 'Is There a Doctor in the House', suggests that he was one of the numerous medical staff stationed in Oxford. Monica attended first aid classes as her war work in her first weeks at Oxford. The affair with Arnold began in 1940 when, as she told Larkin, she was a 'romantic 18-year-old' and newly arrived at university.

Looking back in 1943, Monica recalls that during the early, heady days of their romance:

We thought our loves and thoughts and fun
Too fragile to survive the war
But now two years of war are done
And we are richer than before
We looked for death but there was birth.

In spring 1942 – a year and a half into the affair – she was more reflective. They have lost something:

I sit by the fire, I light my cigarette
And I think how we are the same stuff
As the dustman, the young soldier,
The woman in the café drinking tea
And you and me.
Give me vision – what we thought we had
Oh, me in you and you in me,
Let the eyes of the blind be opened
Let me see!

By the Easter 1942 vacation there had been a break-up. She thinks about it as she hikes (with her mother, presumably) in her northern hills during time out from Oxford:

I said that I would think of you no more
And find oblivion where you never came
But in the valleys you were there before
And when I sought the hills they spoke your name.

In October, on her return to Oxford, she is distraught. The affair is over, they are thrown back on themselves alone:

My mind has escaped where you cannot follow
Never peace for me comes again.
There is no room in my life here for you.

Who broke it off? Arnold did, as a poem by a clearly lovelorn Monica tells us:

I ask no cure; I understand
How all our lives are lived alone
Only touch my groping hand
Just a moment with your own.

But she understands. If they meet in the street, 'you will not look my way'.

The affair was clearly intense enough to inspire floods of poetry (which he, evidently, did not see) and it lasted getting on for two years. One guesses it was Monica's only such relationship at Oxford. Given relaxed wartime mores, and the plentiful supply of prophylactics among the military, it may have been consummated but, in light of the course of the first five years of her relationship with Philip, probably not.

6

Teaching for England, 1943–1945

'we left and were glad to be going'

Philip to Monica, 1975

In her final year, Monica dedicated herself to hard work. Among the handful of women in her year she gratified her tutors and college(s), gave her parents bragging rights, and boosted her own sense of worth with a 'top' first. This at a time when the degrees were not handed out, as the wartime phrase was, with the rations. They were printed in *The Times*, the paper of record, as national events. As a graduate of distinction, Monica could have gone on to do a B.Litt – a short dissertation. But she did not want to. There was something oppressive to her about Oxford. She did not, in 1943, like the place, although, in later life, she could be sentimental about it. One of her friends, Yvonne, put her dislike in a 'brilliantly metaphorical' way that pleased Monica: 'You have gained the laurels while you disdained the tree.'

Larkin, like her a first-class graduate, also elected to put Oxford behind him in 1943, rather than enrolling for a B.Litt as his closest friend Kingsley would do. He wrote a congratulatory poem on their rejecting Oxford to Monica in later life:

City we shared without knowing
In blacked-out and bitterless days

Till we left and were glad to be going
(Unlike the arse-licker who stays).**

She too wrote a poem about being glad to leave Oxford. It opens

Oxford: Ite missa est†

Know then enchantress I am not for you
Many as you have taken in your net.

Monica Jones declined to be netted. Why these two young people who had excelled there should be so resolute to shake Oxford's dust off their shoes is odd. But evidently they felt out of place, grammar school products as they both were. But if they did not belong at Oxford, where then did they belong?

Something happened to Monica after gaining her first in summer 1943: pupa became butterfly. Not a British cabbage white, but one those giants, the size of bats, that flutter through the Amazon rainforest. Her dress became flagrant. She told Philip, aged twenty-eight: 'it is only recently that I have stopped thinking of myself as a depressing ugly duckling'. Her sartorial swanhood was the more remarkable in the era of clothes rationing, which lasted from 1941 until 1951. The clothes ration book's 66 coupons allowed a woman, annually: 'lined mackintosh or coat' (14 coupons); 'dress, or gown, or frock' (11 coupons); 'blouse, or cardigan, or jumper' (5 coupons); 'skirt, or divided skirt' (7 coupons); 'nightdress' (6 coupons); 'petticoat, or slip, or combination, or cami-knickers' (4 coupons) and a pair of stockings (2 coupons). That, Miss Jones, was it for a year.

Monica recalled how she and her mother once fell on a length of puce velvet like a couple of shear-wielding furies and ran up a skirt apiece in no time. A large portion of Lily's letters to her daughter are about making and mending clothes. Wartime habits die hard.

---

* He wrote this and gave it to Monica in 1975. It is quoted in biographies in a less frank version.

† The liturgical quotation means 'go, it has ended'.

Monica wore her unimportant underwear until it was falling apart. Philip, perversely, found the threadbare perforation exciting. A later, 1954 reminiscence, at the height of their early affair, is relevant:

> *You and your bottom* . . . I lay in bed one morning last week remembering one after-breakfast time when you were looking out of my kitchen window, and let me tuck your skirt up round your waist to be admired. You were wearing the black nylon panties with the small hole in!

He liked watching his lovers dress and undress. His lingerie expertise was sometimes lacking. Monica despised the 'synthetic silk' nylon which does not 'hole' but runs. She would mend the garments with deftly applied nail varnish.

Thanks to her skill with needle and sewing patterns (trained by her mother) Monica contrived to defy the ration book and be 'flamboyant' in defiance of state-stamped Utility. Monica's dress code was never utilitarian. Her clothes were expressive of herself. Her letters to Philip describe, in *couturier* detail, what outfit she is at that moment wearing and what she has worn earlier that day. A picture of her at Oxford catches her dressed to kill.

Monica spreads her wings

When I knew her, she wore high heels in the country walking from the station to her Tyneside cottage. It was agonising, she told Philip. Larkin cautioned her to tone down her clothing in the country; her town clothes suggested 'promiscuity', and it might be dangerous to be regarded as the 'hot bit' at the end of the village street.

The Parisian 'New Look' was the Anglo Saxon Utility brand's post-war challenge: Monica embraced it and makes reference to Christian Dior in her letters. Her wardrobe was *Résistance*, flaunting the new-look wasp waist and full bust. The first was more easily come by under ration-book austerity. It was harder to maintain when, as years passed, the shops were bursting with appetising edibles. Diet books helped after the ration-book years, as did the 'girdle' (less poetically the 'roll-on' corset, mentioned from time to time in Monica's letters). Her hair was exuberant and carefully dyed: many thought her a natural blonde.

Women sometimes disliked her dress in her prime. Anthony Thwaite quotes one stern critic, 'a former student now [2010] in her late seventies':

> In my then opinion, Miss Jones was very suspiciously blonde, very highly made-up . . . her tops were much too low at the front.

Despite such disapproval, which she must have sensed, Monica declined to dress down.

Having chosen not to stay at Oxford, Monica, in return for her 'real degree',* was contracted to teach school for two years. Larkin, after failing to get into the Civil Service did public library work. It counted, like Monica's schoolteaching, as reparation for his third year. Her teachers, Ethel Seaton and Helen Gardner, encouraged Monica to serve out her time in the classroom and then apply for university jobs, not specifically Oxford, when her time as a teacher was up. While thinking out her future and doing her national service she found

---

* It was a matter of private satisfaction to Philip that Kingsley, unlike him and Monica, got a 'short', two-year, first-class degree.

employment at Brereton Hall, a fine Grade One listed sixteenth-century mansion and estate in East Cheshire, which was in the process of transforming itself into a girls' boarding school.*

Brereton Hall is 70 miles from Kidderminster, so she lived in. This was no hardship, for she loved the northern landscape and Brereton had extensive grounds and farms. By the standards of the last years of the war, the accommodation was comfortable bordering on luxurious. More so by far than St Hilda's. Lily was amazed to learn that on the night of Monica's arrival they were served chicken – something at that time you were lucky to get once a year at Christmas. Having grown up sharing living quarters with a dozen family members, Lily sounded a warning note: 'It is usual in these old places that there are never enough bathrooms.'

Monica enjoyed the teaching and the power to devise a syllabus. She made extra money by giving personal tuition on elocution. A letter to a friend – also teaching to pay off her third year at Oxford – catches her upbeat mood at the Hall. Kay was teaching 'great louts' and having to hit them to preserve classroom order. 'Thank goodness I have girls,' wrote Monica, 'I don't think I could bring myself to clout them.' The letter contains chat about other former members of her small cohort at Oxford who were also teaching, and Ethel Seaton who, she says, has written a 'very, very horrible' letter to her: 'she says I have to go and do some research after the war.' Go back and do a B.Litt, that is. Monica wanted to move faster. She had started writing a book, for the general rather than the scholarly reader, on Crabbe. An early draft was sent via Seaton to Lord David Cecil, the master of light, high-table, Bloomsburyish scholarship. Cecil pronounced it too light.

Towards the end of her indentured schoolteaching Monica began applying to every university advertising a junior vacancy. Bedford and Kings College London, Birmingham and Durham all interviewed her. Her mother, while telling her what hat to wear and advising her to use her Oxford contacts, ordered the *Times Educational Supplement* to pick up any job advertisements Monica might have missed. She was

---

* It opened fully in 1946, by which time Monica was at Leicester.

offered nothing. Three things were against her. Firstly, she was now a schoolteacher, not a freshly brilliant graduate. 'Don't call yourself a teacher,' her father advised. But what else could she call herself? Secondly, she was too easily abashed and not a good interviewee. Thirdly, and most damagingly, by the time she put herself on the market all the men were returning in their demob suits to reclaim their jobs or claim, as heroes, any new posts which were going. Monica was being interviewed to the clamour of VE/VJ street parties and 'welcome back' banners. Should she hang on for a university job or settle for a cushy teaching job? Brereton Hall would certainly take her. There was, however, too strong a whiff of spinsterhood about girls' school teaching.

In some desperation she finally applied for a job at lowly University College Leicester in November 1945 and was appointed in January 1946 to an assistant lectureship with the prospect of tenure after a probationary three-year period. If, God forbid, she stayed that long. Philip Larkin was appointed eight months later as an assistant in the college library. For neither Oxford first was it a grand start in the university world.

7

Turbulent Leicester, 1946–1947

'the only rose in the bush'
                    Monica's mother to Monica, 1947

What, then, was this institution where Monica would spend the next thirty-seven years? University College Leicester, when she joined it, was an outpost of the University of London, along with far-away places with strange-sounding names like Rhodesia and Hong Kong. Such 'colleges' operated under the imperial sovereignty of London University's Senate House, that building in Malet Place which Orwell immortalised as the Ministry of Truth, John Wyndham pictured as the only place in the metropolis Triffid-proof, and Hitler wanted to make his chancellery once he'd stamped the jackboot on Britain.

UC Leicester was initially privately funded – as a tribute to the fallen of WWI. It was taken on by London in 1929 as a degree-awarding institution. It was, at the time, distinctly not Oxbridge. The core building had originally been a lunatic asylum. In my day a favourite undergraduate jest was '*post insano sano*'. Those up, as was I, with the 1960s sage R. D. Laing – famed for his (mad) theory (expounded in *The Divided Self*) that madness is the higher sanity – might think it the ideal site for a university. At least they'd taken the padding off the walls. There was even a Victorian cemetery across the road (and there were jokes about that, too).

Monica was interviewed, in late 1945, by Dr Arthur Collins, head of the UC Leicester English department. He was, in point of fact, the department in toto. With Monica's appointment the staff would consist of a senior lecturer in charge (him) and a probationary assistant lecturer (her). Leicester could thereby claim to be the first gender egalitarian English department in English university history. Five years on, when I arrived in 1960, Monica was still the only tenured female staff member, one among fifteen. It was clear gender bias (most of the students were female) but Monica never yearned for sisterly comrades. She later waxed furious about a sixties newcomer being young, aristocratically connected, and daring to wear too fashionable clothes.

By any objective assessment Monica was, in 1945, too good for Leicester as it then was. In his interview Collins must have been impressed by grande dame Helen Gardner's stately reference but also by the candidate. Her lively mind and . . . something else. There may have been some impropriety. Thirteen years later, on his deathbed in hospital, he recalled inquiring of the newly arrived Miss Jones whether what she was wearing so alluringly were red stockings or red tights. A strange thing to have on your mind as you prepare to meet your maker.

The relationship of the years that followed was surely innocent. But Collins's family evidently did not approve of Arthur's fondness for Miss Jones. They prevented her from seeing him in his last days, when he was dying in hospital. She was devastated and told Philip that Arthur meant as much to her as her father, who died at exactly the same time.

A piece of Collins's conversation with Monica survives. She was upset when Philip chided her for not knowing something about Coleridge. 'Ask Philip if he knows all the contents of the books on his shelves,' Collins told her. After his death, one of his daughters wrote: 'Of Philip he used to say "An honest man but quite mad in some ways".' 'He loved you very dearly', the same letter tells Monica. Lily had been aware of Collins's affection for her daughter, noting sardonically: 'One thing about Dr Collins, he doesn't hold the crime of youth against you.' She wanted Monica to find a young man to marry, not a father figure.

What Monica joined was, as has been said, not a university but an extramural college accredited and supervised by the long arm of London University. It had no independence. The college (as Monica always called it; it did not warrant the word 'university') was, in 1946, village-sized. In his obituary of Monica, Dick Watson describes her recalling that 'on Tuesdays the staff lunched together and the Principal gave out the pudding'. The 1946 English department comprised some thirty students.

Monica, alongside Collins, had a free hand on syllabus matters within London's broad parameters. She scorned the 'cabbage patch' approach to literary study. Her vision was generous and encompassing. The 'amateur tradition', Larkin called it. And for a few months Monica was queen of the roost as regards curriculum. Pedagogically they were the happiest months of Monica's life. The Monica and Arthur double act came to an abrupt end in 1947 with the arrival of Arthur Raleigh Humphreys.

UC Leicester, enthused by the country's victory, resolved to get full university status. To this end, from 1947–57 the emphasis was on growth. This was professionally the unhappiest decade of Monica's life. 'More will mean worse,' wrote Kingsley Amis in his albatross prediction for British universities. By 1950 Leicester would be five times its 1946 size and still growing. For Monica it meant bureaucratisation – not a word which would have come easily to her lips. Her colleagues in the newly created Sociology department could have explained it to her. In classic Weberian antithesis, Gemeinschaft had become Gesellschaft. Community had become corporation. Village had become office block. 'Worse' was the word for Monica. And in her view it got ever worse over the thirty-seven years of her university service.

The first stage in Leicester's big bang was a layer of professors, big men (all of them) tasked with the institutional mission of founding research. New departments were established. By 1960 Sociology had proved to be a national winner and, oddly, extraterrestrial rocketry under the dynamic Ken Pounds. The English department, too, was expected to aim for the stars, though at that time it was in truth a departmenticle whose staff (another male lecturer was appointed in 1947) could have been contained in a Gilbert Scott phone box with room for one more. True, too, there was nothing that could be called research emanating from Leicester's English department. But Monica, as letters from her mother reveal, was still seriously considering the book on Crabbe. And, as her lectures throughout her career witnessed, she was phenomenally well read.

The incumbent head of department, Arthur Simons Collins (b. 1899), was not Oxbridge but London. His doctoral thesis was published in 1928 under the title *The Profession of Letters: 1780–1832*. I read it on Monica's recommendation. Collins's scholarship had dated, but it was a creditable effort. Morally, he deserved the prospective chair in English. After all, by 1946 he had been running the department for twenty years. Instead, he was humiliatingly required to reapply for the headship he'd occupied since 1929. Who was Dr Collins going head to head with? It was a shortlist of two. Professor (already) Arthur Raleigh Humphreys was bright blue Cambridge. He was younger than Collins, in the early height of his career, and had published strongly.

Collins was as provincial as a Melton Mowbray pork pie: Humphreys cosmopolitan. He had studied pre-war at Harvard and come back to serve his country. He had a good war in Intelligence. Collins did not serve. In the year after the khaki election, that was unhelpful. Monica in later years was spiteful about Humphreys lapsing into 'officer mess talk' when he wanted to bully her. He was coming from a chair at Liverpool University and a department he had, in no time at all, put back on its post-war feet.

There was no real interview. Humphrey's appointment was wired in. And Leicester was lucky to get and keep him for thirty years. The students, however, did not see it that way when he was foisted upon them. A number of them were returned servicemen. They liked the glamorous teacher with the infectious literary enthusiasms. They liked fatherly Collins. They liked village-sized Leicester. Humphreys arrived in January 1947 to be met by a mutinous three-day strike, all the English students picketing the student gates. Was Monica with them? She was: shoulder to shoulder with the strike leader, Norman Sharpe.

Sharpe was a returned RAF pilot, glamorous, and nicknamed 'Bish' because he intended to be ordained after graduation. He recalls:

Monica and I had a mildly romantic interlude – not surprising, since I was almost two years her senior . . . it was quite a strain. A daunting encounter, and it did not last.

Monica, young lecturer, looking for love

Letters between Monica and her mother reveal the interlude was more than 'mild'. It occurred between autumn and winter 1946–47. Bish took her to a rugby game every week and church the day after. 'I grew to like it very much indeed,' Monica recalled of the rugger. She always relished the spectacle of men bashing men, on the pitch or in the ring. Monica's mother dearly hoped she would marry Bish. But, shrewd as ever, Lily suggested she might turn the crisis in the department to her advantage.

Don't set your mind against this new Head of the English Department. He may be a very nice young unmarried man . . . Never mind whether he is Cambridge or not. If you go the right way about it you'll probably get much of your own way about what to teach . . . There will at least be some rivals for Larkin and that other eligible young man [Bish]. They had better look out.

The student uprising blew itself out. Humphreys was the future of Leicester, the university to be. It was a mission he accepted and fulfilled. Collins's health collapsed and he took time off for what was officially described as shingles. Compounded, Larkin later hinted, by drink. But he accepted his wooden spoon and trudged on, unpromoted, to retirement in 1957. When he died, in his late fifties, Collins's daughter wrote to Monica:

> Nobody knows the cause of cancer but I feel that grief can cause it . . . he was desperately disappointed at losing the Chair but more grieved at the treatment by some of his colleagues.

If Collins paid with his life, Monica paid for her dissidence, in his cause, with her career. At the end of her three-year probation, Humphreys delayed making her a tenured lecturer. She brought it on herself. Her defiance took the form of declining to publish. It meant that later she was held at the bar (i.e. denied her grade increments on grounds of scholarly non-performance). For nearly four decades she shouldered more than her fair share of teaching. There were no complaints on that score. She believed in teaching but disbelieved in the careerism which was nowadays increasingly propelled by scholarly publication. She rationalised silence as protest. Against what? I've thought about Monica's life a lot and I think her willed refusal to publish, initially on principle, was an error. But I admired the way she diverted her intellectual creativity into what, when you come down to it, higher education in humanities is centrally about: knowing your material intimately and lecturing as an act of intellectual communion.

Her lecturing talent counted for nothing against the rattlingly empty CV and her original sin at the college gates in 1947. Her letters echo bitter complaint that she is lumbered with heavy classroom loads to free up colleagues to pursue their research. They were granted sabbaticals and promotion while she was the departmental galley slave, tied to her oar, lecturing on everything from Havelok the Dane to E. M. Forster until field specialists – always, until the 1970s, men – came along to filch those topics from her.

It rankles with me to this moment that for close on four decades Monica Jones, the most senior lecturer by age in the department, was denied the minimal promotion to Senior Lecturer: which at least would have been nominally appropriate. It was mean. The permanent denial cut a slice off the pension she lived on for her last nineteen years. The defence of Humphreys, from his wife Jean among others (who recalls what a good cook Monica was), is that Monica's promotion was turned down by the 'powers above'. As someone who ran English departments, I find this unconvincing. In those days heads of department were potentates, not middle management.

Humphreys had his reasons: and they were, it must be grudgingly admitted, good ones. She did not publish, therefore perish it must be. Humanely, of course. I understand his rectitude and acknowledge his good manners to her over the years. He was a just man. A redbrick Aristides. Miss Jones did not do what she was paid to and took half the year off not to do it. Larkin occasionally grizzled about the same delinquency. She had twenty-eight weeks a year free to broaden her mind with reading and (literally) cultivate the two gardens she had in later life. Philip, as head of an explosively expanding library at Hull University, was at work five and a half days a week, forty-nine exhausting weeks a year. Writing poetry was pushed to the side as something for evening hours.

Humphreys decreed Miss Jones could keep her job to the expiration of her contract. He would be kind and courteous, ensuring that colleagues followed his example. But she was the bad example. What would a department of twenty Monica Joneses be? What it had been in 1947. Lily congratulated her daughter in 1947 for being 'the only rose on the bush', but shrewdly she wondered whether Monica's stand-up fight with Humphreys over the Collins business had made him reluctant to take on more women. 'Do you think,' asked Lily, 'they have set their face against appointing a woman on your staff again?'

As time passed, Monica was regarded in the department as living-dead wood, mocked in the Staff Common Room behind her back as 'Mrs Larkin' or (for those who knew their Tennyson) 'Lady Shallot'. An exception could and should have been made, because Monica Jones was exceptional. Which of her colleagues is in the *Oxford Dictionary of National Biography* for services to literature? Not Humphreys, Arthur Raleigh, but Jones, Margaret Monica Beale.

8

Enter Larkin, 1946–1950

'When you first came to College do you remember how we talked and talked and did you think me a queer girl – you made all your own work – those were the nice hours'

Monica to Philip, 1952

Larkin arrived at Leicester, his first college post, in September 1946, as the Collins-Humphreys imbroglio was coming to the boil. He befriended Collins with his 'pipe-gnarled face' through Monica. Larkin was a connoisseur of defeat and Arthur Collins had been ruthlessly bested. What had the man given the best years of his life for? A belief in higher education which was now so much fuddy-duddy. A Collins/Jones novel formed embryonically in Larkin's mind. It was never finished, but its frame and details survive. They are less than flattering.*

Historically, Humphreys was the best thing that had ever happened to the Leicester English department. But in 1947 it was the worst thing for its sole woman member. Humphreys had a sense of the dimensions of English Studies, its new post-war directions, the growing strength of non-Oxbridge redbrick, and the subject's core energies. There was in this vision no room for Jacks-and-Jills-of-all-trades like Monica and Arthur Collins who merely *loved* literature and could

---

* The partial narrative is described by James Booth, JB 127–131 and printed as a supplement to his edition of Larkin's *Trouble at Willows Gables* (2002). See below, pp. 52–53.

communicate what they loved to students destined to get second-class degrees, with luck, from London University.

Humphreys trawled the profession for first-class appointments. He had an eye for quality. Richard Hoggart – author of the bestselling polemic *The Uses of Literacy*, which had triggered a national debate on 'culture' – was snaffled from Hull, who had underpromoted him. G. S. Fraser, a man of letters who had drunk with everyone in the London literary world, was high metropolitan – the polar opposite to Hoggart's crusading provincialism – and another constant butt of Monica's malice. Philip Collins, working in further education, had made himself the country's leading Dickensian. Tom Craik had been exposed to the stern doctrine of Leavisism* at Cambridge and as sternly rejected it. Ronald P. Draper brought Lawrentian provincial earnestness from Nottingham. Linguists, mediaevalists and Americanists were recruited. A full hand for ARH to play with. He made himself the department's leading Shakespearean and established a reputation as one of British universities' pioneer Americanists. That ARH had written a monograph on Melville inspired Philip to have a go at *Moby Dick*. It was as dire as he knew it would be.

Monica could never forgive what ARH had done to the department he 'stole' from Collins. Why, she asked me in 1965, does Arthur not go and get himself a Regius chair somewhere and leave us in peace? He could have done but didn't; he had dedicated himself, body and soul, to Leicester. And he left a first-class department behind him. They should name a large building after him.

Monica and Philip had arrived at Leicester within a few months of each other. She to a department of two, he to a library staff of three full-timers, serving a student body of 220. An academic Lilliput. She caught Philip's eye and ear before he knew her. Who was that *talkative* girl? is the first known thing he said about her. Monica's first conscious sight of Philip is recalled by a librarian friend, Pamela Hanley. It was early spring 1947: they were in the Tatler – a coffee shop in the London Road for whom the word percolator probably suggested a

---

* i.e. the school of F. R. and Q. D. Leavis and their journal, *Scrutiny*.

surgical procedure. It was still serving its dreary brew in my day.

'Who is that man sitting by himself?' Monica asked Pamela one lunchtime. When told, 'Her acid observation [was] that he looked like a snorer . . . a characteristic remark, made probably because of his large nose.' 'Snorer' is Hanley's mishearing for 'schnorrer': slang Yiddish for worthless Jew. Monica was casually anti-Semitic in her conversation. As she would later be in her letters to Philip.[*]

Larkin's first visual impression was that she 'had fair hair, black horn spectacles dresse[d] rather specially and was . . . quite small'. They had, they were delighted to discover, cohabited Oxford over exactly the same war-disrupted years, a few hundred yards apart, their names jostling in 1943 on the same first-class list. How could she be so invisible at Oxford and spectacularly visible – and audible – at Leicester?

To those around them 'they embodied the glamour of Oxbridge', Hanley recalls. Larkin was soon seen 'walking out' with Monica, his long (6ft 1in) lope and her short (5ft 4in) high-heeled trot. For the first few months Philip had kept his spirits up with funny, angry, despondent letters to his absent mates, notably Kingsley and Jim Sutton. Gradually he slipped into the group centred round Monica and discharged a greater portion of his wit in conversation over evening pints.

Looking back, he described himself as a 'time wasting young swine' but he manifestly enjoyed wasting time in company with Monica and her pals. Some of the male company, having lost seven years to the war, were older than their teachers, on first-name terms with them and used to mess bonhomie. Gradually Philip alienated Monica's affections from Bish. Monica's mother's interest had been raised by the reported fact that her daughter now had two highly eligible young men interested in her: a poet and a warrior-priest. For a while the three of them went to Saturday rugby games together. Rugby was not Larkin's sport, but he told better stories, made funnier jokes than Norman, and drank well. Monica despised men who got 'tight' too

---

[*] See the Afterword for Monica's anti-Semitism and Larkin's disquiet on her prejudice.

fast. Bish finally gave up and married another student in July 1948.

From the start, Philip and Monica had a livelier relationship than current biography records. In 1946 their letters began: 'My dear Monica' and 'My dear Philip'. He called on her (by day, not night) in her lodgings, but was careful. He would hide if anyone else dropped by. The fact that his bicycle was propped up outside rather gave the game away.

The first extant letter from him [26 December 1946] to her is a courtly request that she cast an eye over the proof-copy of his imminently to be published novel, *Jill*. It was too late for correction, but comment would be valued, and pray, Monica, be frank. The novel is set in the exact three years they were both at Oxford. Philip reminds Monica, however, that it is a 'lending copy' – the true Larkin touch. He wanted it back. The exchange was, nonetheless, a masonic handshake. They had a bond above Leicester. They were Oxford dark-blue in heart and mind.

A four-year relationship followed, as elegant as an eighteenth-century minuet, from that imaginary handshake to the first act of love in July 1950. Letters were largely unrequired: they saw each other whenever they felt like it at their place of work. But for his first published novel, enshrining 'their' Oxford, Larkin wanted a presentational ceremony. A courtly letter.

Ceremony and Oxford likewise figure in Monica's first surviving letter to Philip. Five years after graduation she was now eligible for her MA. She writes to tell him she is going up to the university (from whichever point of the compass you approach Oxford it is always 'up'). She apologises for not having said goodbye, but 'things mounted up' and she has forgotten to bring her 'gownery'. Will he kindly, as an Oxonian favour, take it down from the hook on the back of her office door, parcel it up and post it to her?

The request wouldn't have been much of an imposition, given that he made regular visits to the post office to send his washing back to his mother. But for Monica to set off to Oxford for a degree award only to discover she'd forgotten her cap and gown seems an unlikely amnesia.

The letter continues, informing him that she will be attending the ceremony 'in the company of a friend I hate'. Not 'someone I hate' but a hated friend. Like him wanting his lending copy back, it's a telltale detail. Philip, already, was a friend she didn't hate. She has, she tells him, decided to skip the celebratory 'Gaudy' (college feast) and that 'chattering soulless mob' she found *utterly* hateful. Like him, she still resented Oxford.

She includes what will be leitmotifs in their epistolary relationship: principally what she was at that very moment wearing, or about to put on. 'I have new winter shoes of yellow suede', she tells him, 'and £5 they cost; isn't it outrageous?' And, another refrain through future years, she shudders at the thought of the imminent socialist government: 'It is all terrible and makes me *sick*' that they will have to pay 'A. Bevan's five shillings a week' for a National Health Service.

Larkin was captivated by her mind and offered the corrigible proofs of his forthcoming novel, *A Girl in Winter*. It was an act of singular trust. But what did he, privately, think of Monica in the years after first meeting her? During this period Larkin saw himself as a novelist in the making, not the poet he became. And he used his current fiction-in-progress to look from different angles at the women in his life. There were currently two of them, each with a never to be published novel featuring them as heroine.[*]

Monica was portrayed in the clandestine work called provisionally 'A New World Symphony'. The draft survives in substantial fragments. The patchy narrative opens in Easter 1948. Vacation. Augusta Bax is showing her mother round the campus – identifiably twenty-five-year-old Monica and Leicester. The reader is given a disagreeable pen portrait of both women, particularly Monica. She is 'febrile, red-haired and jewel wearing'. In the early morning she looks washed-out, a 'slum brat'. But when made up she achieves a fragile prettiness, light-boned and thin-wristed. Her great fear is lest her front teeth should give out: she is calcium-deficient and the back ones are far gone already. She talks too much and hates people she

---

[*] The other woman in his life, Ruth Bowman, is discussed later, pp. 58–62 and 76–77, and the unpublished novel about her that he was writing along with 'A New World Symphony' on p. 64.

lodges with. 'Slum brat' strikes a harsh note. Monica had told him (the son of Sydney Larkin, OBE) about her working-class parental origins. He sniffs, snobbishly. But privately.

Augusta Bax is, as was Monica Jones in Easter 1948, an 'assistant lecturer', up for tenure after three years' probation. Her hopes are pinned on Dr Butterfield (transparently Arthur Collins) landing the English department's headship. Butterfield has a soft spot for her. They are like-minded about life and literature. But chances are Butterfield will not be able to get Augusta, or himself, over the stile. Her future does not look hopeful, though the novel hints (not least in its title) it could be triumphant if she were to escape her dull, second-rate college. Which she does. 'A New World Symphony' was, as much as anything, Larkin getting things straight in his mind as regards Monica. The portrait of Augusta Bax has a devil's advocacy feel to it: what was the case to be made against this woman? If completed and published as its existing fragmentary form predicts, 'A New World Symphony' would have been, as Booth says, libellous and hurtful.[*] But Larkin kept 'A New World Symphony' on the go and as late as 1953, after Monica had become his lover, he was thinking of doing something with it. It raises an aspect of him which is seen recurring through his life: he could be fascinated by a woman, ostensibly love her and be devoted to her for years, but never, entirely, admire her. Or even, sometimes, entirely like her.

Monica did not know what Philip was secretly thinking and writing about her, any more than she knew four years later he would joyously collaborate with Kingsley Amis on lampooning her in a novel called *Lucky Jim*. 'Augusta Bax' and 'Margaret Peel' were both versions of Monica Jones and expressions of Larkin's apparently unresolvable ambivalence about her. It's something hard to untangle psychologically but part of him, one suspects, resented her for making him love her.

---

[*] For the reflections the fragmentary text contains on Monica and anti-Semitism see pp. 246–247.

9

Love, Life and Letters, 1946–1950

'You are a brilliant letter writer'
Philip to Monica, 1972

There are only a few letters between Philip and Monica in their Leicester years. But they grow increasingly intimate as they saw more of each other face to face. In summer 1947 he was in Oxford taking his librarian exams and catching up with old friends. She sent him a many-thousand-word, three-day serial letter. She has, she tells him, been 'deported' on a retreat for women staff. She must give a talk on Crabbe. She'll dutifully 'churn out' the required 'dreary stuff'. The jaunt convinces her, surrounded as she is by yahoos, that the arch-misanthropist Swift 'is the greatest mind of all time'. Humanity is awful. She lets rip on the theme. The journey on the train (British Rail, nationalised!) coats her in filth in the first half-hour and her colleagues' chatter means 'I have only managed 10 clues of my Times crossword'.

Already in the train she sees herself, self mockingly, as 'rather a picture of helpless femininity or summat'.* What Galahad will rescue her? The countryside is too lushly Du Maurier's *Frenchman's Creek*, green marshmallow, for her hilly northern taste; 'what a place to be brung to!' There is a comically gloomy letter from him awaiting her. Playing the psychiatrist, she advises him, mock-seriously, 'to turn the

---

* In her early letters to Philip, Monica often affects a cod Yorkshire accent.

bad into summat positive'. Sod 'Dover Beach', she continues. The sea
round where they are billeted like wartime evacuees 'has a black soul
. . . Oh Philip, this bloody sea! It keeps coming in and coming.' The
noise is 'hellish'. Pubs? 'Nary a one.'

She is 'incarcerated in a Cornish cove in a congeries of cretins'. One
of the company – Marie by name – calls her, to her face, 'an affected
little bitch'. Monica smiles. The letter strikes the keynote of what will
be her side of a thirty-five-year correspondence: occasionally hilarious, written to the lived moment, and calculatedly disgraceful. 'You
have style: and that is sufficient,' was Larkin's later judgement.

As regards style, Monica's eye is always on the latest, post-war,
fashion. 'Do you', she asks Philip, 'have any opinion for the great
forum on the length of the new [i.e. Parisian 'New Look'] skirt?'.
Monica rejoices in the release from the years of wartime 'sacking'
and uniformity. In 1949 she tells Philip that 'it seems strange to be
wearing anything of silk at all'. But, when it comes to stockings, 'these
false laboratory silks [nylons] do not count as anything'. Her mum
has made her a pair of pyjamas in 'aggressively slimy satin . . . I do like
to indulge my gaudier tastes in bed, & that sounds a bit equivocal'.

In three years she has come from discussing Oxford gowns to silk
pyjamas. 'Equivocal' is not the word. Mainly quotidian matters are
dealt with elsewhere. Shall they go with Bish to see the Wallabies
[Australian rugby team] in 1947? No. In summer she keeps up with
the test matches – 1948, against Australia for the Ashes, is a nail-biter;
Hutton and Compton vs Bradman and Miller. In one of his (lost)
letters, Philip in 1949 declares he wishes he could throw it all away, in
a grand Lawrentian gesture, and take up the peasant life. 'How right
you are about farming,' she jauntily replies, not meaning a word of
it. 'I feel it is the only honest life; real good-earthish I feel. Do get a
small-holding & I will come as a hired girl so long as I am not asked
to do anything on poultry' (a reference to her lifelong ornithopho-
bia). It requires a heroic effort of imagination to see Monica Jones in
land-girl uniform unless Dior designed it.

She gives him her illicit copy of the forbidden lesbian classic, *Well
of Loneliness*. Is she? No. She isn't. He gets his first camera – a Puma
Plus – precursor of the famous second-hand Rolleiflex five years later.

She would like some 'really classy photographs' from him. She will, over the years to come, get to know Philip's lenses well, and they her. She writes to thank him for a 1949 Christmas present – perfume. Always his favourite present for a woman he was sexually interested in. Collins has given her a tartan stole which she will, doubtless, wear when lecturing on *Macbeth* and Sir Walter Scott. ARH gives a less welcome present. She has now been in post for three years: the normal probationary period. But she will not be tenured to the rank of lecturer. Why not? Because she has defiantly given ARH no plans of future publication. 'Before Christmas', she tells Philip, foot-stampingly:

> I received a letter from Humphreys which annoyed me a good deal. I have just now replied, in a style which made it a letter I should not care to receive. But I do doubt that he will perceive any sting in it. You'd need to say to him plainly that his letter was insufferably impertinent & indeed insulting, as well as being totally without consideration.

Looking back over the slender surviving correspondence between them during the years 1946–1950, what signifies is that Philip kept her letters and she his. Significant too is the gradual warming of their terms of address and farewell. To begin with it is 'Dearest Philip' and 'Monica' or 'M'. A year on she signs off 'Yours till the stars lose their glory'. By Christmas 1949 her farewell is 'Yours always'. Prophetic.

10

'A Perfect Friendship', 1946–1950

'I am not a philanderer'
Philip to Monica, 1967

The title of this chapter is what Monica, looking back, called the four years, 1946–50 that followed her and Philip's first encounters. It was the only period in their thirty-five-year working lives when they were able to see each other, should they want to, every working day. They were something more than colleagues but as yet something less than lovers. Neither was sexually experienced or adventurous. On a trip with her to the Lake District in summer 1948 Philip, in drink apparently, made a move and was repulsed. The episode resurfaces as Jim's drunken bedroom lurch at Margaret in *Lucky Jim*.

Why, though, did Monica not let herself 'go all the way', as the phrase then was? Philip, one suspects, would, after a hesitation or two, have been willing – particularly with drink inside him. Ambition must have been one of Monica's reasons for being 'coy', as their admired Marvell put it. She had hopes of an academic career. Oxford, preferably. Helen Gardner had spent six years labouring in redbrick before being called back. Marriage and children did not combine with academic achievement for a woman. Cyril Connolly's pram in the hall was more doom for them than men because women pushed the damned perambulator every day to and from the shops.

What Monica meant by 'perfect' was passionate celibacy. Evidence suggests she did not make love to a man until the age of twenty-eight

(1950).* Larkin was virginal until he was twenty-three. Not from timidity on her part but policy. Not from lack of desire on his part but ineptitude. Why didn't Larkin push more resolutely to go all the way, as brash Kingsley Amis would have done? Because Philip was otherwise engaged. Literally. Monica must surely have suspected there were things he wasn't telling her. And, in fact, he never did tell her the unvarnished story. Philip Larkin was not a confessing kind of man.

Philip's undercover fiancée, Ruth Bowman, was, from 1945–1949, a student in London, reading English and taking a diploma in education, aiming to teach school after graduation. Their relationship, as Philip paid restrained court to Monica and she was falling in love with him, was clandestine but, since 1945, fully sexual. In his Leicester years, Philip saw Ruth on weekends in still bombed-out London. The melancholy townscape was appropriate. They made furtive love, fearing the vigilant landlady's eye or too loud creaking of the bedsprings. He wrote to Ruth twice a week – she as often to him. All his letters, four hundred of them, were burned later by order of her grandfather. He had never liked that Mr Philip Larkin messing about with his young Ruth.

It's useful, for Monica's story, to review Larkin's idiosyncratic sexual practice. He was evolving it in the four years of 'perfect friendship' with Monica in Leicester and premarital sex, in London, with Ruth. Larkin had been a highly sexed, but furiously frustrated, schoolboy: he was shy, stammering when nervous, poor-sighted, not handsome, prematurely balding, no sportsman, and lacking in daring. His schoolboy fantasies were carried into his university years. As late as 1943, aged twenty-one, staying with his parents in Coventry, he could write to Amis:

I would give all I possess
(Money keys wallet personal effects and articles of dress)

---

* I make the assumption that the Oxford relationship with Arnold was not consummated.

To stick my tool
Up the prettiest girl in Warwick King's High School.

This is not – to be blue-nosed about it – mature adult desire. And if ventured, even as a tentative fumble, in the real world it would have landed Larkin in jail.

Larkin's first completed works of fiction were written at Oxford. He was still sex-starved and they are fantasias about girls' schools in which cricket, spanking and underwear figure.* In the days of gender-segregated education many boys' imaginations ran that kind of riot, although few wrote novels about it. As pornography, this juvenilia with its hole-in-the-changing-room-wall peeping seems innocuous compared to what schoolboys share on their iPhones nowadays. Their interest is that in the period of their 'perfect friendship' Monica weaned Philip from juvenile into adult sexuality. She grew him up. She involved his mind, not his mental fantasies, in sex.

It was a major achievement. Larkin had met Ruth Bowman during the summer of 1943, in his first job as a twenty-one-year-old librarian in a Shropshire public library. Like Monica's schoolteaching, the work qualified as public service in return for his 'full' three-year degree course. In 1943 Ruth was a sixteen-year-old schoolgirl: possibly younger. She was far from being, as Philip had lusted, the prettiest girl in school (in this case, Wellington High School for Girls). Larkin's municipal employers would have been displeased at a girlfriend so close to the legal age of consent (sixteen); her schoolteachers, when they picked up what was going on, disapproved. Ruth defied them.†

In Larkin's novel *Jill* the schoolgirl object of desire, based on Ruth, is fifteen – the hero is labelled by his Oxford mates a 'baby snatcher', sexually criminal. Fifty years later, his letters to Ruth were long gone, as was Philip, leaving her in control of the narrative of their relationship. In age, with a sad life behind her, she romanti-cised her first love. She and Philip were two naïve young people,

---

* The first description of Larkin's juvenilia was by Andrew Motion. James Booth gives a fuller description in the chapter 'Brunette Coleman' (JB 58–81).
† Larkin delayed full sexual relations with Ruth until she was eighteen.

feeling their way towards physical completion. Ruth was, Larkin told his friend Jim Sutton, at the time 'the only girl I have met who doesn't instantly frighten me away'. It was low praise. While moving, as he promised her, towards marriage with Ruth, Larkin was enjoying a relationship on a higher plane with years older, degrees cleverer, Monica Jones. She did frighten him a bit and always would. Monica could hold her own, and sometimes trump him, on Hardy, Katherine Mansfield, Lawrence or whoever Philip's latest literary god was.

Monica was sexy. That was her campus identity at Leicester. When their relationship was fully established Monica posed, both for Larkin's many lenses (specs and camera) and private delectation, as a Playboy Playmate. Philip's interest in Monica 'posed and photographed' was a central pleasure to him in their early relationship. Larkin was an early reader of *Playboy* magazine. His taste in pornography was connoisseurial, not brutal. But by no stretch of even a fifth-former's fantasy could Ruth Bowman have posed as a 'Playmate of the Month'. She was shy, NHS bespectacled, thoroughly nice, and partially disabled. Nor could she yet talk sophisticatedly about literature. Monica won out as regards glamour and mind.

'Heavy petting', as Larkin called it, was the sexual regime with Ruth for two years. It was safe practice before the 1960s pill, when only married women could acquire the contraceptive diaphragm, and backstreet abortion was criminal and dangerous. And heavy petting represented commitment, unlike the buccaneering sex of the Kingsley Amis kind. As Larkin protested over and again: 'I am not a philanderer.' 'All the way' had risks: unwanted children and unwanted marriage. That was what happened to Kingsley during Philip's relationship with Ruth. Monica would have a couple of pregnancy scares in the early years of her later full relationship with Philip. Heavy petting, however, was never on her menu.

Ruth had a wracking pregnancy scare after the couple's first sex. It took place as she left school to embark on her undergraduate studies in English at King's College London, in October 1945. Kingsley offered to get his mate condoms 'if that's what worring [sic] you'; they were hard to come by at that time without embarrassment. Kingsley should have heeded his own advice: his teenage girlfriend Hilary got pregnant in December 1947, forcing them into marriage a couple of months later. The child was named after his godfather, Philip.

As a prelude to his and Ruth's inaugural love-making Philip wrote 'Wedding-Wind' about a young woman waking in bed, her first morning as a married woman. Monica told him 'Wedding-wind I like extremely', not, apparently, knowing its inspiration or that it had coincided with a fearful pregnancy scare, which, had it not turned out to be a false alarm, would very likely have meant forced marriage – assuming Philip did the right thing.

There was a cascade of life-changing events for Philip in 1948, in the same period as Kingsley's marriage. Philip's father died on Good Friday. He wrote informing Monica with the emotional frigidity, born of dread, which marked all his engagements with death. 'Is it natural to like work?' he pointlessly inquired, before mentioning the passing of the most important man in his life. Ruth, the most if not increasingly second-most important woman in his life, had a twenty-first birthday in mid-May. She could now marry without parental consent. Philip proposed, was accepted and gave his now fiancée a ring (cost: ten guineas). As he told his confidant, Jim Sutton, it was a 'rather odd' thing to do. Having given him her all for three years, Ruth may not have thought so.

In August, Philip, now the man of the Larkin family, helped buy a house in Leicester, to set up home with his widowed mother. She paid for the house. It seems Eva did not know of Philip's intention to set up home with Ruth at some vaguely future point. Or bring her to Leicester. This life-death-love maelstrom was the prelude to two of the most miserable years of Larkin's life.

In future Larkin would scrupulously avoid the ring wrangle, or proposals. Such things implied going somewhere in the relationship, and love with Larkin was a journey without destination. You became, as Monica later put it, a 'situation', fixed, like a developing photograph, at midpoint. Philip was never an engaged man again. A later cagey remark to Monica clarifies his love policy: 'I would sooner marry you than anyone else I know'. But to actually place himself behind 'the wallbars of matrimony'? Never. Larkin, after the 1940s, loved women plurally. There was always, with and after Ruth, more than one love of his life to juggle train tickets for and exchange letters with. These visits and letters kept on the go conflicting relationships, which never went, in the larger sense, anywhere.

II

Monica Boxed, 1949–1950

'He didn't half keep his life in compartments'
Kingsley Amis, 1986

The above observation by Kingsley Amis, on Philip's death, was shrewd. Philip boxed and coxed everything in his life. The two largest boxes were Poet and Librarian. Philip joked about it: looking up at his years of collected departmental meeting minutes on his office shelf he would point to his 'collected works'. Fat ring-binders and slim volumes. In his *Who's Who* entry he designated himself 'Librarian and Poet'.

The boxes into which he segmented his life contain starkly different pop-up Larkins. He was, Monica realised early on, chameleonesque:

When you say how alike you and I are I think of the many respects in wh we are unalike. Old chameleon Larkin. All things to all men indeed!

In this respect he was like Kingsley, who, on one of their rare meetings with Monica, tried to win her over with a show of his faces like Jim Dixon's in *Lucky Jim*. It misfired. Monica judged his performance as substanceless masquerade. Philip and Kingsley were, both of them, hollow men, one of whom Monica had chosen to love. And it was in his letters to Monica that Philip was most nearly himself. As Jonathan Raban observes: 'It is in the letters to Monica Jones that Larkin seems to be writing without the aid of props, mask or accent.'

In the four years he was coming to know Monica the literary box most important to Larkin was 'novelist'. He told Jim Sutton he 'went on trying in the 1945–1950 period' to complete a third novel: but couldn't beyond drafts. 'Why I stopped', he said, 'I don't really know, it was a great grief to me'.* I would like to think it was Monica who helped push him towards poetry, his true métier. She never thought supremely highly of his fiction and made no secret of it while correcting the text of *Jill* for its reprint in 1963.†

There was a shock for the women in Philip's life in the 1940s when they discovered what, as aspirant novelist, he had written about them and stowed away in the novel-box. In 1999, James Booth showed Ruth the depiction of her as the 'cultureless provincial girl', Sheila Piggott, in his fragmentary novel 'No for an Answer'. The poor, now aged, woman crumpled. How could Philip have done it when she fondly believed they were at the time all in all to each other? Had he secretly despised her?

When Booth came 'barging in' on Monica at around the same time – shortly before her death – to introduce grossly unflattering Augusta Bax, her reaction was laconic: Philip Larkin had never been 'straightforward'. 'He lied to me, the bugger, but I loved him,' she had told Motion. Had the biggest box of all been opened, the one containing his journals, it might have been the key to all the others and the revelation of the real Larkin under all the chameleon colorations. Or the fact that there was, *au fond*, no real Larkin. Like Joanna Southcott's, that tell-all box never will be opened, even at the end of days. Monica destroyed it: leaving her fifty-four boxes in its stead.

Did Larkin, as Alan Bennett pungently proclaimed, merely 'use' his women as a necessary box of sexual disposables? The defence case, which I find persuasive, is that Larkin really did love the women

---

* James Booth deals with this stoppage in Chapter 7 of *Life, Art and Love*, 'Just too Hard for Me'. One possible reason is that in collaborating with Kingsley Amis he realised his friend was better than he at fiction, but not, most critics would say, as a poet.

† See below, p. 164.

in his life, even concurrently. He was not a philanderer (like Dylan Thomas); nor a predator (like some modern-day Earl of Rochester); not a satyr like Kingsley. He was, to use the word he never would, a polyamorist.

Modern life is not set up to accommodate male polyamory. Larkin formed his own doctrine on the lines of the folkloric rhyme:

Hogamous, Higamous,
Man is polygamous,
Higamous, Hogamous,
Woman's monogamous.

Men, the ditty avers, can love (genuinely) more than one woman, multiply, simultaneously, or serially. Female monogamy is nonetheless de rigueur – at least in the man's world which was the world Larkin lived in and strongly resented losing in his later years. He avoided married women because you only got a slice of them. He broke that rule only once, disastrously, with Patsy Strang in the early fifties. It produced an unwanted pregnancy. Had the child not died unborn, Philip might have been moved (after Patsy's inevitable divorce) into marriage and a less poetic life. A boxed-in existence of no interest to Larkin whatsoever.

What would a man of his disposition rather leave? Children or poems? Larkin gives the uncompromising answer in 'Dockery and Son'. Larkin's sexual praxis is selfish, and at times cruel. Monica saw that and, with recurrent distress and breakdown, accepted it. It was, together with the positive things she did for and with him, part of her contribution to the great poetry of her nation.

Larkin was a selfish lover. Ruth had no recorded relations with anyone else while with Philip – not even, as best we know, at university. Maeve Brennan, Monica's great rival for seventeen years, had to dispose of her fiancé before partnering Philip and thereafter never seriously strayed. Larkin's organisational rule was dispersal, on the 'wife in every port' principle. He could keep his relationships with Maeve and Monica alive for nearly two decades, and Ruth and Monica for five years, because they were in different places. But they were never so distant from him as to make them hard to reach at weekends when convenient. Frequently exchanged letters were as necessary as the diver's airline.

Larkin's pockets were tight. It was imperative his women should have an independent income. The letters with Monica over the decades record tiny cheques, and banknotes as small as ten-bob, being repaid by her for expenses run up on holiday or borrowed at weekends with the banks closed. Larkin needed women, but he never supported a woman: not even his widowed mother. Her dead husband's insurance paid her way. Philip's correspondence is peppered with penny-pinching complaints about the incidental costs of love. An early, but typical example, writing to Kingsley, is an account of his taking future fiancée Ruth to a jazz club, picking up the tab, and being later denied sex:

> Don't you think it's ABSOLUTELY SHAMEFUL that men have to pay for women without BEING ALLOWED TO SHAG the women afterwards AS A MATTER OF COURSE? I do: simply DISGUSTING. It makes me ANGRY . . . It's all a fucking balls up. It might have been planned by the army, or the Ministry of Food.

The total for the night's entertainment came to 11/3d (51p). Apparently Larkin was not making fun of himself. In his memoir, written after his friend's death, Amis claims Larkin told him that if the night out cost as much as fifteen shillings, masturbation was a better deal than a date. And took less time.

It was vital that the women who shared Philip Larkin should never cross each other's paths – or, worst of all, talk about him between themselves. Judgements about Larkin the lover were never compared by his sexual partners. Ruth and Monica never met. Monica didn't have a mutually knowing relationship with Maeve until Larkin's last days. She suspected 'bloody Patsy'* but was given nothing firm to go

---

* Patsy Strang, one of his lovers, along with Winifred Arnott, when he was working in Belfast in the 1950s.

on. Philip almost had his cover blown when, during an accidental meeting of Monica and Winifred Arnott in Belfast, he realised he had given both women the same perfume.

For some time neither Maeve nor Monica knew that Philip's last lover – for ten years – was yet another woman who worked in the Hull library. By this stage of his life he was as skilled in covering his tracks as a cat burglar. Wearily at the end of her life, when she knew enough, if not all, Monica concluded he was constitutionally 'unstraightforward'. And her? She had been faithful but not unconditionally loyal. 'His mother', she told James Booth, 'gave him loyalty. But I don't think it's good for anybody, that kind of thing.'

12

Unhappy Family, 1948–1950

'Mum is at the bottom of all this'
Philip Larkin, 1957

As Monica says, there was another, inertly powerful, woman in Larkin's life: his mother Eva. After his father's early death in 1948 – an event of psychic shock for Philip – he was the man of the family. Manhood released him into finally proposing marriage, to Ruth. The patriarchal inhibitor was dead. But with manhood came responsibility. His sister, Kitty, could look after herself, but not his mother. Eva was well pensioned but emotionally needy. The rational thing was to put his ducks in a row. He did so by bringing Eva from Coventry where his childhood and, perhaps her marriage, were – to borrow the word he uses in the poem 'I Remember, I Remember' – 'unspent' to Dixon Drive, Leicester (the street which gave lucky Jim his surname).

The ménage proved disastrous: his mother was a muse killer. It produced one fine poem: about the huge gulf yawning, all the time, between them.

'That was a pretty one,' I heard you call
From the unsatisfactory hall
To the unsatisfactory room where I
Played record after record, idly,

Wasting my time at home, that you
Looked so much forward to.

Oliver's Riverside Blues, it was.

Monica was walking distance away from Dixon Drive; there were friendly meetings but Miss Jones was never introduced as Philip's soon-to-be-wife, any more than Ruth had been. Of his women, Eva liked daughterly Maeve Brennan best. Maeve's life, other than Philip, was caring for her aged parents. Maeve was unthreatening. Monica and Eva did not get on beyond cool politeness. As early as 1951 Eva was uneasy about her son and Monica's attraction for each other. Even when later in life she was living in Loughborough and Philip was in Hull, Eva did Philip's washing, which he brought by suitcase. On one occasion a basque of Monica's was accidentally mixed with his underwear. There is no record of Monica ever washing Philip's clothes.

Philip made no effort to warm his mother's and Monica's relationship. It was a small blessing for Monica that she did not have to eat too often at Eva's table. After one of Mrs Larkin's meals, she said the unlucky diner needed to lie down: not to digest, but to recover. She herself could play the kitchen range like Yehudi Menuhin. Philip was careful to tell his mother how much better her cooking was than Monica's. It was a hollow compliment.

Eva's widowhood was thirty years, and many meals, long. While she lived, Philip gave Monica to infer that he could not, with the burden of his mother alongside 'the toad work' on his shoulders, think of marriage. But the way might be open after Eva died. Monica had her own reticence: she wanted to get married, she said, but she hated the idea of 'getting married'. That awful ritual of bondage and relegation to handmaid status revolted her.

In June 1960 it was Eva who introduced Maeve to Monica when all three were assembled to watch Philip officiate at the Queen Mother's opening of the new library. Eva had taken to Maeve, and Maeve recalls, plausibly '[Eva] hoped he would marry me'. There was no such hope recorded about Miss Jones.

When Mrs Larkin did die, in 1977, aged ninety-one, Monica lamented that she was now too old for Philip to take to wife – advantage to seven years younger Brennan. It would pain Monica over the decades they were lovers that she was not an entirely welcome guest on the two big Philip 'festivals' in Eva's house: Philip's birthday and Christ's. But at least she was spared the meals.

13

Happy Family, 1946–1959

'lots of love from we two'

Monica's father to her at university, 1943

When she left home for Oxford, and then Oxford for Brereton Hall, Monica was, her letters confirm, close and loving with her parents, and they mutually with her. Neither of her parents had had more than nineteenth-century early-school-leavers' education, but Lily was, culturally, self-improving. In January 1954 she listened solemnly to the BBC recording of Dylan Thomas's *Under Milk Wood*, Richard Burton's noble baritone gracing it. She discussed it with Monica who, like Philip, had a soft spot for Dylan. Lily also made a stab at Eliot's *The Waste Land* – and listened to Benjamin Britten on the Third Programme. The Joneses attended WEA (Workers' Educational Association) classes.

After Monica met Philip in 1946 her stated feelings about her parents accommodated over the years to his phobia about home and family and his much-quoted belief that they 'fuck you up, your mum and dad'. Monica gradually bought into his jaundiced domestic opinions and echoed them. Whether her views honestly changed in her thirties or she put it on to humour Philip is unclear. I believe the latter. In her letters to him, after she and Philip first made love in 1950 and before her parents died in 1959, she is severe, sometimes snide about Lily and Fred: she was a less fond daughter than she had been – at least in her letters to Philip. The letters between her and her mother remained fond and daughterly, judging by Lily's surviving return mail.

Larkin's views were clear and intransigent. 'Home', 'Mummy' and 'Daddy' were something to escape from and marriage something to avoid. Larkin's prejudices on the matter are expressed most thoughtfully in 'Dockery and Son', most forthrightly in 'Self's the Man':

> *Oh, no one can deny*
> *That Arnold is less selfish than I.*
> *He married a woman to stop her getting away*
> *Now she's there all day,*
>
> *And the money he gets for wasting his life on work*
> *She takes as her perk*
> *To pay for the kiddies' clobber and the drier*
> *And the electric fire . . .*

The poem continues in the same marriage-hating vein for six stanzas.

Monica still saw a lot of her parents in her early Leicester years, spending every vacation and break in Stourport on Severn. In the 1950s, her parents' last decade, Monica scatters observations about them in her letters to Philip. Designed to please him, one might assume, they can be harsh. Her father was 'jocular' but abrupt with it, both to her and her mother. He had a workman's sharp workplace wit. 'Father', she said, 'is not an easy man.' He always wanted to put her and her mother in the wrong, parroting 'What did I tell you?' She blamed her automatic response to think ill of herself on her 'upbringing' and particularly her father who, poor man, came in for complaint in her letters to Philip.

After retirement in 1957 he watched TV all day and wouldn't let Monica watch the cricket, she said. She longed to see Compton dancing down the pitch and Typhoon Tyson and 'old butterfingers Graveney' who could never hold a catch while, like a fat seal, Cowdrey in the slips held them magically. When Philip was also watching or hearing the same match it gave her 'an odd feeling of companionship'. Her father came between them.

Fred Jones liked his food – but nothing fancy. On her weekends home in the 1940s and 1950s the adult Monica would prepare grub-up boiled beef, mash and carrots. Occasionally she might venture devilled kidneys for breakfast. His favourite dinner was 'stew and potatoes' with 'sc*ld*ng tea'. In the fictions he was writing privately about Monica in the first phase of their relationship, Philip portrays her father, whom he did not know, as a brewery agent and drinker, a depiction at variance with what we know of Frederick Jones. In retire-ment he was, as Monica recollected, a great reader: but in his fashion. He would borrow his six books a fortnight from the local public library. But, from Monica's schooldays on, he resolutely refused to read anything she was reading or that he was aware she had read. His clever school child, later the brilliant Oxford graduate and academic, made him feel, she suggests, smaller than he, as a man, wanted to be in his own house (in fact largely purchased by his wife).

Fred was a football fan – his team was the Kidderminster Harriers at whose matches he could shout to his heart's content. It's hard to imagine Monica going with him, scarf and rattle at the ready. She records a fight he once got into in the grounds with a drunken fan. She was, in later life, a sports fan herself, but never soccer. Her sports were cricket and boxing, both of which she was converted to by Philip. 'My family', she gloomily concluded, 'is so ignorant'. And she could have added uncultured, compared to what Philip's had been. Her deprecation strikes a rather sour note and does not chime with the hundreds of fond letters from her mother and father she kept till her death. It does, however, chime with Philip's parental, marital, familial, home-life phobias.

Lily Jones was devout. Monica describes accompanying her to Sunday school, where she helped with the instruction. The Bible Monica was given for her own Sunday study was on the bookshelves in her room at Leicester. She subscribed to the *Church Times*, occa-sionally sending cuttings to Philip. She would mischievously suggest that there, not the *TES*, was where the department should place its appointment ads. It would, God willing, improve the quality of new colleagues.

From Monica's letters one can pick up next to nothing about her extended parental families. Her paternal grandparents remembered her birthday and sent as much as a ten-shilling note. There was an aunt on her mother's side who settled in the Highlands of Scotland, and holiday trips, early in life, planted the seed of Monica's lifelong love of Walter Scott. She persuaded Philip to holiday there alternately with Sark. Other than her parents and, one may suspect, her uncle Wilfred ('Wilf') who lived with the Joneses until 1940, Monica resolutely cut off connection with everyone else, declining invitations to visit and attend funerals. Under Philip's tutelage she was making herself in the 1950s into the woman alone in the world I would know in the 1960s.

It was the gentleness of her mother which stayed most powerfully with Monica and came back to her in later life: 'I am thinking of my Mother & how easy she was to look after when she was alone. When Father was in hospital [with cancer], she made no trouble of it. I came to her each weekend.' Her grandmother and mother were both 'rotten cooks'. Lily's 'greatest virtue' was 'adaptability'. She would do what she was told at the oven by her daughter. You could, of course, adapt too far. Monica thought her mother too much the Patient Griselda. Mrs Jones did not stand up for herself. Lily never complained – even when a moan or two about aches and pains, in her fifties, might have meant treatment for the heart condition that killed her and robbed Monica of the family member who meant most to her.

Monica's intimacy with and eventual subservience to Philip had good and bad effects. Both testify to the fact that he was all-important to her. Some people whose opinions I respect venture the term 'coercive control'. It seems evident that he stripped away connection with her living family to have sole dominance. I don't believe he was a tyrant, but he had the inscrutable knack of making you want to please him. Stretching a point, I would call him by nature kind – except in the perennial messes his two-timing got him into. Still, it is credible that his near pathological opposition to home and family, in any form, drove an emotional wedge between Monica and her parents in the last decade of their lives. His similar opposition to marriage distorted her life in more subtle ways.

14

Imperfect Love, 1950

'I am bloody-minded'

Monica to Philip, 1950

The 1950s began with what seemed like a continuation of the perfect friendship. Philip wrote a 'pretty little short story' as a New Year 1950 present for Monica. It was called 'Roger'; about a man whose friends 'teach him to sneer at Munnings and to admire but not to love Modigliani'. These trend-hounds talk about 'The Battleship Potemkin and very likely Chagall'. Larkin liked Sir Alfred Munnings for the same reason he liked Beatrix Potter. Both featured nice animals. He also – along with Monica – disliked fashionable Modernism. She fortified that prejudice in him.

They saw each other 'all the time' that summer. But July began badly. Monica's Oxford tutor, Ethel Seaton, was retiring and she went back for the farewell celebration at St Hugh's. It was horrible. Monica's Oxford was gone; and she hadn't altogether liked that 1940s Oxford. Now it was much worse. The college ablutions were still filthy. The hall was 'full of Americans – gangs of girls all alike with I think matt khaki complexions and enormous mouths and feet' all braying 'school-marm scholarship'.

Seaton was being replaced by young fashionably dressed Molly Mahood (later a distinguished Marlovian). 'Naturally I disliked her on sight,' Monica told Philip. She added 'I am sure the food has been poisoned.' Her college was now something out of Hieronymus Bosch.

Particular venom was directed at the college gardener, 'a deformed, red-eyed, half-wit, DROOLING & SLAVERING . . . leering, staggering, slobbering . . . I have never seen so many deformed & crippled in one place.' There might, one thinks, have been a few such around in the years when St Hugh's was a military hospital and she an aid worker.

The surviving letters of 1946–49 show Monica at her best: vivacious and no one's fool. This letter shows her at her worst: vicious and loathing everything, including, sometimes, herself. She realises that Philip will by now have seen Monica Jones as she really is:

> It's silly to say all this to you like I work off all my bad temper in telling you; and then I am sweet and nice to those whose opinion I don't care about at all and I do care what you think of me and always show you all the bad and then you think I am bloody-minded and 'hard and competent' like you said the other evening. Oh, well, well.

Monica was a woman of many parts, some attractive and some, as she admits, repulsive. That was part of her charm for Philip. He, like her, was complicated. At the end of May 1950, around the time they first made love, Larkin brought to publishable form* a poem about Monica: 'If, My Darling'. It portrays Monica (his darling) transported into his mind – half wonderland, half abyss – struggling to make sense of him. It was an impossible task.

Summer 1950 ended with crisis on all fronts. Ruth remained the fiancée but university and London had broadened her mind. She was currently a trainee teacher in Newark with a career ahead of her. She wanted more than letters, occasional sex, and a ring on her finger to frighten away other eligible men. She was no longer the schoolgirl twenty-three-year-old Larkin had led astray. The 1950 long vacation was imminent (but not for librarians). Why, Ruth must have wondered, did Philip never invite her to Leicester? The answer was, firstly, Monica; secondly, he no longer loved Ruth unconditionally.

---

* James Booth's useful dating. The poem would not be published until *The Less Deceived*, 1955.

His solution was flight. He would put the Irish Sea between himself and his three woman problems. In May 1950 he had applied for a librarian post at Queen's University Belfast. He was accepted after an interview in June, the post to be taken up in September. He did not integrate Ruth, Monica, his mother (with whom he was living in Leicester), or his sister into this move out of their lives. Philip, nonsensically, again proposed marriage to Ruth. But marriage where? Belfast? He had not invited her to join him there.

He did not mean his second proposal. After three days he withdrew the offer. Ruth returned the ten-guinea ring with a dignified farewell. His 'misengagement' was over. In the same hectic weeks, Philip sold off the house in which his mother and he had lived for two years and arranged to move her to where his sister lived, Loughborough. As he candidly told his friend Jim Sutton: 'I do realise that my mother must live with someone – only I'd rather prefer it not to be me.' His contact with Eva would henceforth be occasional holidays, weekend visits, bleak feasts on high and holy days, and twice-weekly fond letters. Their relationship, which was in its way loving, endured till death did them part, which would be a long time coming.

This headless-chicken period in Philip's life climaxed on Friday, 17 July when, they both having drunk too much, Monica made an overt sexual advance. He had, presumably, told her he was leaving Leicester – and her. Her move may well have been a desperate attempt to hold him. Had he not wanted sex on that ill-fated 1948 Lake District trip? Had his timing been better chosen then, and his address more tactful, she might well have assented.

He, on this occasion, rejected her. The Ruth commitment, about which Monica knew nothing, was paralysing him. She, distressed beyond words, thinking she did not, despite all the signs, attract him, fled back to her parents' house (it was now the long vacation). There it was that the words, a flood of them, came. She wrote to Larkin, in barely controlled fury and self-hate, over the weekend. The following are the salient points of her 2000-word letter.

You say to me you are sorry to have upset me – look, you haven't upset me *yet* but you *will* if you keep on and keep on about your own unspecified inability to deal with things, all of this veiled in a heavy gloomy *mysterie* leaving me in a pleasing fluttering state of uncertainty as to whether your *real* character is like the Marquis de Sade or Bulldog Drummond . . . It would be ridiculous for four years perfect friendship – it was for me anyway – to be up-set by an hour's stupid folly, for that's what it is. I was exhausted and miserable and overwrought, it was hysteria. Surely you under-stand that? What you shd have done was give me a good shaking, saying 'here, none of that', or if you preferred it you could have uttered the film classic, 'Please – don't let's spoil it', you ought to have done so. I don't know why you didn't.

She did not know the whole story. He had a couple of weeks earlier proposed marriage to a rival she had never met and had applied for a job across the Irish Sea – departure a few weeks on.*

So, more Miss Prim than Bulldog Drummond or the Divine Mar-quis, Philip had declined Monica's offer of herself. At the end of her letter she suggests they return to their 'usual' relationship. 'I like you better than anybody I've ever met, but just as usual, just as always, so don't read things into what I say, or write; do feel that's all the same as ever it was'.

She was, the letter records, where in the future she would often be in her dealings with Philip: on the edge of breakdown:

On Monday a bird came into my bed-room! I screamed [&] ran out. It got out in its terror. I was helpless on the stairs because I could not stand. Even my heartless Mother said 'you'd better have a drink', gave me gin, which I accepted.

She signs off coldly, 'Yrs as always, M.'

But 'usual' and 'perfect friendship' were now impossible. In the interval between awful July and farewell at the end of August, Philip mended bridges with Monica, explaining his career move but,

---

* In Belfast, retrospectively, he seems to have told Monica something more detailed about his 'misengagement' to Ruth.

apparently, not everything, or anything, about Ruth's ring. And he had an insurance policy: he would soon be in Ireland. Separation would give him an opportunity to let his relationship with Monica wither into friendship: or, one way or another, develop into something lasting. The details were as yet unforeseen. There was no suggestion Monica should look around for some position (schoolteaching would have posed no problem) in Northern Ireland.

With Ruth off the scene, Philip and Monica first made love, by best guess, on 19 July 1950, and repeatedly, in the time remaining, thereafter. 'By the end of summer', Monica told Motion, 'he had come to me'. Philip, in Ireland, recalled wryly the setting: Monica's lodgings bedroom:

> I hope . . . your room doesn't look sad & lonely now my lethargic cadging figure isn't in it. Truly I shall always remember the fire-place & the cricket-bin & all the battery of things on the man-telpiece, Fifi & blue Neddy & the flowered lamp. Your life there has come into extremely sharp focus for me now: heating milk, singing in the kitchen, drying stockings . . .

In the space of three months in summer 1950 Philip Larkin had freed himself of an engagement which had gone two years stale; freed himself of domestic cohabitation with his mother which had proved creatively stifling; and made love to the woman with whom his future might lie. And then run off to Ireland leaving her behind for pastures, and women (it would prove), new.

His flight inspired a poem, 'Single Ticket', commemorating his shrugging off his past 'like gravecloths'.

15

Loved and Left, 1950–1955

'Letters are the only comfort in a voluntary exile'
Monica to Philip, 1950

Monica and Philip spent the night together before he left for Belfast. She and his mother saw him on the train to Liverpool. Monica tearfully consoled herself with her favourite sweets, Peppermint Charms, feeling 'like the kind of woman they write about in *Woman's Weekly*'. He gave her a copy of Yeats as a farewell present – not her favourite poet.* She signs off the letter, which she sent ahead of time to greet his arrival overseas, 'Beloved child, beloved star . . . love of every kind there is. M.', adding a little cartoon of their imaginary cat, Pussy. Her letters over the next weeks are 'an endless babble' of love. His are a mite too polite for her taste – she craves passion, not 'thanks' for her 'kindness'. She writes libidinally in bed at midnight – smoking Gold Flake and drinking. The 'usual woolly vest drying in front of my fire . . . I look nice in my blue nightie and blue bedjacket'. He has shown her a poem, 'In the Spring'.†

She hates the new 'worthless and unnecessary courses' ARH has brought in. 'That man's presence is like being in a room with a broken gas-pipe.' In the 'awful' staff meetings she lets Collins speak for her. He, ever loving, 'called me a fawn in a maze'. Let them, she

---

* Ruth had given him a volume of Yeats as a token of her love.
† 'Spring' in *The Less Deceived*.

suggests, devise a Swiftian 'Little Language' for their letters.

> If you die before me I will absent me from felicity awhile to tell
> your story: I mean edit your letters. I find them full of interest,
> layer upon layer.

As a move towards making the department university-worthy, ARH
had drawn on a friend with patronage from Cambridge days, Boris
Ford. Ford – a Leavisite – was general editor of the *Pelican History of
English Literature*, an ambitiously authoritative project. Humphreys
was invited to sub-edit a volume. He recruited his department to
contribute. Monica he instructed to 'put a chapter on Crabbe and late
C18 poetry in his book'. *His* book, as she saw it, containing, as ARH
intended, the harvest of *her* mind? The notion disgusted her.

What should she do? She cannot tell ARH 'that it'd shame me to be
associated in *his* work, Lord! Lord! What am *I* doing in this – this sort
of thing is for *other people*.' What to do about ARH's 'damned book'
will haunt her for two years. Philip sympathised with her vexation: 'I
know all one wants is to be left ALONE', he reassured her. She might
have preferred him to add 'with you'.

In their far-apart letters of this period she and Philip conduct a
quantity of literary conversation. They exchange views on French
poetry; she knows poems he doesn't. She mounts a dismissal of D. H.
Lawrence. He is streets ahead of her on him, but she has her thought-
through criticisms:

> Of course, the trouble was, [Lawrence] had this damned *ambi-
> tion*. He wanted to *be someone* . . . I shd probably have detested
> him if I'd met him, but reading about him makes me terribly sorry
> for him – so uncivilised, so incapable of coming to terms with the
> world, & he learned so little; it's like a child of two abandoned in
> Piccadilly Circus to look after itself; and a spoilt child screaming
> and kicking, for something it can't possibly have – a repulsive
> spectacle, but a very pitiable one. So unwise, *I suppose*, in short.
> And so doubly sad for it to be a grown man and a talented one.

Philip sends her drafts of his poems. These years, after they became lovers, he in Belfast she in Leicester, are the closest she came to him creatively. She was not a collaborator apart from occasionally suggesting the right word. Nonetheless her opinion on whether a poem works is freely given. He respects her judgement. More importantly she confirmed his sense of where the main tradition of English poetry, which he intended to lead, lay: Hardy not Eliot. Rhyme and half-rhyme not vers libre. Small not grand subjects. Self not world. Most importantly she bolstered his morale in the hard years before his name became known and he famous as a poet with *The Less Deceived* in 1955. She earned his dedication of the volume to her.

He finds it hard to write in Ulster. His rooms are noisy – 'do like Keats said, *become a clod*', she advises. She's put 'Dior's autumn face on' – a picture for his mind. Her farewells are love-making on paper, 'Goodnight sweet chuck. Golden slumbers kiss your eyes,' ends one. She goes cod Elizabethan with complaint against 'these roaring hugy [sic]* waves' that separate them. November 1950 closes in and she tells him to go watch the Pope being burned along with Fawkes on the fifth by the Protestant militants and, with winter coming, does he want her to send the thick pully he left with her?

* From John Heywood, 'To Her Sea-faring Lover', 1557. Larkin would have known it from its inclusion in *The Oxford Book of English Verse*.

16

Life Sentence Leicester, 1950–1955

*'I go on living but everything gets deadened & toned down . . .
till I'm just a dull unleavened lump. How often have I sought
for your simple & feeling phrase about wanting to commit
simultaneously murder and suicide. Exactly'*
Monica to Philip, 1950

In the weeks which followed Philip's going to Belfast, Monica realised
that, whichever way she looked at it, she had been loved for a few
weeks and left for years. Left with what? Leicester and Stourport, half
the year apiece. It was a dreary axis. According to Dick Watson, her
long-time friend in the sixties and after, 'Monica loved the Leicester
that she knew in the 1940s and 50s'. But there are no kind words
about her home-from-home city in her letters to Larkin. There is
indifference at best, urbicidal rage at worst. And there is ubiquitous
contempt for Leicester's *espèces de canaille*. When it comes to Leicester
it is an unlovely, unloving Monica that one sees.

She loosed the following diatribe, in a serial letter of 16 October
1950. She has now been in Leicester five years, and Philip has been
gone a fortnight:

I went shopping this afternoon. I'm again struck by the *bitterness*
of my feelings – I *hate and despise* the harmless good-tempered
people on buses or loitering in the street *in my way*. If some poor
tottering old woman lays a hand on me in the bus to stop herself

from being flung headlong *I could strike her*; if somebody fat sits
next to me and squashes against me I want to *insult* them. Their
talking, their laughing, that awful Leicester whine – I feel my face
screwing up into angular contempt; their coughing, even their
breathing, disgusts me to the very bowels. *Just* the same feeling
as when you squash a very fat juicy insect; like you did that last
evening in my room and wiped it up with a face tissue, remember?
No it wasn't the last evening either – it was lovely Tuesday.

The lovely Tuesday refers to the day of their making love before he
packed his bags for Belfast. The mantelpiece figurine of blue Neddy
was looking down, and her stockings were drying on the kitchen line,
which amused Philip. The squelched bug rather blights the romance.

But where was the romance leading? A few months after leaving
Belfast, Larkin laid down the contractual rules for the next thirty
years. There was to be no ring:

I find it . . . puzzling to know what people *think* they are doing
who get married. To me the strain would be the constant lack
of solitude, the never-being able-to-relax, not at midnight, or
3 a.m. . . .

And where does that lead thirty years on? A bitter poem ('Love Again')
of September 1979 gives the answer:

Love again: wanking at ten past three . . .

17

Love and the Tuppenny Stamp,
1950–1973

'As soon as we came together we parted'
                                    Monica to Philip, 1964

With his woman problems a country away, Larkin bloomed in Belfast. He cultivated a circle of intellectual equals and played (in his sombre fashion) the dandy, sartorially and intellectually. Socially his 'sub-sarcasm' amused his new friends, as did the art of comic mimicry he'd perfected with Kingsley. In his Ulster cosmos Philip Larkin twinkled. His sexual range extended with two women who did not strain his conscience. Patsy Strang was upper crust; a privately super-rich, Sorbonne-educated poet, novelist, and the wife of a philosophy lecturer, himself a top person. Patsy was the first cosmopolitan, sexually appetitive lover Larkin would have – and the last. Women of her kind were, he eventually discovered, dangerous.

He formed what would be a long, confidential, friendship with safer Judy Egerton. There was also the anything but cosmopolitan Winifred Arnott – an EngLit graduate working as a temp in the library, who cheered him up and went cycling with him. Their relationship was on that margin between intimate friendship and physical love. She (reportedly) was tempted but stopped short. She would, she told James Booth, have gone to bed with Philip if she could have trusted him to marry her. As it was she enjoyed him until someone she could trust came along, which they soon did (to Philip's vexation). His memorial of their relationship is the opening poem in *The Less Deceived*, 'Lines on a Young Lady's Photograph Album'.

As Andrew Motion puts it, Philip cast off the 'drab influence' of Leicester. Monica was never drab, but she was pushing thirty and would be three years past that milepost before Philip returned to England. Patsy and the other women in Belfast were seven years or so younger than Monica. That kind of age difference with her rivals would always worry Monica. She felt she and Philip should have clinched things in the 'perfect friendship' years and her mid-twenties.

From 1950 until 1955, Larkin, in his Ulster fastness, wrote a series of his finest letters to Monica and showed her more of his poetry in progress than he ever would again. Absence and guilt made his heart – or, at least, his pen – grow fonder. Monica was a fixture in his life. She was his 'steady'. In absentia, he laid down the terms of their love: they would meet seldom and enjoy unconstrained sex when they did. The connecting filament would be handwritten letters.

His library work required Philip to type and he used the keyboard for the final drafts of his poems. His life, he said, depended on 'that lowly mechanical thing . . . my Olivetti'. His poetry workbooks are crammed with laborious poems in progress – sometimes written over years. For them he used erasable Royal Sovereign 2B pencils. His poetry was carved into shape. By contrast his letters flowed. Some of Monica's letters to him would have the accidental imprint of lipstick on their envelopes. 'Sometimes', he said, 'there clings about your letters a faint redolence of perfume'. And his? Probably a faint whiff of Craven A.

In his letters Philip was not hindered by his lifelong stammer and, by the mid-sixties, deafness. Letters were arenas where his verbal wit and her eruptive emotions had free play. One hears their voices in these letters. Monica liked to tell her students that 'our language is like the *Chinese*, in so much of its meaning'. Martin Stannard makes the shrewd observation that 'when they met, he and Monica often found it difficult to talk. At a distance they "spoke" voluminously'. Half a dozen voluminous runs of Larkin's letters have survived.* Anthony Thwaite and James Booth have made substantial samples available in print. Their three edited volumes are Larkin writ large. They constitute multitudes more pages than Larkin's *Collected Poems*, and his prose miscellanea. Two runs stand out as paramount – those with Kingsley Amis and those with Monica. For each Larkin co-created an epistolary theatre in which the relationship could enact itself and evolve over years.

The epistolary Larkin(s) were not Larkin in the flesh. 'Sometimes', said Monica, 'your letters are so unlike the person I last saw . . . I suppose because you are not being that person when you write'. She by contrast is personal. Larkin, in his letters, was reincarnated by those he wrote to. He drew breath from them and his chameleon changes were not play-acting. Kingsley Amis, the wittiest writer of his time, drew emulous wit from Philip. Maeve Brennan, the nicest of women, drew reciprocal niceness from Philip. Robert Conquest, the destroyer of grand illusions, awoke the ironic disbeliever of everything. Colin Gunner roused a comradely, foul-mouthed bigot. And Monica? Her raw honesty drew the least inauthentic Philip. In his letters Larkin was a one-man dramatis personae, but most himself with Monica.

Larkin's letters breathe on the page, printed and holograph, as pneumatically as a runner's lungs. The frequency, at its height, of three-to-five-day interchange with Monica generates a drum-beat reciprocity. Their epistolary modes dovetail. His is one of instrumental control, with mastery of pace, tone of address, phonic volume, stylistic bathos, daring figures of speech, literary allusion. His letters rise into prose poetry or slump, artfully, into slang.

They are en masse brisker than Monica's, befitting someone working as hard as he was in, and for, his library. Monica's letters can extend to fifty sides in days-long series: diurnally and nocturnally variable. They both hand-wrote legibly – near calligraphically, in his case – and retained the wartime habit of using whatever paper came to hand. The overall climate created by Larkin's letters to Monica is one of

---

* See the appendix on Larkin's will – all but chosen runs of letters, including mistresses other than Monica, he instructed to be destroyed 'unread'.

politesse, solicitude, humour and attentive love: shot through with an odd kind of nursery infantilism. The last sometimes embarrasses Larkin critics and biographers who pass it off as quaint.

Their parental instincts discharged on little furry animals – particularly those created by Beatrix Potter and, as postcard art, by Racey Helps. Potter was an author Philip said he would sacrifice the whole of 'Proust – Joyce – Mann' for. Peter Rabbit was a favourite and he nicknamed Monica – after they were lovers – 'Bun(ny Rabbit)'. She called him her 'big huggy bear'. In the fonder parts of their letters one sees them as their own children. The bunny rabbits scampering, big huggy bears stalking, and ducks waddling across the pages of their letters give the impression of Philip and Monica petting each other. In the fully sexual phase of their love, he would lecherously praise her 'bunny haunches' and she his 'ursine hugs'. Philip made Peter Rabbit so real to her that at one low point Monica toyed with the idea of taking advertised work at Potter House, near Hawkshead.

Larkin was as gifted a sketcher as he was a photographer and wooed Monica in their early days with sub-Potter and erotic drawings (those haunches) as, later, he wooed her with love-photographs. Although she accepted the reduction of herself to a *mascotte*, Monica was not as adept as Philip at using the 'Bunny' motif in the body of her letters and would more often sign herself 'Bun'. Monica's postcards were ingeniously appropriate. As the annual visit to Lords loomed, in June she sends a postcard with a nineteenth-century picture 'The Scorer' on the front. One closed card, alarmingly, has a pop-up pin-up when opened. Unlike Ruth and Maeve, she knew Philip liked soft porn. She, herself, would do Playboy pics for him. None, apparently, survive but a description of one does. In 1966 she asks, 'remember the Playboy pose which you arranged; do you? Bra & sweater pushed up, just enough to show breasts. Does it rouse you? I bet not'.

The animalism and Playboy eroticism went along with their mutually confected 'little language'. Virginia Woolf's description of what lovers' patois meant for Swift and Stella fits the Larkin and Monica epistolary dialogue:

In any highly civilised society disguise plays so large a part, politeness is so essential, that to throw off the ceremonies and conven-
tions and talk a 'little language' for one or two to understand, is as
much a necessity as a breath of air in a hot room.

Equally apt is Swift's own rumination on the intimacy of the Little
Language and its function as lovers' code:

methinks when I write plain, I do not know how, but we are not
alone, all the world can see us. A bad scrawl is so snug . . .

Occasionally there was a third voice in the Monica–Philip correspondence – Kingsley's. The Amis–Larkin letters make play with
cacography – comic insults against King's English. They breathe the
sweaty intimacy of the student room – a skinful of beer and Eddie
Condon's Chicago All-stars on the wind-up and hilarious 'joke-
swapping'. The mannerism continued when they were distinguished
men of letters. The joint tone was anti-authoritarian 'Kikkng agst the
prix' (to briefly talk Amis). Horspiss and Bum were epithets. Bougar,
or Buger, expletives. Grunting expostulations – Ogh! Argh! Gob! –
Billy Bunterish punctuation. The two students eternally attempt to
outdo each other, and it can be very funny. There is Kingsleyism, on
both sides, in the Philip–Monica correspondence.

There is stylistic unison in Amis–Larkin letters, but none in the
Philip–Monica run. They are like two performers in the same or-
chestra playing different instruments. Larkin emulated the golden
age of letter writing; Horace Walpole – the master of epistolary form
– was his model. Larkin did not write letters to Monica, rather he
composed them. Even when dashed off, they have the grace of the
speeding skater. And their pleasure, for him, was how easily composition flowed.

He laboured to produce his poetry – it could take him years of
drafting to produce a print-perfect poem. He could compose and
recompose fiction – but it lay, too often, never quite as good as he
wanted it to be on the page. Letter writing, however, like his jazz
columns, emancipated the wordsmith in Larkin. He could, like his

beloved Pee Wee, Wild Bill or Fats, improvise. Fountain pen in hand he was, literally, fountainous. He could converse incommoded by his lifelong stammer, and his progressive hardness of hearing. His letters poured out in a way his brain could never get his mouth to work.

As Martin Stannard points out, both their letter-writing styles were 'voiced'. Monica's loud voice and barking interruptiveness irritated Larkin in oral conversation and company. In the early fifties he gave her a stern lesson on her elocution.[*] She proved incorrigible. Philip solved the problem as he saw it by rarely taking her into society. Letters lowered Monica's volume, and Philip could skim her long effusions, which he often did. On the page no one can hear you bark.

Monica's megaphony contrasted with Maeve Brennan, Monica's longest-lasting rival. The other woman was soft-spoken and well-spoken, trained as a librarian to institutional hush. She, unlike Monica, was taken into company by Larkin. Three of the half-dozen significant Larkin women were librarians.[†] Like Lear he believed that a soft, low, gentle voice in a woman was an excellent thing. But he stuck, faithful in his fashion, to foghorn Monica.

Monica is a letter writer streets ahead of Maeve, whose prose, as her memoir testifies, is plain. Routinely Monica's letters are fifteen to thirty sides of fluid chat, complaint and anecdote. They resemble a literary stream of consciousness. At times, it is more surging flood than stream. They have odd disjunctions: after a savage diatribe against Maeve that runs to several pages, Monica suddenly reminds Philip to water the flowers. One might suspect irony, but it is more like a needle jumping on a 78 rpm shellac record. It's still the same record.

For Philip and Monica the fountain pen was the tool of choice. They despised the Bic which, when infirm, they were obliged to use. Ballpoint did not inscribe with chisel bite. Theirs was a relationship founded on Waterman and Quink. 'Letters', Monica said, 'only feel *real* with pen and ink'. She, typically, served; he, typically, returned serve. There is an unfailing courtesy in his returns. He was ever solicitous ('how is that cold / tummy upset / running cistern /

---

[*] See below, pp. 94–95.

[†] Maeve Brennan, Winifred Arnott, Betty Mackereth.

cystitis?'). She seldom corrected what she had written. Interlineations and crossings-out are rare. Her letters were not composed, like his, they gushed, geyser-like. Occasionally, in crisis or her later years, she would tear out a page, or a whole letter, on the grounds it was raving, hysterical or (when she read it in the morning) drunken. Her letters, in vacation and sometimes weekends, were a major work of the day and in term time of the night.

Monica Jones's letters create a hologram of her. They envisage Monica for the absent Philip. To this end she describes how, at that moment, she is dressed ('that beige dress, pink slacks, new blue night-dress', etc). She describes the floors she is scrubbing, the plates she is washing, the linen she is ironing, the interminable departmental meetings 'beastly' ARH inflicts on her, the scent she is wearing. She made herself different (snack-sized) meals when alone and describes the food in detail. Not a sprig of basil, or a pickled walnut (the one pickle she allowed into her kitchen), blade of chive, or leaf of parsley escapes mention.

The runs of the couple's letters have their large climatic characters. En masse, from beginning to end, Monica's are a thirty-seven-year span of uncertain, too often bad weather. They chronicle pain, loneli-ness, acute emotional deprivation, rage, physical suffering and, in the end stages of her correspondence with Larkin (which gives out in the 1970s, when they turn to the phone), lowering disease (alcoholism, sadly) – all of this chequered with shafts of sunshine, wit and learn-ing. Larkin's overall tone is weary, ironic and stoic: if one could find the right words in the right order – as Coleridge defined poetry – life could be handled. Just about. Best not to get excited: 'My mind', he said, 'is a pool: if stirred, it grows muddy'.

Monica's darkest moments are Kurtzian. Philip's are more Marcus Aurelius. As T. S. Eliot said of Larkin, he could make words mean what he wanted them to mean. Monica left words to speak for them-selves. Their letters, in their reciprocal totality, are a unique literary duet. A genre for which we have no name. Of Philip and Monica's intercourses, physical and social, that of their letters was the richest and most durable. What will survive of us is letters, Larkin might have paraphrased his most famous last line.

In fact, he foresaw it as early as 1956:

I was reading about the Carlyles tonight . . . 'Their worst agonies seem not to have come from their common hypochondria, her jealousy or his monstrous selfishness, but from not getting letters from each other on the day they were expected when they were separated.' Do you think people will write like that about us when we are dust? My dear rabbit!

The other long-enduring love relationship of Philip's life was with his library assistant Maeve Brennan. He secretively wrote and posted letters to Maeve when on his fortnight's holiday in a shared or adjoining bedroom with Monica, in Skye, Sark, Wessex or wherever they had gone that year in their annual holidays after he returned from Belfast. Places where he and Monica could sign in as Dr and Mrs Larkin.

Monica in whites, on holiday with Philip

Larkin evidently got an illicit thrill from epistolary infidelity. Richard Bradford hails as 'formidable' that while in the furthest Highlands, tramping the glens with Monica, he is writing to both Patsy and Winifred. It is even more formidable when you consider that on those same holidays, he and Monica wrote duet letters to each other on facing pages of a diary. And, of course, there were the postcards for Mother.

Over his four years in Belfast Philip adhered to Monica by the postage stamp, occasional holidays, trips to his mother in Loughborough with Leicester as a briefer second stop, and rare reciprocal trips by her across the Irish Sea. In April 1951 she visited Philip in Belfast and went on an excursion to Dublin – her first 'abroad'. She did not intend to make a habit of it. Philip wrote a detailed chronicle of the jaunt to his mother, climaxing on Monica's opinions (negative) of self-raising flour.

18

Monica Muzzled, 1952

'you've no idea of the exhausting *quality of yourself in full "voice"'*

Philip to Monica, 1952

Something momentous happened at this 1950s stage of their relationship. Philip discovered that Monica embarrassed him in company. Such a thing had never happened when he was at Leicester. But her provincial star was outshone in Belfast. Someone, most likely Patsy Strang (he was 'rather dazzled by Patsy' at this time, Philip confessed), mocked Monica's garrulity after meeting her. Philip wrote Monica a long, cruel letter. It was written shortly after he had impregnated Patsy and been released from the consequences by miscarriage – things Monica did not know.

He and Monica had taken their annual summer holiday that year in Grasmere and had, as an act of affiliation, visited the Beatrix Potter house in Sawrey. He had, the letter said, something he must tell her:

> It's simply that in my view you would do much better to revise, drastically, the amount you say and the intensity with which you say it. You are vaguely aware of this already, aren't you? You say you 'chatter like a jay' . . . I don't say that exactly: what I do feel is that you've no idea of the *exhausting* quality of yourself in full 'voice'.

He expands on his exhaustion before laying down rules:

> One, *Never* say more than two sentences, or *very rarely* three, without waiting for an answer or comment from whoever you're talking to; Two, abandon *altogether* your harsh didactic voice, & use *only* the soft musical one (except in special cases); & Three, don't do more than *glance* at your interlocutor (wrong word?) once or twice while speaking. You're getting a habit of *boring* your face up or round into the features of your listener – *don't* do it! It's most trying.

He goes on in this vein for another paragraph before finally ending the lecture and turning 'To things pleasanter': he has filled in his football coupons.

Another woman would have told Philip bloody Larkin to get stuffed and buy himself a mynah bird. Monica was not for reforming, but, deeply hurt, she simply went mute in company with him. Larkin solved the foghorn problem by very rarely, until the 1970s, taking her into company. Soft-spoken Maeve, a few years later, he did extend a companionable arm to. In the context of the 1950 corrective letter, James Booth quotes a painful judgement on Monica:

> Anthony Thwaite remembers being baffled, when he first met [Monica] a few years later, that the urbane Philip should have paired himself with so socially inept and ungracious a partner.

There is an *amende honorable* in Thwaite's judgement in *Letters to Monica* that she inspired some of Larkin's very best letters. And Thwaite, one notes, later became her supportive friend. But that ugly first impression sticks in the mind.

Larkin's Belfast loves, liaisons and romantic friendships are chronicled in the biographies and throw plentiful light on him. What they show less clearly is how Monica, the absentee lover, got through the Philip-less years. After one visit, Monica wrote that she thought she might be pregnant. Larkin airily told her he nowadays trusted his contraceptives. He was by now knowing about such things. She, perhaps, wished she were pregnant.

If Monica had made a man of him, after his schoolgirl loves and lusts, Patsy Strang sophisticated the man. Philip tried the Beatrix Potter trick on her and was roundly bollocked. She wanted none of that infantile Jemima Puddleduck nonsense:

> I had a sort of difference of opinion with P. Strang about the Potter books: she condemned them as 'anthropomorphist': further she accused me of not liking animals at all, only Potter ones & ones on my mantelpiece. I was at somewhat of a loss. I do sometimes feel ashamed of liking these sweet little bunnies.*

In one sense Philip went all the way with Patsy, and in another he didn't. According to Andrew Motion, Patsy proposed divorcing her husband, marrying Philip, and stipending him from her plentiful wealth to write poetry. Philip would be allowed to sing in a golden cage. He was unwilling and let the relationship go cold.

He and Monica enjoyed at this stage of their fractured relationship ritual summer holidays in locations like the Scottish Highlands alternating with Wessex and the Lake District; distant, literature-rich regions where they would not be recognised and could check in as Dr and Mrs Larkin. It was not until 1955 that they discovered Sark – their village in the sea. 'I did enjoy that [Sark] holiday – just like abroad without any of the trouble and dysentery and swindling and embarrassment', Monica wrote after the happy summer break.

Larkin was happy in his new life but, perversely, Belfast stifled his poetry for a few months. Andrew Motion notes the well ran dry in 1952. He wasn't unhappy enough, Motion suggests: deprivation, as Larkin much-quotedly said, was to him what daffodils were to Wordsworth and west winds to Shelley. Other things went happily. Ireland was a sexual template; for the rest of his life, Philip would routinely have two, sometimes three, irons in the fire. Some involved, as with Winifred, loving friendship: there was little if anything carnal. Others might be kissing, cuddling with climactic love-making. Still others had the physicality of a contact sport. Monica was at the sharp,

---

* Patsy did allow him to call her 'Dearest Honeybear'.

fetishistic end of his spectrum of love. Her muzzle could come off in bed. 'I think', Larkin told Monica in 1951:

> someone might do a little research on some of the *inherent qual-*
> *ities* of sex – its *cruelty*, its *bullyingness*, for instance. It seems to
> me that *bending someone else to your will* is the very stuff of sex,
> by force or neglect if you are male, by spitefulness or nagging or
> scenes if you are female. And what's more, both sides *would sooner*
> *have it that way than not at all*. I wouldn't. And I suspect that
> means not that I can enjoy sex in my own quiet way but that I
> can't enjoy it at all. It's like rugby football: either you like kicking
> & being kicked, or your soul cringes away from the whole affair.
> There's no way of *quietly* enjoying rugby football.

Love, in this machismo style, was a hard, low tackle. With Maeve, ten years later, it would be caresses.

On occasions he complained that Monica was too passive in the act of love. There was not, for him, enough 'act'. He never made such complaints to Maeve, and with Patsy he never had to. Monica called herself a 'Quivering Coney' (a trembling rabbit – 'coney' as they both knew, was Elizabethan slang for vagina) when confronted by the brunt of Philip's demands.

But over the 1950s the epistolary relationship was at its most mutually rewarding and compensated for incompatibilities. They had constructed themselves into a twentieth-century Heloise and Abelard.

19

Monica Lampooned, 1955

*'I am best described in Arthur Askey's words just an ordinary
little worm wiggle wiggle wiggle squirm squirm squirm'*
Monica to Philip, 1952

November 1954–November 1955 was the year when the love chalet
Monica and Philip had created came tumbling down. It had begun
well enough in January 1954. There was a flow of bubbling letters from
her in their Swiftian 'little language' of love and daily news. Snippets
catch what an elated Monica now felt their relationship to be: 'Well,
hello, pig, monkey brand catnip', 'O, lamb, O, lamb I am missing
you'. 'Dearest Cabbidge'. She has, she tells him, a new 'welweteen
top' which will make her look 'Lady C. Lamb' not 'yr little rabbit'.
She's lecturing on Cowley, Milton and the Faerie Queene; 'how can
you ask a rabbit to do that?' He sends her 'At Grass'. She tells him 'it
falls below the real stuff . . . the real inevitable poetry'. 'Powerful hugs
and loving blows and cuffs' for him when he next comes, she vows.
'O, I could swallow a large dish of juicy fruit salad this minute'. 'Best
kisses 20 doz. [and] pinches and blows'. 'Mumping mule' she calls
him when, as always, he moans about work. 'The toad work' has not
yet been invented, but it was spawned in this amorous jabber.

There was for Monica, darkening this flood of fondness, an occasional fear that the relationship was becoming infantilised. 'I am
either being a rabbit', she wrote, 'or Jane Carlyle all the time – these 2
things almost amount to serious hallucinationism within me. I mean

this. It is not a hallucination I mind having.' It was a way of saying she was fooling herself, but she was love's happy fool.

Larkin returned to England (but not, directly, Monica) to take up a job at Hull in 1955. His return coincided with two high-watermark publications for him, *Lucky Jim* by Kingsley Amis (January 1954), on which he collaborated, and Larkin's own *The Less Deceived* (November 1955). Both would impact on Monica.

Larkin and Amis had met, both of them reading English, at Oxford in April 1941. It was a dramatic introduction: Kingsley did an imitation of a man shot, and graphically dying. 'For the first time', recalled Larkin, 'I felt myself in the presence of a talent greater than my own.' When it suited Kingsley his forte was a burlesque talent, it was sublime tomfoolery. Philip's '40' (his joke) was 'sub-sarcasm'.

Early ideas for *Lucky Jim* were tossed around between Kingsley and Philip when they were still on the joke-swapping, room-sharing footing they had cultivated as students. From the first, Amis's novel was conceived as attack comedy. The institutional target was the redbrick university. It rankled that Philip, Kingsley (particularly when he found himself in Swansea) and Monica each found themselves condemned to work in these lowly not-Oxford institutions. The Candide *du jour* hero Jim Dixon and *femme* (almost) *fatale* Margaret Peel were pictured as lecturers at Leicester (clearly identifiable). Jim is nothing like Philip; Margaret is, as her detractors claim, spot-on Monica, laced with spite. Three things are fundamental in the composition of *Lucky Jim*. The first is that a main inspiration for the novel was a visit Kingsley made to Philip in Leicester where he resolved 'something ought to be done with this' when left alone in the college Senior Common Room. The second is that slander of Monica ('Money-cur' as Kingsley called her) was a primary motive – possibly even preceding the above SCR epiphany. Thirdly, it is clear that Philip was collaborative – arguably at times co-authorial – in the project. 'I hope you didn't tell those poor girls the awful wounding things you told me,'* Kingsley said.

---

* The other 'poor girl' was Ruth Bowman.

Five years on, after a string of rejection and continuous honing by Philip and Kingsley, the 'something to be done' was given to the world as *Lucky Jim*. Amis had told Philip it would be 'a comic novel featuring Monica' and 'a marvellous welter . . . of derisive hatred'.*
Andrew Motion says Philip only half thought the novel he and Kingsley were concocting would ever be published. Amis, the evidence suggests, had not yet met Monica while writing the novel which would render her eternally ridiculous. But references in the novel to Margaret Peel's tufts of hair overhanging her glasses suggest that Philip showed photographs as well as passing on a wealth of detail. Philip, when he saw drafts, asked: 'you weren't actually there taking notes [of our conversation] were you?'

Philip passed along to Kingsley, among other 'wounding' things about Monica, the details of a weekend they spent in the Lake District, when she apparently denied Philip sex – a cardinal sin, as they saw it. Monica was, in the brutal slang of Oxford blokes, a 'PT', a 'prick tease'. Although the novel merely honours 'Philip Larkin' as dedicatee, he was seriously contributory. He was the 'ideas man'. The 'fun' in what Larkin called the 'funniest novel I've ever read' has a ring of him about it. And, of course, Philip gave Kingsley – for sacrifice on the altar of comedy – Monica Jones. Why? One perceives again that cruelty which sometimes cross-veined his love when he had a pen in his hand. Doubtless the journals Monica destroyed (after reading them, most likely, with what reaction one can only imagine) were full of it.

Kingsley's first intention was to call *Lucky Jim*'s villainess 'Veronica Beale'. It was, Larkin thought (as would have done every fee-hungry libel lawyer in England), too close to Margaret Monica Beale Jones. Kingsley's second choice, 'Margaret Jones' was worse. Philip prevailed on Kingsley to again change the name of his harpy to 'Margaret Peel'. Still a tissue-thin pseudonym. Martin Amis describes his father's 'attack on Monica':

---

* The pitch of hatred Kingsley and Philip brewed up between them against Monica is spelled out in Chapter 4, '*Lucky Jim*', of Richard Bradford's *The Odd Couple* (2014).

Monica is remade as the unendurable anti-heroine, with her barn-dancer clothes, her mannerisms and affectations, her paraded sensitivity, and her docile-hostile adhesiveness.

'Adhesive . . . not quite predatory, but still . . .' was how Kingsley also described Monica, on first meeting her. She stuck to a man, it was implied, like Sellotape on the fingers. Margaret Peel comes close to entrapping the novel's ingenu hero Jim Dixon. But finally Jim escapes the harpy, and her sub-Oxonian, redbrick slum with a beautiful popsy and the prospect of lots and lots of dosh in the City of London.

While he was collaborating on *Lucky Jim* with Kingsley in the late 1940s, Larkin was also privately working on his own 'Augusta Bax' novel which also took a cruel look at Monica Jones. In Belfast in 1953 he gave up 'A New World Symphony', citing as his reason to Patsy Strang (a rival then unknown to Monica, with whom he had days before holidayed in Skye):

You know, *I can't* write this book: if it is to be written at all it should be largely an attack on Monica, & I *can't* do that, not while we are still on friendly terms.

Monica, over the sea to Skye

Not, one notes, 'loving terms'. The phraseology indicates that Larkin did not foresee anything other than a 'friendly' connection with

Monica. And 'still' suggests it would not last forever. Kingsley and Philip were best friends. But perhaps they were something closer than that as well. As Martin Amis puts it:

> It was always clear to everyone that Kingsley loved Philip with a near-physical passion. Philip probably felt the same at first.

'He thought that Philip was his property', Monica recalled at the end of her life. Other people had made that mistake. In the long run, Monica won. But Kingsley got the first low blow in. His Monicaphobic comic masterpiece was a bestseller in its day and has been in print ever since, as well as being made into a film and a TV drama. *Lucky Jim* made Kingsley Amis a household name. It made Monica Jones (alias 'Margaret Peel') a lifelong figure of fun. Or, in her self-lacerating word, 'ridiculous'.

Monica was kept in total ignorance about *Lucky Jim*'s contents and Philip's co-creative role. He forwarded her a bound copy a couple of days before publication. It was too late for changes but not too late for legal action. Gollancz were unaware of how riskily libellous Amis's novel was. Philip was clearly nervous. Philip had written a letter (now lost) with the volume, apologising for what was coming Monica's way. He explained that his involvement in the project was the result of passing 'irritation'. Against her, presumably. It seems that after reading the novel Monica destroyed his letters of the period in a Medea rage, and, it's clear, some of her own letters as well. As Thwaite notes, between 30 December 1953 and 3 August 1954, there is an 'inexplicable' absence of Larkin letters to Monica.

She read *Lucky Jim* through the night of Friday, 29 December at her parents' house. The three-day, two-thousand-word letter which followed is written in a storm of alcoholic rage, Ophelia-like mental derangement, and cold, well-aimed, fury. And finally, capping it all, there is moral hauteur. She forced herself to rise above the vulgar yah-boo lad-lampoonery of these two overgrown schoolboys.*

---

* James Booth, who owns Monica's copy, notes there is no mark in the book. She kept it in her select personal library to her death, however.

In summary this is how the massive letter erupts and runs.

Friday, 29 December

She will read the work in bed, 'beautifully arranged' in a nightdress. Philip is, before she opens the volume, not knowing what it contains, her 'darling pig'. She begins with a pre-emptive compliment – he is worth twenty Kingsleys, she avers, 'who suck so much from you'. But she will not attack his friend, that would be to play the 'disagreeable female'. 'Goodnose [God knows] I'd hate to seem like that – you know I don't assume a property in you . . . I am an unattended female, and really you ought to know me better, See?'

Already on high moral ground, she is, she says, 'in the mood of a love cat'. She will, she insists, be fair:

> I can't read for you – I have to read for me . . . I'd hate to seem to want to be one of those who like to think they 'think like a man', pah! . . . I don't think sex ought to come into it.

Philip, at this point, was probably bamboozled. He expected cat claws not cat love and a lecture on *Rezeption und Kritik*. With one of the abrupt chord changes common in Monica's letters she suddenly slips from high critical to orgasmic:

> O I *do* like you and I *do* tonight! My brown bear! O my stroky fur one! O hugs! Plenty of nice soft cuffs you'd get.

She is manifestly drunk.

Now, at last, for the novel. She 'gallops' through it during the night hours.

Saturday, 30 December

The letter breaks off and is picked up the next morning – she describes her clothing in great detail. Then, 'all right piggy', she goes into a pages-long narrative riff inspired by the 'smallest glass of sherry Jim had seriously been offered' – one of the novel's smart wisecrack lines about Jim's reaction to the exiguous refreshment offered him by Professor Welch.

Monica riffs on Kingsley's narrative – Jim being visited by a group of women, led by popsy Christine. There is no booze; Jim offers her the smallest glass of nothing. Monica lets her imagination rip into Dadaism. She recalls Philip getting drunk on a bottle of Beaune he has brought to a BYOB party – she standing alongside him in her sheepskin coat. 'Shall these dry Beaunes have life?'

She is drunk again.

At last, she gets to the point. 'Well I'll tell you a bit about L.J. Some of it really is very funny – Oh I can't list all the bits that amused me.' But the total impression is that the novel is 'forced'. It doesn't flow into its own story. The ending is a 'clumsy huddling up'. These are legitimate critical points, which others will later also make. But those other critics, unlike Monica Jones, are not lampooned in the novel.

So far Monica has not mentioned Margaret. She now, preparing for a second sleepless night, goes for the kill:

> From you I imagined something much more damaging – *really* monkey* – what *do* you take me for? *Really* I sometimes wonder. Do you in your head think me fit to be certified? For I would be if I got stirred up by the like of that. O monkey! twenty kisses, plenty kisses . . . O my silkie one, Goodnight and one more kiss and one more kiss.

Sunday, 31 December

She has waited two days to strike, and she does it coldly and soberly. The first snow has fallen outside, and its chill laces her prose. She describes the scene poetically, and then goes back to the novel. 'Oh',

---

* Al Read, the radio comedian's catchphrase was 'Right Monkey'. He was a favourite of Philip and Monica.

she inquires, in *faux naïveté*: 'is "Margaret" some lady who didn't find K. attractive? I thought it must be someone he was punishing.' It can't, surely, be an actual study from life. 'Margaret may be admired by some critics but she seems very hollow to me.' She goes on in assumed perplexity:

It even occurred to me that it's the kind of fantasy he'd probably like to make up upon myself, except I am not so egotistical as to think everybody wants to put me in a book and I do not believe you would be so treacherous.

She exonerates him, though they both know he was double-dyed treacherous. The blame is shifted to the scapegrace nominal author:

K. would love to make himself believe that I am the sort of character who pretends to do in herself with sleeping pills and uses the wrong lipstick and dresses with fatal wrongness.

This, one might think, was the moment when she could / should have broken with Philip and sued the backside off Gollancz, rendering Amis an untouchable author.

She merely wrote a letter. It puts Philip on the spot. He surely *cannot* have betrayed her. What is he to say, in the words of one of the blues songs all three of them loved, 'Frankie and Johnny' – 'I was your man, but I did you wrong'? Monica was yoking Philip to herself while embarking on her long, and eventually successful, campaign, to sever him from Kingsley. That mattered to her more than ridicule.

In the thirty years of life which remained to Philip the two erstwhile inseparables can scarcely have met thirty times. Not once did Kingsley come to Hull after Philip moved there in 1955, except for his (once) dearest friend's funeral. Philip's and Monica's letters are peppered with derogatory remarks about Philip's once-upon-a-time best friend.

Monica left the novel at Stourport for her parents to read, telling them that Philip had pulled Amis's narrative into shape. They, gallantly, denied seeing any satire of their daughter – though they must have done. Lily wrote, having seen the fifth edition of *Lucky Jim* noted in the *Observer*:

> I reckon that quite 1/3 of the proceeds should be given first to P. Larkin for putting it in good shape. Mark my words that book will die. The material is poor and ordinary. Your Pa says he hasn't seen anything funny yet. Much love, Mummy.

The reading world, alas, disagreed. And will, it seems, forever more.

Less Deceived, 1955

'*Not even a rabbit can like humiliation*'

Monica to Philip, 1955

On his Christmas 1954 trip to England Philip gave Monica a present doubling as an amend: could he dedicate his forthcoming volume of poetry to her?

> I don't mean any great fanfare of trumpets, just a note 'inscrib-ing' (rather than dedicating) it to Monica Jones. No subordinate clauses about 'remembering that sundrenched auberge in Picardy where we drank that exquisite bottle of Chateau Margarine . . .'

He did not however undertake to invite her judgement on the vol-ume's content, nor had he asked her to read proofs. That stage of their relationship had passed. But the dedication witnessed to her importance to the poet.

They had a New Year holiday (a regular high-day event for Monica in New Years to come) in Winchester and Salisbury. Monica was always softened by cathedrals. 'How's horrible work?' she asks him. Boring, he might have replied. Larkin was making definite plans to return from Belfast to the mainland. Not to Leicester (Monica had earlier brought to his attention a library headship going there) or Loughborough, to be near his frail mother, but Hull – equidistant (but distant) from mother and lover. As usual, he did not consult, beyond informing those who loved him of what he had irreversibly decided. Why did he want to come back? 'In 1950', he reflected, 'I ran away from England & the problems it held, but really they're still there unchanged & now I'm going back to them.'

There were personal reasons. Winifred Arnott, the library assistant with whom he almost but not quite had a consummated affair, had become bored with the life-stultifying love of Philip Larkin. The wild Patsy affair, pregnancy, and her divorce – in which his affair with her may have been a factor – had frightened the life out of him. Yet again his solution was flight, to live and love another day in another place. There was also something nobler. Philip Larkin wanted to make his name as a writer and take charge of a major library. He was bigger than Ulster's little magazines, no reviews and book-shelving assistantships. The fact that the Hull salary would be twice as large was another inducement. As a librarian he was on his way. At thirty-two, Philip Larkin would be, he boasted, the youngest university head librarian in Britain with a very big toy to play with. But he did not delude himself: 'How little our careers express what lies in us, and yet how much time they take up.' Monica could repeat that with even less joy than he.

After the *Lucky Jim* furore, Philip and Monica had talked seriously about their future: 'Wd I like to be married to you?', she asked, 'Well of course . . . but the awful vision of *getting* married appals me'. She was hurt when he pondered 'possibly' living with his mother (in Hull); 'not even a rabbit can like humiliation'. She was not now, she realised, his paramount concern. Not, indeed, in some ways even a person: 'I know you just think of me as a SITUATION', something to be fixed.

'Margaret Peel' continued to be an issue – *Lucky Jim* was the book of the season. Monica loftily dismissed it as 'old stuff'. Kingsley Amis, she condescendingly observed, 'is basically a good simple decent chap who's gone the wrong way'. The wrong way into literary stardom, Philip might enviously have thought, looking at edition after edition of *Lucky Jim*. Monica would soon be able to put her verdict on Kingsley to the test. ARH, to raise the profile of his department, had set up a conference on 'Angry Young Men' writers. Star attendees would be Kingsley Amis, Malcolm Bradbury and John Wain. Monica had yet to meet the man who lampooned her. Bradbury, whom she thought 'terrible' – having known him too well as a Leicester student (1950–53) – was in the process of depicting her as Viola Masefield in *Eating People is Wrong* (1959). The hero of that future novel, Professor Stuart Treece, was transparently ARH. The scene in which Stuart / ARH helps Viola / Monica remove her brassiere is evidence of the planetary distance between fact and fiction.

'I feel a bit afraid to meet Kingsley,' Monica told Philip. 'I don't shine in company, being shy as a rabbit.' Kingsley and his wife Hilly were staying with Monica's college friends the Evanses: 'suppose they bring the baby?' Monica asked, nervously, fearing the de rigueur single woman's requirement to dandle the other woman's bundle of joy. To her relief, Hilly proved cheery. To her glee, Kingsley 'looked terribly broken down and had a baby's napkin safety pin to fasten his right cuff . . . his jokes wear thin after a time . . . he asked for fried eggs at breakfast so [the Evanses] had the experience of seeing him eat one.'

Not a pretty sight. 'I don't approve of K.', she went on, 'and considered in cold blood he is awful, but for a spell any way short I can't help liking him'. It was added joy that 'ARH was furious at the talks'. He would have been more furious had he known why young Bradbury was regarding him so closely. The conference made Monica think. She was increasingly disillusioned about the way the British university system was changing. 'I agree with you', she told Philip, 'about "English Studies", the only alternatives that I see are pretentious distortions or feebleness. I now do the feebleness.' The 'increasing nastiness of the department', its 'corrupt standards' make things worse. Philip returned to England and Hull in March 1955. His calls were first to his mother and, second in line, Monica. 'I do want you to like me best,' she told him. He now has a secretary at Hull, she learns – 'is she the sort who will sit on your knee?' Not yet.

Larkin's breakout volume as a poet was *The Less Deceived* (1955). The scent of his women wafts over its pages. The dedication is, plainly, to 'Monica Jones'. Monica could see she had inspired poems in the volume and – in some places – could claim a hand, by earlier praise, in their inclusion. She, more than anyone, had kept Philip in heart through the low moments of the years when the poems laboriously came to their perfected form. Monica had been privy to drafts of Larkin's poems in his lean years and her moral support, and their shared belief in the kind of poetry that mattered, was vital. He wasn't getting much of it anywhere else. As Booth wryly points out, the first of the five slim volumes on which Larkin's reputation rests, *The North Ship*, when published in 1945, received one review in the *Coventry Evening Telegraph* – which 'gives every sign of having been written by Larkin himself'. Without Monica, he might have ended up a mute inglorious Larkin. But without other women the slim volume would have been even slimmer.

The lead poem in *The Less Deceived*, about the young woman's photograph album, was a delicately lecherous compliment to Winifred Arnott. Other poems dated from Philip's love affairs with Ruth and Patsy – who admired the volume hugely; 'you're a real maker,' Patsy told him. Monica was sharp enough to see that other women were involved in the collection. But Monica Jones, the dedication asserted declared to the world, was *prima inter pares*.[*]

After *The Less Deceived* and his major inclusion in his friend Robert Conquest's *New Lines* anthology, Philip was elected spearhead poet of the Movement, as it was banally called – with the implication that all post-war English poetry needed was a good laxative.[†] His verse, and the tradition for it he created five years later with his contextual *Oxford Book of Twentieth-Century English Verse*, co-produced with Monica, laid out the battleground for the specifically *English* tradition – the line of Thomas Hardy versus supranational modernism.

Monica could bathe in the glow of *The Less Deceived*. 'Oh, I am sure you are the *one* of this generation,' she told him. 'Darling,' she said, 'I feel as I should if you had made a century for England and saved the rubber.' But now that they would be seeing more of each

---

[*] It is a pity this primacy, and that of Winifred, is necessarily lost in the *Collected Poems* (2012).

[†] The authoritative study of the Movement is Blake Morrison's 1980 monograph, which led to one of Larkin's later life friendships with the young author and editor.

other she warned: 'it would be dishonest not to let you know the worst about me . . . I am rather touchy lately.' He has, she notes, made 'this enormous change in his life': Hull. She 'had nothing to do with his decision'. She is aware 'you wouldn't make such a decision for me.' He must know, however, that the last thing she wants is 'power' over him – the idea 'revolts' her. Nonetheless she will protest his tactlessness. 'Do you know what you wrote? (I'm not offended) that yr Mother would think, if you married me, that it was in order to get away from her?' Did he not have a more generous description for what, she conceded, would never happen?

When he came back to England his mother and sister had put pressure on Philip to move Eva to Hull. He resisted and her mental state collapsed. She was hospitalised. James Booth is harsh on Monica at this stage of Philip's career: 'Monica was doing her best to persuade him to marry her by the well-calculated strategy of sympathising with his misogamy.' Her letters suggest to me that what she wanted from him above all was more presence, more public appearance together, not the ring on the finger. She was willing, if not happy, to accept a morganatic role to a man who wanted no wife in name. What did they expect? To 'live in a house called "Oakdene" & advance sound parish views? That wd be awful wouldn't it? . . . The kitchen audible in the lavatory and vice versa?' Their union would be something else.

I Am Nothing, 1955–1957

'Professors despise women'
Monica to Philip, 1954

After *The Less Deceived* Larkin went up like a rocket, as had Amis after *Lucky Jim*. The pals were on their way. Monica was falling like the stick into oblivion – or, worse, something to be poked fun at. 'Margaret Peel' was sniggered about by every knowing student on the Leicester campus, her gulag. Philip's reassurances were not always heartening: 'You at least adopt a motto of "Non Serviam" . . . I don't think you're absurd *at all*'. His contradiction rather implies that others may well think it. Professionally Monica's prospects were already shot: she was belatedly tenured, but ten years' research sterility meant, at best, a standstill career. And at worst it might mean the dead-wood chop. ARH, she tells Philip, is increasingly 'as rude and overbearing as he dare be. I am sure he is trying to drive me away. He is much nastier than he used to be. He makes me feel slow and stupid.'

'I am the department *ghost*,' she moaned. 'Professors', she bitterly says, 'despise women'. She returned public scorn with smarter private scorn. One day she came in to ARH's office on departmental business. He was working on his Arden edition of *Henry IV*, laboriously collating textual variants. A nitpicking kind of scholarship, Monica thought:

His clothes are appalling not just old, not just dirty, tho' they were both, but so cheap! They'd never been anything but appalling, from the day he carried them home from a closing down sale at a surplus govt. supply store . . . convicts' clothes.

He gave off 'a vapour of pomposity and foolishness'. You would not want to be looked at closely by Monica if you were in her bad books. Many at Leicester now were. ARH's Arden edition, incidentally, is judged superior by Shakespeareans.

ARH had harnessed her as the department workhorse – forty tutorials a fortnight, five lectures a week, hundreds of exam scripts to mark. Departmental stars shot past her to their readerships, chairs and sabbaticals, and Monica picked up their teaching slack. Her one consolation was that 'I spend most of my time in the company of great literature', but with the sense that the walls of her life were closing in on her. 'I hate the direction in which the College and the dept are going. I foresee it getting nastier and nastier.'

Philip encouraged her to be amusingly malicious about her colleagues – even those who were manifestly well meaning. Malice isolated and alienated her. It was sensed by those she scorned. She could, with the kind of co-operation which Philip had shown Kingsley, have thrown off a sprightly article or two for the *TLS*: a monograph even. She still pondered something between hard covers on her favourite poet, Crabbe, and made notes, but it went nowhere. Nor, in one important respect, did she. She no longer went to scholarly libraries or kept up with the few journals she found civilised. All that remained to her was the company of great literature and the duty, she liked, of talking about it to receptive audiences.

Was Monica Jones badly treated? She was. In its new professionalised, career-seeking form ('enfeebled' and 'nasty' as she put it), there was no respected place for those who 'merely' knew a vast amount of literature, had judged what was good and bad, and could convey what, in their considered judgement, the 'greatness' of great literature was. Her belief that senior men in her profession 'despised women' was overstated but, in the 1950s, not far off the truth.

Philip's love for her was constrained. He could have helped her get a bigger flat where they could cohabit more publicly and for longer periods domestically. But it suited him to keep her a dangling woman.

Theirs would become, in future years, a secret relationship that was no secret. But what kind of relationship was it? Philip could be at times, when not evasive, brutally frank: 'In my heart of hearts, I'm on no-one's side but my own . . . I don't mean, of course, that I don't like making love with you . . .' The word 'like' hangs limply.

Larkin was a maestro of the unprogressive relationship. Monica and later on Maeve Brennan were Philip's lovers longer than many marriages endure: but being 'on the way' to somewhere was all they ever got. He himself liked to tell friends that there were two women in his life: one whom he should marry and one whom he wanted to marry. Some women, Patsy and Winifred notably, declined to be flies trapped in Larkin amber. Monica and Maeve, for all the decades of their marriageable life, accepted his willed indecision. They believed he was worth it.

By 1950 people were curious about Monica, at her age, being 'on the shelf', as the sneering phrase was. Arthur Collins told her, irresponsibly, when she was still two years short of thirty, that there was gossip in the SCR among younger women at Leicester about:

> my ridiculous secretiveness because I never told them how old I was . . . By God! If they ask me now I shall tell them a lie . . . I wonder if there is anything else they want to know – my latest bank statement, perhaps, or my monthly accounts? If there is any insanity in my family? Do my mother's hands brush the ground? Fools! Blast their eyes!

'I keep a kind of padlock on myself because I am not sure of what you want,' she told Philip. 'I feel rather like the secret lady of some king – something like that – whom he visits some times, but can't "own".' She then breaks off, abruptly, to tell him she is thinking of buying a scarlet suspender belt – she knows how fond he is of her 'private clothes'. Such disjunctions reflect a life ever harder to hold together.

He chose to visit his mother, not Monica on her (Monica's) birthday, 8 May. He'd promised he would see her and broke his word. She got herself into 'what you call a working myself up state.' She could tell, as their ten-year anniversary approached, that 'you have changed more than I have in the progress of our "relationship".' 'It's my choice & I made it. I can't take you in my stride; you take up most of me, and that's what I'm like . . . How difficult real life is . . . I wdn't rather have a letter than your presence'. She quite understood 'all you say about your shell you little crustacean. I've put a shell round myself.' It did not protect her, it merely cut her off from life.

In October, another miserable term starting, she burst into wailing realisation:

Do you know that in this January I shall have been IN THIS PLACE FOR TEN YEARS. I cannot bear to think of it–my *best* years they should have been and here am I. What have I got? No I'm really wretched: my best years and nothing to show – surely, surely I ought at least to have a decent place to *live* in, or, at least have my work pretty well in hand; those are the ten years in wh people make a *success of their careers* – you have done so, you needn't mind, you've plenty to show: rapid advance in your pro-fession & very satisfactory advance as a chap that gets referred to in the Lit. Sup. You talk as though you're as badly off as me till I believe it, but of course you're not: you may be as *miserable* as me, but in the world's eye you are a successful man. Success wd not make me much cheerfuller, but I shouldn't feel my self to be so *ridiculous* as well as miserable – I don't deserve the dignity of being miserable, ridiculous is what I am . . . I am simply ridiculous – a reject, an incapable . . . with every year you get a sort of gain – I just get loss and shrinkage . . . Why aren't you coming tomorrow?

She accepts he no longer finds her 'sexually inflaming'. He intimated sex was 'the spur' in their relationship: he is no longer pricked. Her self-laceration goes on for sixteen sides, finishing, 'I think of you all the time.' And he her? 'You don't read my letters,' she alleges later in the year – this one he most certainly did. But nothing changed – the die was cast. How did she become this shell of what was once Monica Jones? At such moments, recurrent in her life, she was paralysed by what she called 'that terrible inertia that comes from misery'.

The scorpion surrounded with a circle of fire will sting itself to death. Self-harm is all it has left. One aches for Monica when she tells Philip she is 'thrilled' by having bruised her shoulder because 'it is a kind of company'. As Art Garfunkel might croon, 'hello painful my old friend'. Their favourite poet, Hardy, put it best:

Though fervent was our vow,
Though ruddily ran our pleasure,
Bliss has fulfilled its measure,
And sees its sentence now.

Ache deep; but make no moans:
Smile out; but stilly suffer:
The paths of love are rougher
*Than thoroughfares of stones.**

The pendulum swung. But, as always now, momentarily. Sark in September 1955 was a blessed ten days' holiday. And, over their three days at Lords in June there had been an exciting test to be determined by the fast bowlers she loved above all cricketers. Momentously on 1 November *The Less Deceived* was published and Philip came to Leicester. Excessive jubilation was dampened by the fact that at the same time Eva, clinically depressed, was being treated with electro-convulsive therapy. She recovered and found solace in the Quaker-influenced Circle of Silent Ministry. Philip now routinely came to Monica after his monthly visit to his mother. Occasionally more frequently.

In New Year 1956 Monica and Philip visited Chichester and its cathedral. This annual 'churchy' visit inspired his most loving love-offering. It was designed as a 1956 Valentine poem for her – 'something special'. But perfecting it required a few extra days. As James Booth notes '[Philip] consulted Monica Jones during the drafting of "An Arundel Tomb" more than in the case of any other poem'. The gift poem finishes with the overquoted last line (inscribed, among other places, on Maeve Brennan's tombstone): 'What will survive of us is

---

* Monica quotes in a letter to Philip with self-reference from Hardy's poem in the second, angriest, Maeve crisis in April 1964.

love'. Booth credits Monica's 'acerbic intelligence' as inspiring Larkin's stringent afterthought: 'Love isn't stronger than death just because two statues hold hands for six hundred years'. But who, on Valentine's day, speaks the whole truth? The poem was a high point for Monica. He loved her: the world would now read the fact.

The tenderness she felt, and enjoyed, had its downside. He nowadays found her too giving in their love-making. He wanted tussle. But the annual pattern of their relationship remained unbroken. Lords came and went again. In high summer there was a holiday, this year on Skye: they were still fit enough to hike and Monica recalled her beloved *Waverley*, bonnie boats and noble Flora MacDonald.

Monica accepted that things would not change other than with the slow wilt of passing time. She was now in her thirty-fifth year. Philip made a point by moving into ostentatiously bachelor accommodation – the high-windowed 32 Pearson Park. This university flat was, says Andrew Motion, 'a declaration of eternal independence'. The faint echo 'from Monica' is thrown back. For a few years, when visiting Hull, Monica booked into a hotel 'to keep up the appearance of respectability'. And, one suspects, to keep her from riffling, as unstoppable Patsy Strang had done, among his most private papers where a private Larkin might be found.

It is not easy for those of Monica's party, as I am, always to feel with Larkin. And one should not indulge the easy condescensions of the biographer 'in charge of all the facts'. But one can, if not sympathise (I don't) at least see where he was coming from. Larkin, as much as Hardy, needed the love, companionship and (to stretch the word) worship of women – as much for his poetry as for himself. It was selfish but that was what he wanted. His best friend, Kingsley, was tormented in middle and later age with sexual impotence. He wrote one of his finest novels, *Jake's Thing*, not about it, but out of it. Larkin suffered what one might call relational impotence – an inability to commit. It was, perversely, a kind of creative stimulus. He wrote a couple of his greatest mid-career poems, 'The Whitsun Weddings' and 'Dockery and Son', out of that impotence. Could he have written his last great ode to death, 'Aubade', had a wife been lying in bed with him? No more than if a wife had been sitting beside him in the train that Whitsun. The cost to both him and Monica in terms of life-loss were large. She, at least, paid it not voluntarily but knowingly. Knowing too how terribly it would hurt. She could complain but never let go of him: or he of her.

22

'Ten Years!' 1957

'I detest to be a figure of pathos'
Monica to Philip, 1955

For Monica January 1957 was a glum anniversary month:

Do you realise that you and I have known each other ten years . . .
The years, 3 Australian tours, 3 General Elections. I wonder for
how many decades we shall know each other?

The word 'know' is loaded. What are they moving toward? Mere
acquaintance? Exchange of Christmas cards? What lies ahead is pro-
pitious for him. 'You may go far,' she says. And her? She dare not
ask herself. 'Sometimes', she says, 'I blame you for destroying my
confidence.' One question haunted her: was what she had sacrificed,
for him, worth it? And, overhanging that, the awful realisation that
it was too late to change things if the answer were no. It was bad but
any alteration would be worse. She had made her choice and must see
it through.

The year began badly with his flouting an anniversary important
to Monica. Larkin's practice was to spend Christmas grimly with his
mother and celebrate New Year for a couple of days with Monica –
typically with a trip to some cathedral town. In 1957 he cancelled.
Monica was cut deep. 'It's a pain you have to give', she concedes –
there are things in his life more important than her – but he always

reserves the right to do such things without even talking to her before-hand. 'It's not a thing I'd do to a child.' She does not have the privilege of acting like a 'jealous wife', but she can be righteously angry.

Her loneliness is, at times like these, verging on borderline psychotic: 'Most people now I don't want to talk to, nothing seems worth saying. Already I've lived alone enough to be a little queer.' It took the form of OCD – there was a housewife imprisoned inside her, shaking the bars: 'You've no idea of the pleasure, the pathetic pleasure a wan little one, but a true one – that doing things with my linen cupboard gives me.' Was this what her love for Larkin had reduced her to? Love's skivvy? Nonetheless, things went on. They wrote Valentine verses to each other – another annual anniversary event. Monica's for 1957 was poignant. It was to be sung to the 'aire of Captain Conie's [i.e. cunny] Fancie' an improper joke of the kind which gave them both a smile:

> *Birds choose their mates*
> *Before they mate*
> *They are not ready*
> *To nest as yet.*
>
> *It's too cold, too dark,*
> *There may still be snows,*
> *Spring barely stirs*
> *But today they choose.*
>
> *Do you want to marry me or not?*

The answer was what it had always been. Yes I want to but no I can't.

Larkin was nowadays ever more preoccupied with his rapidly expanding Hull library. She saw less of him, and wrote massive letters to fill the emptiness. Why, she complained, won't he take her more often to see his mother? Is he ashamed of her? Or, more likely, is he nervous about giving a false impression of impending marriage?

> I am not asking you to marry me, but all the same on reflection
> I can't see why you're so sure that being married to *me* wd mean

an end for you of all the pleasures you value most and find in
yourself.

She is, she prides herself, 'a good deal different from the average
husband-hunting, husband-eating lady'. Then she reminds him she is
not his mother, he is *not* his father. At work all is nastiness for her. But
it is a West Indies test, a real contest for the MCC, and Lord's will be
glorious. He will be hers for five days.

In July Larkin complained again about her passivity in making
love. She wanted mutual 'tenderness' but 'It wd be faked emotion as
far as I'm concerned: I just don't feel personal at that time', he says
honestly. For him, sex with Monica was a rough-house thing. Nowadays he saw his mother and Monica within twenty-four hours on the
same weekend trip. Eva remained in direst straits. At the end of July
Sark was in prospect, but for the second time that year he cancelled
something all-important to Monica. 'I was the more deceived,' her
letter of protest began. Why had he cancelled? Eva's condition was
not the reason. He was going instead to a conference at Portmeirion
where he would meet up with 'bloody Patsy' – now Patsy Murphy.
She has a baby, and Monica, cursingly, wishes it 'will sick on your
best suit'.

She is beyond fury, interpreting the slight as 'not a move away from
me but an act against me'. She realises now why he kept 'tactfully
dropping little remarks', when they were in London,

abt not liking holidays and so on while you have arranged for
yourself a perfect whirl of holidays. I suppose last year you resolved never to take a real holiday with me again, was it? Maybe
it seems a waste of your holidays to see me on a bit of them when
you can see me in term time when you're in Loughboro' anyway?

She has noticed his crueller tone with her and more 'impersonal' love-
making. And of course she realises

that I should be very anticlimactic between the glamour of Portmeirion and the further glamour of your tour of the capitals to

the international smart set.* If it makes yr triumph any sweeter to reflect that yr whirl of excitement goes on in comparison with my retirement into weeding and scrubbing floors for the summer you have that satisfaction . . . I don't know what I mean. I can say this, that if you desired an explosion you could not have calculated a more effective one than dropping me for a holiday in favour of bloody Patsy. How could you do such an *absolute outside* thing? . . . it seems at the moment the utter insult, the absolute Machiavellian Ultima Thule offence beyond credence let alone forgiveness.

Then, with one of the peculiar jumps in the train of her letters of this kind, she goes on to recommend Dulux as the best paint for redoing his flat – 'but remember the sandpaper first'. By the time she writes again a week later, she has swallowed her rage and apologises. He arranges a compensatory jaunt to Yorkshire – conveniently close to Hull for him but not in Hull itself where they could be seen together. He could, of course, have taken her to Portmeirion and be damned about Patsy. But he never nowadays took her into company.

He takes her, as further apology for the Patsy affront, on a trip to London where he buys a second-hand Rolleiflex. Her rage fades: she can even joke about his delinquency as to holidays: 'I meant to have told you before how amused I was by yr remark in a letter – a good few letters ago – that . . . going on a holiday with me was like going with a cross between Gracie Allen and Emily Brontë.' Her spirits were further lifted by the autumn fashions – 'I can't wait to wear the sack line'. Perhaps she will wear one on the September break he has invited her to in Pulborough, West Sussex for a few days.

The American government was, at this period, giving fellowships for British academics to spend periods in American universities as part of their campaign to roll back the European intellectual love affair with Marxism. In late 1957 ARH pushed Monica to apply for one. She met the American consul, who visited Leicester recruiting,

---

* These travels abroad seem never to have happened. Doubtless the invitations were real and mentioned by Larkin.

but the more she thought about it the more she became afraid of (1) the awful loneliness (2) leaving her mother (3) 'politick'. America must realise the whole world was not envying them. What would Dr Pussy say? she asks. She answers her own question: 'No – how could I leave you?' She will not go to 'Yankland'. But then, later, she will note: 'you didn't at all try to stop me'. Larkin interpreted the American possibility as her proposing marriage: 'if I'm prepared to marry you it shouldn't need an American invitation to precipitate the proposal'. He did not, however, say he would *never* marry her. That door he always left ajar. Monica, one suspects, never seriously intended to take up the American offer if it came her way. She was using it to test Philip's fidelity, and he saw through her ruse.

Monica in the late 1950s

23

'My Worst Year', 1958–1959

'It seems to me I am spoiling yr life in a hideously ingenious way'
Philip to Monica, 1958

Monica soldiered on through what was left of the fifties. The one dimly bright light had been Philip's moving to Hull in 1955. They were, at least, in the same country. But in no sense were they together. He was a hundred miles from Eva in Loughborough, ten miles further down the same road from Monica in Leicester. It was a two birds with one stone thing for Philip, 'the professional weekend enjoyer' as she sardonically called him. Their paths crossed: there was no union.

He himself, oddly, saw his weekend stays with Monica as something like gay cottaging: 'It seems . . . to me that what we have is a kind of homosexual relation, disguised.' Homosexual relations would be criminal for another ten years. Whatever it was called, distance left him free over the next fifteen years to cultivate an intense relationship with his assistant librarian Maeve Brennan, with whom he was a professional weekday enjoyer. At this stage his relationship with his other woman was in its early stages. Once it flowered, Maeve, like Monica, would find herself a woman trapped in aspic. The arrangement worked for Philip in the area of his life which mattered to him more than women or libraries. The years 1955 to 1965 saw the bumper crop of his poetry culminating in *The Whitsun Weddings*.

Monica, as always, stayed with her parents in Stourport in vacations. It was from there she wrote her longest letters to Philip. Her colleagues were elsewhere, pursuing their research and prosecuting their careers. Her reading was mind-broadening at best: or merely books at bedtime. There was some gardening and a lot of shopping and cooking with her mother. Monica's parents knew little about their daughter's no longer young man. There are no mentions of visits by Philip to Stourport or any interest in what Monica might have been doing there. In the thirteen years between first meeting Monica and her mother's death, Larkin met Mrs Jones only twice. In the exchange of letters between Monica and her mother, Lily very rarely mentions Philip.

Monica's home life at Stourport was wholly domestic. In moments of exasperation she called her mother 'terrible', but they cooked together for the man of the house, which Monica enjoyed. Her Leicester digs allowed her little more than boiled eggs, tea and toast, and she resided in none of them very long. Mrs Jones, not Fred, made occasional day visits to Leicester in the 1940s and 1950s: she could not stay with Monica as there was no room in her digs. Sometimes the two of them would go on longer trips to Weardale, where there was still Peart family. The region remained dear to Monica.

Suddenly, out of the blue on 11 October 1959, Monica's mother died of a heart attack. She had kept any premonitory symptoms to herself. Monica wanted burial: but Lily had asked, in her last hours, for cremation, 'wh. I hated'. To the end, Margaret Lily Jones did not want to cause any fuss. Philip could have taken a compassionate long weekend from work to comfort Monica. But death terrified the life out of him. And his library was making its major leap forward. He was, he persuaded himself, simply too busy to help the woman he ostensibly loved currently going through hell.

Monica grieved but did not cry at her mother's death. Her widowed father's grief took the form of gluttony. 'My Father was voraciously hungry, I couldn't give him enough to eat, while I just had paralysis of the throat and couldn't swallow'. She catered for his needs, as condolence. Monica's dolour was self-denying. She allowed herself to feel nothing and ate nothing. Her recurring bulimia – the periods of 'tomato sandwich fever' – originated at this traumatising period of her life.

Stress piled on stress. Her father, who had been suffering from cancer, died on 19 December, two months after his wife, of a post-operational heart attack. Philip's letter of condolence was coolly sympathetic, making, as James Booth observes, the bizarre remark that Fred's departure from the world may have been eased by knowledge of the Conservatives entering Downing Street. Philip's softer hearted mother wept sympathetic tears on hearing of Monica's loss. Culminating this winter hecatomb, Monica's beloved Arthur Collins died within a week of her father.

Monica in later years looked back on this last as the crowning blow: 'When Collins died . . . that was the beginning of my troubles.' He was taken into hospital with no forewarning for Monica, and 'lived only a few days . . . He was upset the nursing home people wd not let me in':

The last I knew of it is that he cried when he was told that I had been there and been sent away, and that he asked if I was wearing my red tights. His relatives asked in a joking way how he knew they were tights & he said, 'she told me'. That's the last I know.

What, in the course of this twenty-three-side letter, should she leave Philip in her will, she asked. She would, over the next years, think ever more nostalgically of 'the old old days when it was just Collins and me'. In retrospect she dated 1959 as the start of her drift into alcoholism. It had left Monica a thirty-seven-year-old orphan. Given the size of the Peart brood, Monica had an extended family and she received invitations to spend Christmas with far-off relatives. She declined. Her 'family' was her parents. When they were sliced, simultaneously, out of her life, along with Collins, she accepted that she was now alone in the world. All she had was Philip, and there could be no Christmas with him in 1959. Eva came first.

24

The Sixties

'*I am alone*'

Monica to Philip, January 1960

The sixties, despite his glum verdict in his poem 'Annus Mirabilis' on their lateness 'for me', were the years of Larkin's ascension. Honours, fame and even showbiz glamour (he was now the Ringo Starr of verse, he jested), showered on him. For a man whose *The Less Deceived*, in various forms and parts, had been rejected by virtually every reputable publisher of poetry in London, it was 'manna'. 'And what the fuck is this?' Larkin liked to imagine the Israelites saying when they saw what Jehovah had served them up for breakfast. He felt the same about celebrity.

Success made Larkin amorous. The seventeen-year affair with Maeve Brennan which had been simmering for three years began seriously in February 1961. Both his women were faithful to him; he, necessarily, was duplicitous. He got gratification of a different kind from them: at one pole (Monica's) tough, at times experimental, sex; at the other pole (Maeve's) 'heavy petting'. Larkin called it 'reserved love' in a letter to Maeve from Sark where he was simultaneously enjoying the unreserved variety with Monica.

For Monica, aged thirty-eight to forty-seven, the sixties were a decade of loss, ageing and betrayal. Her letters are, at a level below the sprightly conversational which she still maintained, a chronicle of woe, career failure, and – above all – loneliness. She was, by 1960, existentially solitary. One sees in her letters to Philip a sad awareness that their love had lost its drive. Theirs was a relationship without the conjugal cement of cohabitation. It was a house built on ink, paper and postage stamp. She was more frightened of the relentless calendar than he. Philip was born looking middle-aged. Now famous, he was more attractive to women than he had been, with a head of hair and dandyish proclivities, in his twenties.

Monica could see her future. Intimate letter-exchange punctuated by infrequent sex, rarer with the passing years, short annual holidays, and weekends where the main event was the food she cooked. Her life would be drudgery with flashes of bliss. All the while, 'age and then the only end of age' was ever looming. It was the sense of emptiness which afflicted her in the cold New Year of 1960; 'every smallest thing is too much for me . . . Nothing interests me'. The heart was going out of her, as forty loomed. 'I am almost afraid of making up . . . I am alone' she tells Philip. An uncle, whom she has no time for, tells her, 'get married . . . This is not a proposal even though it's leap year' she quips, gloomily, to Philip.

She takes refuge in chores. There are a couple of pages in one letter on bookshelves for her new flat at 8 Woodland Avenue. But they are for a place which she rents and is passing through with two suitcases of belongings. Why spring-clean for a landlord? But she does play-act at domesticity. She is housed but homeless. So is he, but more comfortably so, in his 32 Pearson Park eyrie. He is earning twice as much as she, denied promotion and annual salary increments for non-performance. Lecturing is not the most important thing lecturers are supposed to do.

On 17 January she notes 'this is one month ago that Father died'. She tells Philip, so he can see her, even though he is a hundred miles away, that she is wearing a Jaeger skirt, size 8 ½, her badger leg stockings, and a brassiere which, she notes, he knows well. Thus outfitted, she will lecture on 'my dear G. M. [*Guy Mannering*] the most cheerful of Scott's books.' Philip has tried, valiantly, but he simply can't get on with Sir Walter.

Monica fantasises how her hero would trounce the department's stage Scotsman 'Guzzling George Fraser . . . odious little vermin.'

She feels all the time that the department wants her gone. Malice, her old friend, eases her pain. ARH 'won't refuse to bow the knee to Baal'. And what did that pagan god demand? Sacrificial female victims. Monica Jones declines to hurl herself into the pit. She mocks the man: 'silly bugger ha ha!'

Richard Hoggart (nicknamed 'HRH' – 'His Royal Hoggart' – and 'Baron Hoggart' in her and Philip's letters), now riding high, she does not wholly despise. He makes clumsy attempts to help her, but she looks down on him. *The Uses of Literacy*, which had (justly) made him famous, is dismissed as a 'silly book', 'Something for the mass mouth to swallow'. In her opinion he's 'a decent man if only he could write in clear English':

> I quite like him, really, but think he is a pernicious writer. George [Fraser] I like less, but a Scotch grammar-school has at least taught him some basic things, I think too that George has more brain than Hoggart if he would not be so lazy and drunken and concerned to earn sums outside his paid employment.

Ronald Draper, the departmental Lawrentian, is a 'beast' and dull with it. 'He is supposed to be clever', she told Philip, but if so 'it isn't a way I know about'.

She rants about her colleagues. Lice on the locks of literature, all of them. Why does she not, as they do, publish and 'advance'? She consoles herself with the thought that she is too honest in a slough of male mendacity. At this crossroad stage of professional life she resolves to pretend no more: 'I am always aware of my limitations, the only thing I can say is I do always try to say *true* things and this it is which inhibits me; this flow of meaningless speech, this is what is wanted.' She will not supply it.

Monica yearns for Collins. When she thinks of what has replaced him 'hysterical laughter of despair overcomes one'. Resolution forms in her with the New Year: 'I don't like wasting my life by not liking most of it.' As usual, amidst this rumination about her life she slips in a snapshot for Philip's inward eye: 'I am decently dressed in striped shirt, lilac skirt, but shall soon change into old trousers again.'

I have to interject here. The academic world would have thought
Monica was wrong about the colleagues she rantingly abuses. All those
mentioned above, and some she doesn't mention, were a credit to
the department Humphreys had built. But there was a coldness and
condescension to her and the weight she was carrying in her teaching
load which drove her, at least in the privacy of her letters to Philip,
to get her own back. Teaching was still, in the sixties, what D. H.
Lawrence had called it in *The Rainbow*, 'A Man's World'. Monica's
rage against the Leicester English department, fair, unfair, or partly
fair was exacerbated by grief in bereavement, the perennial inability
to get across what she believed important in English Studies, and –
crowning it – the awful paralysis of her relationship with the man she
loved. Her mood shuttled between despair and desperation propelled
by spurts of anger. Were she not so clever, so able to see it all for what
it was, it would have been more bearable.

Monica got through winter and spring and by July 1960 her life
began to mend with anticipation of the forthcoming summer holiday
to Sark. She tells Philip she is looking for a swimsuit to buy. She hasn't
swum for twenty years – at Oxford, one presumes. She buys a couple
of suits: 'too small as you directed' accentuating 'the main thing' – her
'figger'. Before Sark in August there is the reassuringly usual three days
at Lords. This year it's England against Pakistan. Philip resents paying
two guineas a day for a walkover. Monica pays her own way happily. It
would, nonetheless, be one of their 'nicest' Lords occasions, she later
recalls. As always, she bought a commemorative mug. Dexter slogged
a lusty half-century, seamer Statham took six wickets. The examiner's
meeting, thank heaven, did not date-clash. And there is pleasure in it
for a change. 'My candidate [Bill Ruddick] scraped his first' and was
duly appointed 'my chap'. He will serve loyally in that subaltern role
for five years. She declares roundly: 'I don't like anything in my life
at present except being with you'. But her life is so overwhelmingly
being without him. She breaks down on the last night at Sark.

The business of disposing of her parents' house occupies the rest of
August. She is a ghost in the home where she grew up, surrounded
by remembered, happier Monicas. 'I feel in rather a bad way – really',
she tells Philip, 'but don't like to write it because that makes it more

real.' A consoling reality is that for the first time in her life she will have, after probate, a sizeable piece of money. She begins to dream of a 'cottage of my own' where, out of the public eye, Philip might spend real, not visiting, time with her. But first there is the dreary labour of clearing Stourport. She has no place to store things that mean something to her. Demolishing her past rouses demons, and she hallucinates. 'I have a hammer by my bed for safety,' she tells Philip. She cannot open the windows at night – although it is August – for fear of burglars and worse. 'In dread of birds' the windows are shut by day and the doors bolted.

Single-handedly she strips her home of all that made it home. An irritating uncle is set up for years with her father's underwear. She saves a pullover for Philip. She wears, while working, her mother's clothes. Walk-in purchasers of fittings and furniture are 'brazen', and make unwanted comments on her spinsterhood. 'The single woman suffers from the married woman,' she says. They impudently instruct her to get married quickly 'or it'll be too late to have children'. She tells Philip, 'I have borne this kind of thing for years.' Why, she wonders, should she want to be like them, 'unthinking mayflies that they are'? Their kindliness insults her.

'What's the most pleasure to me at the moment', she tells Philip, is *The Archers* – the fifteen-minute Home Service 'everyday story of country folk'. Philip listens at the same time. It is a kind of togetherness. But he does not, cannot, will not, come to help her. He could have taken a week off (August is the sleepiest month for university libraries) to help her lift, carry and cheer her up. Every letter she sends him is a cry, and yet he never once visits her in Stourport – such a thing, she said bitterly, years later, 'would never dawn on him'. Was it simply indifference? More probably his thanatophobia, morbid fear of death, kept him away. Whatever the reason, Monica's loneliness was eating through her personality like acid.

She tells him, 'my trouble is I don't eat enough'. For the remainder of her life, stress anorexia will be an intermittent torment. She loses her mother's engagement ring off her thinned finger. The strain of house-clearing, single-handed, comes close to destroying her. There is 'thunder of blood in my ears'. She has bad dreams. She briefly visits

Philip in Hull: staying – distantly – in a hotel so they won't be gossiped about: she knows his attic bachelor flat only by the address she writes on envelopes. On Sunday, when she must return to Stourport, she faints away: 'oh, that was nasty', she recalls.

After the house is empty of everything remembered she feels, at last, she may survive. But for one reason only:

> I never get over the unbelievable good fortune of having you in my life. Life without a man in it would be very narrow, and yet most men are silly in some ways, that childish showing-off, that serious almost ritually religious self-regard, I can't stand that . . .You are absolutely unusual . . . *you remain unusual though being a writer.*

But what was she? His partner? His 'woman on the side'? His 'help-meet'? His 'ball and chain'? His confidante? His inspirational Fanny Brawne?

She can at last, money in her purse, hunt for her cottage. On 14 August she is told, by a bleakly bureaucratic missive from the college, that she has 'crossed the bar' having been held back by ARH, salary frozen, for three years. It also means tenure; she cannot be 'let go'. There is no pleasure in this unpromotion, but there is financial relief. She now earns £140 a month after stoppages. On Thursday, 18 August, as she prepares to leave her family home for ever, she suffers the 'most nervous night I have ever had'. She is convinced she hears footsteps and whispers in the emptily echoing house. Finally it is over. She can put the house on the market: sell her past, create a future.

Preparing for the new academic year she is racked by diarrhoea, vomiting and fainting fits. She is, nonetheless, looking at a house she might buy in Thirsk, Yorkshire – a commutable half hour by train to Hull; and at flats to rent in Leicester, self-contained enough for Philip to comfortably stay overnight. He remains studiously uninterested in her prospective properties. She says: 'I do wish you could have seen them with me . . . I do feel ill.'

He ignores her hinted pleas. The sole experience of 'home', with his mother in 1948, convinced him domesticity would finish him as a poet. Philip, she reiterates over and again, is all that means anything to her. 'I have nobody else . . . Had Collins been living I should have been better about my parents [and] not so awfully dependent on you.' She must go back to Leicester for the start of term 'but I hate it'. 'The awful claustrophobic depression' intensifies her feeling that she needs air. She imagines a windswept cottage with Philip.

Her loneliness is exacerbated by disliked colleagues, a department trying to push her out, and a city with nothing to love in it. 'I do not know how I shall manage when work starts just living seems too hard.' As Philip's 'Bun' she scurries, looking for somewhere 'rabbity' – a safe hole far from Leicester. As always she inserts verbal snapshots of herself in every letter. 'Yesterday', she tells him, 'I dressed up in ladylike fashion, but today I am wearing violet trousers and scarf, white pullover, green jacket.'

When term starts she is smitten with near-fainting dread at the start of lectures, the 'stream of essays' and ARH's damnable crack-of-dawn staff meetings. She switches to autopilot and still lectures with more style than any of the colleagues who look down on her. Hoggart at the epochal Lady Chatterley trial 'sounded absurd' she says, and Philip agrees. The spark of life in her 'is very low', 'Do come', she implores. 'I think I feel as very old people must feel'. But she is not yet, she feels, too old to wear 'Chelsea setter, teenage *weirdies*' clothes'.

Christmas, as usual, is wretched: she declines an offer to spend it with an uncle. The invitation was not 'eager' and she doesn't like him. She declines a half-hearted offer to dinner, on the day itself, with Eva – perhaps put off by the prospect of Philip's Aunt Nellie. Philip, she knew, would never introduce her as his 'intended'. And not even as a friend of overriding importance to him. She gets by on soup on the day itself. Her last written words for 1960 are: 'I dread the whole of the rest of my life'. At the end of the 1950s Monica's relationship with Larkin was more than a decade old, and yet she was continually at a crossroad with him. I was at my own crossroad at this point, and the path I chose would lead me close to both Monica and Philip, and change my life.

25

Lecturer, 1960–1961

*'Every time I put on my big black gown I feel an indefinable
frisson at being a life-size member of Oxford University'*
Larkin in *Jill*, 1946

I had first entered Leicester's precinct in 1957. For me, in my way,
as for Monica in hers, it had been a troubled year. I'd expertly drunk
myself, timidly drugged myself (purple hearts, Preludin), and ne-
glected my studies into unworthy A-level results. Only one institution
cared to call me to interview: University College (for such it still was)
Leicester. The interview was conducted in one of the cellular rooms,
unchanged in layout from the college's distant lunatic asylum years.
I was looked over, one-on-one, by a 'moss-covered' ancient as I've
unfeelingly called him elsewhere; a very civil, visibly beaten-down
man as I now see him with the blurrier, more generous, eyes of age.
He was 'Dr A. S. Collins'. Not 'Professor Collins': whereby hangs the
sad tale told earlier.* I liked the old codger – twenty-five years younger
than I now am. And he liked me. He offered me a place on the spot.

But I did not immediately take up my place, choosing instead to
volunteer for National Service. It was the summer of 1960 when, after
serving my country for two years, I first walked up College Road, and
my spirits were not high. I've summed them up elsewhere:

---

* See pp 43–45.

When I arrived there, the campus air was porridge-thick with inferiority complex. The university on Cemetery Road (immortalised in *Lucky Jim*) was, if not [the university] of last resort, then at best the hopeful undergraduate's third, 'safety net', choice. Unlucky Jims, all of them. To be accepted at Leicester was to have failed everywhere else in academic life.

'Could be worse', a friend said. I could have thrown back Philip Larkin's witticism: 'you can't fall off the ground'.

I was plumb wrong. I had struck it lucky and didn't yet know it. Monica Jones was the main stroke of luck, but it would be a year before I knew that. My first acquaintance with her was ocular. That was how she was publicly known: the flamboyance (floating flame) of her dress. 'Apparel oft proclaims the man', says Polonius to his son, spinning proverb into platitude. Apparel proclaimed everything and more about Monica Jones in 1960. She caught the eye: yanked it out of its socket practically. Who's that? I asked a friend on first seeing her walk by on campus. 'Margaret Peel,' he said. I'd read *Lucky Jim* but it took some jogging of my memory to get what he meant.

My tutor in the first year, Tom Craik, was the only colleague Monica got on with at the time – even though he was a trifle too 'Cambridgey' for her Oxonian taste, and a *Guardian* reader to boot. They bonded over the *Just William* books, *The Wind in the Willows*, and *Jemima Puddleduck*. Monica forgave his being anti Oswald Mosley. She and Philip fondly nicknamed him 'Tom Vole'. He had a hamster called Flip, a wife called Wendy ('a fearful basking shark', Philip thought), and a baby called Roger who grew up, Monica was glad to see, 'rational': i.e. unchildish. He is the only child to whom Monica is known to have given toys; one assumes they were rational toys. As an act of friendship Monica took on Wendy Craik to do a doctoral thesis on Jane Austen – an author Monica proclaimed 'no great favourite of mine [she] upsets me'. Reticent spinsters were not to her liking, although neither were child-bearing wives. She shared Philip's 'Herodian' views about little strangers.

Monica entered and left her profession a lecturer. That is what she did idiosyncratically well and was how her department used her – as a beast of podium burden. It is as a lecturer I had my first real sense of what Miss Jones was. She hated the new lecturing style of tossing out 'a few bright ideas' to spare students the effort of thinking. She threw pepper in the eyes of her listeners – 'proper lectures', she called them. 'I can tell you I wish I could attend your lectures!' said Philip. I was obliged to attend them but, after my first experiences, would have crawled over broken glass to hear them.

Monica's podium performances stick vividly in my mind from my time at Leicester. There was one, I recall, on *Wuthering Heights* in which she spent twenty minutes on Yorkshire landscape pausing only to excoriate American Brontë 'experts' who knew less about moors than Mars. One felt the angrily whipping wind over Penistone Crags. Her annual Hardy lectures enjoyed intramural fame among students. Once when I went into her bedroom (to fix a jammed window – 'Sutherland is strong', she told Philip in that night's letter) I saw the collected Hardy poems on her bedside table. She lived with the authors she loved. Her *Vanity Fair* lecture made me a Thackerayan for life. I hear in my mind as I write her loud clear voice (about which Larkin was so cruel) inflecting itself to uncover the sexually hinted innuendos which only an ear attuned to the clubman Thackerayan voice could catch as they wafted, tobacco-laden into print. She was the sharpest-eared of listeners to literature I've known.

I relished, too, the lectures in which she raged at issues raised by the text. One such virtuoso performance I'll allow myself to describe at length. She gave a lecture on *Hamlet* in November 1960, days after the 'Lady Chat' acquittal, when Richard Hoggart's verdict-changing testimony made the Leicester University English department famous. Monica was not impressed. She liked neither Hoggart nor D. H. Lawrence. *Lady Chatterley's Lover* she thought 'absurd'.

Miss Jones was renowned for *vêtements littéraires* matching the subject of the hour. A touch of tartan when the topic was *Macbeth*: swinging pearls when it was Cleopatra. On this parky November morning in 1960, at nine o'clock, there was a nipping and keen air outside. Duffel coats and donkey jackets were worn inside the lecture hall – cold weather *vêtements*. Miss Jones swept in wearing her black Oxford MA gown. Freshmen like myself had been obliged, in October

1960, to purchase gowns – enriching the coffers of those ornamenters of the university body, Ede & Ravenscroft, and reminding students of an Oxbridge they weren't good enough to know. The Dean had, in an introductory address, instructed the year's newcomers on dress code. Gowns were obligatory for lectures. No trousers for women – then with a jest he'd uttered in the same place at the same time of year since dinosaurs roamed the earth – 'any more than skirts for men. Bona fide kilts are [pause] admissible: the *skean dhu* not . . .' That year something happened. The student body, en masse, without any ostensible protest, simply stopped wearing the black shrouds – the FU sixties had begun. Somewhere a dean died of apoplexy.

Nonetheless Monica wore her Oxford MA gown on the lecturer's platform to the end of her days, by which time lecturers (including me, I confess) took to the lectern looking like beach bums. The gown certified, for an hour, her superiority over Leicester and Oxford's superiority over everywhere. Beneath the gown could be seen a black cashmere pullover and black tights in acknowledgement of the gloomy prince's first-act funerary garb. Whether she had a bare bodkin about her, I doubt.

Prompt upon her hour she slammed down a Westclox alarm clock alongside her handwritten text. The timepiece normally lay by her bed alongside, as I discovered recently – a hammer. She feared what might come in the night – not ghosts, but burglars and worse. Living in an empty house for months on end, with only a sherry bottle for company, does strange things to your imagination. There was a curious tension to her lecturing, a kind of nervous thrill unrelated to the text in hand.

Miss Jones's theme throughout the lecture was that Hamlet, contra Gielgud et al of the 'lilac establishment',* was an unspeakable slob. He loved Ophelia more than forty thousand brothers, did the brute? Balderdash. He robbed Ophelia of her virtue by invading her closet, like rapist Tarquin; shamed her reputation at court by making jokes about her (clearly unvirginalised by him) genitals ('country matters');

---

* A term she used in letters not lectures. Monica was at times homophobic, see p. 179.

slaughtered her father as he would skewer a 'rat'; and then went on to do likewise to her brother, having driven her in the meantime to maddened suicide. 'I loved thee not' he brutally told her, by way of dismissal. 'I was the more deceived,' the misused pubescent girl (a 'darling bud of May', now plucked) murmurs in reply. Larkin had juggled that line for the title poem of *The Less Deceived*.

Hamlet, Miss Jones reiterated, was a lout. The word was duly scrawled in fifty notepads and would likely resurface in fifty finals papers: including mine. The student banter ('her privates we', etc) between Hamlet, Rosencrantz and Guildenstern, was the crude stuff of male university students through the ages. Transfixing her audience through those fearsome horn-rims it was clear she thought the same about the slovenly masculinity ranged in front of her. In a letter to Philip that same month she described the current crop of Leicester male students as: 'Uncouth, aggressively unshaved, street-bully clothed, crude minded'.

Miss Jones would, on occasion, become so impassioned at the lectern that she ripped the pages of her handwritten text. On other occasions she would be so moved by the beauty of the poetry she was reading out that she would break down, croakingly, in tears and be unable, for a minute or two, to continue. The joke was that Miss Jones was the only lecturer at Leicester who needed a St John's Ambulance crew in the back row. It was not histrionic: the lecture stage was one of the few places – the other was letters to Philip – where her emotions were unpadlocked (one of her metaphors). Miss Jones's lectures made a statement. Her views did not come from fashionable 'tripe' in the latest 'Yank book'. I was sufficiently up with the critical times to sense that she was years behind the latest wave: Clemenian image-hunting, Empsonian polysemies, Schoenbaumian archival documentation. There was, for her, something more important. The connection with *Hamlet*, she asserted, must be felt, carnally, through the whole body and mind aided by the resources of high native intelligence. She did not say that: she expressed it. She was it.

Monica rarely went back to her Oxford college but the last time she did, she'd been disgusted by trend-hounds spouting about 'ideology' in Shakespeare – as irrelevant as saying the meaning of a double-decker bus was the advertisement on its side panel, 'Go suck a Zube', etc. Shakespeare wasn't a vehicle for anything but Shakespeare. Monica's lecture on *Hamlet* is with me whenever I watch a performance of the inescapable play. Thereafter I sat close in her lectures. They were, and I speak now from half a century's listening to many of the best lecturers in my business, tops.

The *Hamlet* lecture, like all Monica's lectures, was a sexualised performance. That had been Monica's style since the 1940s. A student, Maureen Paton, said of her: 'Her dress code was always in tune with the times: in the Sixties, her black-and-white Op Art mini-dresses would attract cat-calls about Newcastle United . . . She even wore those red suspenders under mini-skirts (no namby-pamby tights for Monica), sometimes revealing them to the front row of an unsuspecting student audience.' It made her point publicly and loudly: 'I am a woman: I matter: look at me.' And, more importantly, 'listen to me'.

26

Rooms of Her Own, 1961

'Shall I ever feel better again'
Monica to Philip, 1961

There was much going on in Monica's life in my first year at Leicester. What I know now is that she was pulling herself back into a more bearable accommodation with herself and Philip. Her New Year's resolution for 1961 was 'I must get a home soon & a country house'. They will get her out of her 'swimmy' lethargy. But it is not easy; she feels she is wriggling like a worm on a pin. Her mother's beloved brother, Uncle Wilfred, the only relative who has known her all her life, has dropped dead. She comments that 'My tummy feels awful' and that people 'aren't very nice' to her at his funeral. It is the last such family event she will attend. Henceforth she has no family.

But through it all she was desperately intent on housing herself. Patrimony in hand, her first thought was of something large in Queens Road, Leicester, for £2,850. But, she decides, 'I must get a country place first.' She does some serious looking around Corbridge, near where Scotland parts from England – as Hadrian decreed – and twenty-odd miles from her beloved Weardale. Her final choice was a terraced cottage near there in Haydon Bridge. It had good rail connections (with both Leicester and Hull) and a little garden at the back, overlooking the South Tyne. She offered £1,250 to the retired Merchant Navy captain who owned it: 'The river frontage is what really attracts.' She wished it were 'prettier'. The village itself is not pretty but the nominal bridge is fine and historical.

Monica with Haydon Bridge behind her

Philip had been politely interested, but no more. He had not helped choose the cottage in Ratcliffe Road, or even come to look at it. Perish the thought he might have kicked in money. He made it clear he did not intend in any sense to 'live' there – he did not have the luxury of three-month-long vacs. 'Visit', 'short stay' and 'drop by' was all that was on offer. And no dinner parties, if you please: there is absolutely no one in Haydon Bridge or Leicester, apart from her, he has the slightest interest in meeting over a dining table or in a restaurant.

There would be happy moments at the cottage over the years. Monica treasured them like Silas Marner's gold under the floorboards. One Boxing Day morning Philip arrived, from Loughborough, and heard the Haydon Bridge Silver Band playing round the village. Monica got them to play 'Lead Kindly Light', his favourite hymn, which brought tears to his eyes. They walked Hadrian's Wall and found old pubs to drink in. There were a few such moments.

Monica had insufficient cash left to buy in Leicester but enough to afford more rent. The flat she chose was 1A Cross Road in Leicester's

snooty Stoneygate. The flat was ambling close to the pub she particularly liked, the Clarendon ('my local' she called it) with a bracing
walk to College across Victoria Park. The ground-floor apartment had
a small, pretty, garden and a separate entrance. Both properties had
kitchen ranges, so Monica could now cook ambitiously.

She was, at last, handsomely housed and could buy real furniture.
Nonetheless she told Philip, 'It's just a very empty life what with
nobody except you that I care about or that cares tuppence about me,
but nothing either that I care about doing . . . I find it hopelessly
flat'. 'I hate the terms', she told him, 'but dread the vacations'. Her
colleagues parroted half-baked ideas. The students reparroted them.
Only her loyal student Bill Ruddick, she told Philip, 'is worthwhile
– I suppose because he likes me.' Leicester University she said, for the
umpteenth time, is 'a social & moral slum'. 'I am absolutely fed up
here.' She brought another advertisement for a senior library position
at Leicester to Philip's notice. He ignored it.

Their annual New Year break was churchy as always. She nonetheless began 1961 in her now dangerously usual condition – a woman
teetering on the brink of nervous breakdown. On Valentine's Day she
told Philip 'I have eaten nothing for nearly 2 days . . . I can't really
see the page I am writing and have had to send a class away.' At this
point in 1961 something very odd happened – Larkin had a total
health breakdown. He collapsed at a library meeting on 6 March. He
was rushed into intensive care and subjected to a bombardment of
ECGs, lumbar punctures, brain scans, ophthalmic, urine and stool
tests. They revealed nothing. His inscrutably sick body was shuttled
between Hull and London hospitals. Specialists scratched their heads
in both places.

His crisis pepped Monica up no end – she had a Nightingale mission. She will, she told him, put on her yellow suit and pink shoes to
come to Hull. 'The first time I wore them', she tells hospitalised Philip,
'was when we went to dinner at Hoff's [novelist William Cooper] to
meet [C. P.] Snow.' She adds 'If you want me to come at any time
at no notice at all, I will come like a shot'. She advises him to read
Shaw's *The Doctor's Dilemma* for a curative dose of scepticism. When
visiting she stayed in Hull hotels. He was insistent she not go to his

flat. As always, he did not want anyone riffling through his papers. It worried him momentarily even more than his mysterious maladies:

> One thing that makes me ashamed is my refusal to let you use my flat. This . . . springs from the fact that I had left a few private papers & diaries lying around. Such things, which I suppose I keep partly for the record in the event of wanting to write an autobiography, & partly to relieve my feelings, will have to be burned unread in the event of my death . . .

The inner Larkin must never be known: even by Monica.

She kept him company for hours in the London hospital he was transferred to from Hull, the two of them doing *The Times* crossword together. As the diagnostic mystery thickened, Monica fussed about Philip's taking too full, too hot baths on his discharge – a sybaritic habit she had noted in him when he stayed with her. She is reassured by the news that he has eaten a plate of hospital rissole and chips. 'I don't know whether I cd do that even in good health,' she quips. He was evidently on the mend when he could grump about well-wishing visitors picking the shrimp out of his pasta.

There is a non-medical explanation for Philip's hypochondriac collapse. Maeve Brennan, under his coaching, had passed her library exams. He had tutored her. She was now permanent in the library. It was in the anaphrodisiac setting of Hull General Hospital, Maeve recalled, 'our friendship ignited into love'. Monica was unaware of any such ignition. He hid Maeve's love letters from her. The other woman was sending them daily to London and had visited him (in his Hull hospital) regularly, avoiding any brush with Monica. Maeve knew all about Monica. He was writing to Maeve from his bed, signing off 'with gentle affection'. Maeve, devoutly Catholic, prays for him but wonders whether 'God has, or rather might have, inflicted this on you to arrest any interesting developments between you and me.' As her memoir records, their daily work together had become amorously physical, when alone in his office or in the evening. Maeve did visit his flat and ate there with him. At this stage the relationship did not, on the face of it, warrant divine punishment. The Hull University authorities might have frowned on it. Monica would have been wounded to the heart.

Monica continued to worry – but more cheerfully when it was clear Philip was not knocking on death's door. 'I thoughtfully got rather bad eyes in sympathy. If it was liver you would be yellow,' she wrote; adding, 'You don't *look* ill.' Bowels perhaps? A very slight stroke? Sometimes he complained of 'heart failure' after drinks. Hay fever? She reminds him 'how terribly frightened I was when I had that lump in my breast'. And it will cheer him up to know she has bought a new pleated skirt.

Larkin's health crisis left a company of the best physicians in the country nonplussed. One theory was that it was a malfunction of his new spectacles. The truth is both he and Monica were world-class *malades imaginaires*. She was fit enough by the end of the spring term to tolerate even an ARH sherry party at which six guests were served from one bottle of 'Cyprus'. Even her irritations had a new energy to them. She describes to Philip how she was quietly reading her papers in SCR to be driven out by:

> A gibbering mob of foreigners, papists, pansies, Scotchmen, local historians, Jews etc. All coming to a tasting. Oh, & of course, members of the Dept of French who see it as a professional duty.

In Monica spite was a sign of life. In Philip his nervous, probably hypochondriac, collapse was a sign of guilt at now having two lovers.

Grateful for Monica's care over his hospitalisation, he sends her two dozen yellow roses for her birthday in May – yellow being her favourite colour. She would have preferred him to the blooms: 'I hated my birthday, walked the streets all the afternoon and went to bed at 9 to escape it. I had got something to drink but did not seem to want it. I just felt awfully lonely.' She nonetheless drinks the something: Crème de Menthe.

The cottage in Haydon Bridge finally costs her £1,600, leaving her money to refurbish. She sends Philip a ten-page description with diagrams: down to where would be the best place for the electric kettle. She dreams of getting a dog. 'A bitch . . . A boxer wd be nice, but I think the breathing might annoy me.' Four pages on dogs follow, but then realism breaks in: 'what a lot about dogs I shall never have'. He does not yet come to inspect the cottage. He always believed she ought to buy in Leicester: more convenient for him, being near Loughborough once a month, for his mother. He does not yet have a car.

On to Lords, this year the Australians – a tense rubber. Then, in July, Sark. An attack of cystitis furnishes another reason for disliking Leicester: 'there is no town anywhere with so few lavatories'. Her mother had suffered likewise. 'Do you know what fibroids are?' she asks Philip. Her letter becomes detailed. As regards her innards, Monica is mildly annoyed at his having told his mother that her stomach is 'as sensitive as – what was it? Old leather suitcases?'

Her later summer letters mount to a long cry of pain: 'Oh darling, do forgive me & send me a letter . . . Darling Philip comfort me . . . Darling, darling Philip – I like nothing in the world but being with you.' She fears she is pregnant, after Sark, 'or could it be the start of the change of life?' It is neither, she confirms three days later. There were, Larkin told Robert Conquest, 'drinkingly' and 'shaggingly' long nights on the holiday. James Booth suggests that the blooming relationship with Maeve renewed, collaterally, Larkin's attentions to Monica. Unknowing of the reason, she appreciates his amorousness.

Monica remained lingeringly dispirited and enervated after awful 1959: 'I keep drinking gin instead of having lunch . . . dear lovely gin and tonic'. She can get through half a bottle on one letter. She keeps body and soul together with cups of soup; 'I daresay if I were making a supper for you I could make one, & eat it too', she forlornly tells Philip. 'Have you any advice for me, how to feel better?' she asks, even more forlornly. No reply is on record.

In September she at last moves into her new flat, 1A Cross Road, with a flurry of painting and furniture from Stourton brought out of store. It is self-contained, fenced round the still in bloom garden with a herb patch. She relishes the thought of a proper kitchen – 'I can cook reasonably, I think, tho' not Elizabeth Davidly'. This news in a twenty-three-side letter written on her birthday. Alone. She had, she

confessed in a letter the next day, 'a lot to drink' and can't remember
what she wrote. 'I used to like writing letters to you', she says, 'felt
it kept me company, but now it seems to emphasise my loneliness
almost'.

At last, on 16 September, Philip comes to look at the cottage in
Haydon Bridge, staying in a single hotel room. She returns in October to Leicester. 'The new young lady in the Dept', she tells him, 'is
not much to look at. She addressed me by my first name at our first
meeting. You can imagine what I thought of that.' She makes him
a sirloin dinner in her new flat – but, at the last minute, he cannot
come. The examiners' meeting this year was unusually grim: 'I am
almost weeping at the badness of the finalists' scripts.' But she did
'find one real star turn among the First Year set that I had', namely
myself, and Monica booked me as one of her thirty-four tutees for the
coming October.

Finding Monica, 1961–1962

'I could have kissed him'
                                    Monica to Philip, 1961

My first up-close meeting with Monica was in a second-year one-on-one tutorial. By way of getting to know me, she gave me free rein as to what I wrote to see if there were any meeting of minds. It turned out that there was. Nine weeks into the winter term 1961 she told Philip:

> My star turn man in the 2nd year – he is really excellent, a very tough man, and great boozer, but with a most sensitive judgement, &, you'll be interested to know, the real root of the matter in him; his essays & tutorials have revealed him as an independent Crabbe-reader, & [William] Barnes-reader & Hardy-reader* and dotes on all these excellent poets. I could have kissed him. I rub in, to Ruddick, the interest I feel in this man – I think it's a sensible thing to do, as I have shown, and still do, interest in *him*; just as I'm always rubbing in – in a kind way – 'at your age . . .'

'Great boozer' – it was true: I drank greatly. But what she intimates is that she and I had been boozing together (we had). 'Tough' was a radioactive word. Larkin was vilified as a poet afraid to raise his fist

---

* 'root of the matter' – a quotation from the Book of Job. It was Larkin who enthused Monica on William Barnes.

to life: unlike the truly tough Ted Hughes and Thom Gunn. One couldn't imagine Philip Larkin writing an ode to the Hell's Angels or Elvis Presley, or wrestling with the largest pike in the pond.

'Crabbe' was Jane Austen and Monica Jones's favourite poet, and one of mine too. Monica declaimed from memory, after a Crabbe essay I'd written, his last depiction of Peter Grimes, the paedophile-murderer Aldeburgh fisherman. As always with poetry that moved her, she became emotional. She read a passage out to me:

> *And the loud bittern, from the bulrush home,*
> *Gave from the salt-ditch side the bellowing boom.*
> *He nursed the feelings these dull scenes produce,*
> *And loved to stop beside the opening sluice,*
> *Where the small stream, confined in narrow bound,*
> *Ran with a dull, unvaried, saddening sound.*

I knew it and read it back to her in a Suffolk accent. I had been brought up on the county border and had served in the Suffolk Regiment.

If she liked your essays Monica entered into hectic marginal intercourse. It was a side-wind that blew your ideas all over the place. Harking back to Brereton Hall, the school-mistress's ferule was always invisibly in her hand. Alongside the phrase 'different to' in one of my later essays on Thackeray's *Pendennis* she wrote in the margin: 'You're not one of *those* people are you'. After that rap across the knuckles, I ensured I was different *from* those people. I still am, and in later life I spent a year lovingly editing *Pendennis*.

That year I also got to know Bill Ruddick – another young man much mentioned in Monica's 1960s letters to Philip. She had taken Bill on as a PhD student (work she did not like) a year before I came along. He had been her undergraduate tutee and she nursed him to his first. He ingratiated himself with her – 'my chap' Monica called him. In deference to Monica's known passion, he chose as his doctoral topic Lockhart's *Life of Scott*.

Bill was intensely loyal. On one occasion, when Monica was decorating her second home in Haydon Bridge, he travelled two hundred miles round trip to bring her a can of Snowcem she needed. He was a *cavalier servente*: there was no muddy puddle over which he would not throw the Ruddick velvet cloak to protect Monica's shoes. Not that he was well dressed. Monica complained that he let her down when they were seen together. 'A bit of a scrounger', Philip thought him. But for his purposes a serviceable scrounger.

Monica mentions 'Bill' over and again in her letters. She always hinted there might be something more intense than servility in Bill's attentions. She does it in the letter about me above, with its play on the word 'interest'. Why did she discuss Bill and me in her letters? Because Monica knew, of old, that Larkin – far off in Hull – was revolted by the idea of any man coming between him and any of his women. Not for him his friend Kingsley's 'career adultery'.* That was 'sharing' another bloke's property. In the examples of Larkin's pornography collection which survived Monica's flames,† there are no depictions of copulation – an act necessarily involving a partner. Was there another lover? What the letters I've read confirm is that Monica was never tempted – even to flirtation. Except, possibly, once: and that, to a 'coloured communist'.‡ And that too was quite likely her Cleopatra wiles rather than genuine passion. What Monica wanted Philip to know was that 'the old bag' (as she routinely called herself in the 1960s) could still pull young guys were she so minded.

I fell in love and out of it a couple of times at Leicester. 'You're good at making women love you,' one lover told me, 'it's what you do next which is the problem.' Another girl who felt bad about dumping me too hard went to Monica for advice. Women students with women problems often consulted Monica: she was the only female staff member in the department and she wasn't – as she ruefully noted – offputtingly senior in age (yet) or rank (ever). Monica's advice for students with love problems was invariably the same: scrub floors, do the laundry, and clean the house. 'I like doing things that I know I can accomplish properly,' she told Philip, 'like scrubbing a floor'. You washed that man right out of your hair, just like the song said. It was

---

* His son Martin's term.

† See below, pp. 237, 258.

‡ See below, 'Dipak', pp. 199–205.

the remedy she resorted to during tough patches with Philip. There is a lot of floor-scrubbing chronicled in her letters. Monica never told me about this episode.

My year with Monica was formative mentally and intellectually. I perceived how a passed-over, mocked, spinster lecturer of a certain age could be so inviolate: untouched by the unkind gossip she knew she attracted. Monica, in herself, knew that she mattered more than the careerist big men on campus. 'Nonentity professors', as Philip called them. How did she matter? By being in touching, sleeping, talking, loving, joking, and, yes, creative connection with the man she knew, and others were coming to know, was a great poet. She was of more consequence than the middle management in the Eng. Lit factory. She drank at the Pierian Spring: they were selling bottled literature.

Monica offered a way through my confused life, universe, literature and everything maze. Her clarities – some would say prejudices – did it. First was Monica's Razor: as sharply divisive as Occam's. On the one, larger, side were authors of high reputation who were silly. Top of the silly heap were Lawrence and Yeats: syllabus giants both of them. Ted Hughes ('Tough Ted'), soon to make the syllabus, was moving towards silliness. With Lawrence there was all that supreme silliness about savages in loin thongs sacrificing naked women to the equinoctial sun. Lawrence lacked the 'central stability' that a writer like Hardy had. Yeats was a prime exemplar of the higher silliness. Those 'nine bean rows' on the Isle of Innisfree. Had the man never used a dibble? (Monica was a knowing gardener.) 'And imagine,' she said to me, 'a grown man thinking a wind-up toy bird on a branch represented poetry.'

On the other side of Monica's slicing razor were the 'gold in your pocket for life' authors. Elsewhere, 'deathbed' authors – those whom you'd read knowing you only had a week to live. Monica's was the knapsack theory of literature. If you can't pack it and carry it with you for life as a treasured possession, toss it. I was wary about the authors on Monica's silly-list. On five of her 'gold in your pocket' list I would later write books.* Each of them should have been dedicated 'to

---

* Thackeray, Scott, Austen, Hardy, Trollope.

MMBJ'. Her further, clear-as-crystal point, was that you had to earn
your pocketful of gold by wide reading and deep feeling. She hated
field specialism, that leprosy of modern English study. There were no
short cuts. You had no right or ability to pronounce on say *Antony
and Cleopatra*, Wordsworth or even Philip Larkin unless you had read
widely and deeply lesser authors. The way to the great was through
the almost as good. Literature was crossing a field and enjoying the
view, not digging a hole.

Monica's reaction to the writers who were her gold was something
experienced, like love, through her whole being. An effusion in a letter
about her, and Philip's, beloved Hardy, in 1966, makes the point:

> I don't really read Hardy as a *poet* at all: if you see what I mean,
> he's just someone interwoven with 'us' & that means – sometimes
> expressing what we or one of us feels, tied in with us by our almost
> random thoughts of him at some moment when we were together
> – such as your thought of *The Roman Road* at Kyleakin [Skye],
> of all places, in 1957, and our postcards of the rabbit learning to
> walk; or our absolutely – identical – twin thought of *On the Brit-
> ish Museum** when we went to St Paul's once – *not* the last time
> when you were in an extremely sulky mood, God knows why.
>
> Do you remember going down Ludgate Hill & saying, No,
> you tell *me*, what *you* were thinking of, both of us so sure we
> had been thinking of the same thing that we dreaded to think we
> hadn't; but we had! And so tenuous – the voice of Donne, we were
> thinking, while knowing full well that *these* stones hadn't echoed
> it. Darling, I turn quite soppy when I have the mixture of Hardy
> & memory of you & me. Oh dear: I am Heathcliff, that's really
> what it is.

To read the above is to understand why Larkin – despite everything
– stayed unfaithfully faithful to Monica. None other of his 'women'
were, in this passionate way, of his mind. 'Interwoven'. James Booth,
in his authoritative biography of Larkin, wonders, as have others, why

---

* Hardy poem.

Larkin should have made, for almost four decades, a woman as 'edgy, defensive, loud and with little interest in other people . . . socially inept and ungracious' as Monica the primary love interest of his adult life. Letters like the above suggest the reason. There was a meeting of mind, sensibility and literature-lived between the two of them. It gave something to the nurturing climate in which his poetry slowly grew.

What is striking is how primitive Monica's response to the literature she loved was. 'Yank' monographs and Germanic articles in *Neophilologus* or whatever were not, Monica believed, helpful. They were signposts pointing to a desert where a living connection with literature shrivelled. That belief leads to something that every account of Monica makes much of. This eminently clever woman never published a word. She did not bury her five talents, she kept them to herself.

That she would not join the way her 'subject' was going is one explanation. The thinkers in 1960s English Studies were moving towards 'Theory': thinking about their thinking. Monica would not be party to that abstraction any more than Philip Larkin would be party to the poetic Modernism represented by Ezra Pound. Both of them, critic and poet, represented vital traditionalism: the old hat worn with pride. There were other elements in what Philip called Monica's '*non serviam*'. When ARH summoned her to write an essay on Crabbe for the collection he was editing, her response was defiance. Like Zorba, in the film, she danced only for herself. In the larger context of her whole career silence was Cordelia's defiant 'Nothing'. She would not dance to the tune English Studies, in her time, was playing.

That defiance would have stood up better if Monica had gone on to write, in her own voice, something to prove she could. If, for example, she had polished and published a selection of her lecture scripts. They would have found a publisher, as would a critical edition of one of her favourite poets – W. Mackworth Praed (an unusual private passion) or William Barnes. Vanity was in there somewhere. Everyone in university life in Monica's time would have known colleagues who had won glittering prizes at Oxbridge and felt that was it. Nothing more was required, the point was proved. There seems an element of this in the answer Monica gave to a baffled Anthony Thwaite, that publishing was 'a bit showy'. This from a woman whose clothes were the epitome of well-chosen showiness.

If her reason for not publishing is elusive, the one consolation her professional life yielded was crystal clear. Teaching – particularly lecturing – passed her into the company of 'great authors'. And, in her private life, the intellectual freedoms of the academic profession gave her space and opportunity, as Philip's lover, to be in living contact with a great author. Living with and for literature was her 'scholarship'. It didn't need print.*

I took a lot from Monica with me when I entered academic life but the Trappist silence as regards publishing I was not self-denying enough to follow. I made the point in my obituary of her, unsure as I wrote whether I was criticising her, myself or the profession which had been more giving to me than her:

> On her favoured students, her influence was strong but, arguably, risky for those more ambitious than she was for the good things of academic life. She fostered a kind of marching out of step which guaranteed that – like her – one would not get on in career terms. To sign up with Monica Jones for the full duration was, in effect, to commit professional hara-kiri. Honourable, elegant, but suicidal.

Eventually I decided, with a sense of defecting from the true faith, that noble silence wasn't for me. I don't think the better of myself for it.

---

* I make the point later that Monica did have a major publication, in the form of her 'invisible hand' in *The Oxford Book of Twentieth-Century English Verse*. It is, defiantly, Philip and Monica. See pp. 220–221.

Me, Monica and Philip, 1961–1967

'Sutherland? . . . I suppose he does exist'

Philip to Monica, 1967

The first mark of nearness to Monica was that she would talk about Philip. Just casual name-dropping, as if there was no need to press the point. 'Strange', she said to me (this was 1964), 'he's taken his test and bought a car. Never told me he was taking lessons. Poop-poop – not the toad work, but toad on the road. And every time he ventures out he meets a gigantic yellow lobster on wheels.' An image which had the Larkin zing and the forced Monica jollity. Privately, I now know from her letters, she hated that Singer Gazelle, a passion wagon to transport bloody Maeve Brennan about, as she saw it, now that she had discovered about Philip's other woman.

Monica would mention Philip in conversation but would never converse about him. I rooted out hard-to-come-by Larkin poems and tried, vainly, to discuss them with her, but it was a no go. I recall a particularly strained moment about 'Dockery and Son', his anti-marriage ode. It touched her in too sensitive a place. It was off-limits. So too, for all but the most favoured of Monica's acquaintance, was Philip Larkin. The second *privilège de passage* was actually to meet him. Monica carefully arranged my audience. He was not impressed. The highest compliment he could pay me over the five years we occasionally met was 'I don't mind seeing Sutherland . . . he wd be no hardship'. I can be put up with. But not too often and never privately.

After our first meeting he wrote back with witty deprecation:

He himself seemed nice, though clearly not one to put his goods in the window – not willing or not able.

Anthony Thwaite, in *Letters to Monica*, adds a footnote which makes me sound an utter creep. Monica had written in a letter dated 15 November 1962: 'Sutherland was, according to Bill, utterly thrilled by meeting you: he went off saying he was going to re-read all the poems at once, in order to have them and "the man" close in his mind.' If I did set out to find the missing link between man and poetry, I failed. But who, I ask myself, has succeeded?

Philip could never see what she saw in me. There are occasional blandly polite remarks over the following months and years of the 'glad Sutherland's / John's doing so well' kind. She got the message and stopped pushing get-togethers. Shall we invite Sutherland for a drink before lunch, she asks; 'of course he has very little conversation and ½ of that can't be heard.' I recall, from the few times we met, a sprinkling of his conversational *beaux mots*. Was he following the test series? Yes – though funnily enough it was like sex in the head. Listening to Arlott was the only kind of masturbation you could do with a wireless knob. Dexter hitting six was ejaculation in the head. We laughed.

Inside every fat man there were two fat men trying to get out. He told a long, very funny joke about Dylan Thomas – which he must have got from Kingsley, a brilliant mimic, in one of their joke-swap sessions. Dylan on this occasion, as on many occasions, was pissed (Larkin used the bar-room phrase) out of his mind. His eye was caught by a beautiful young thing on the other side of the bar. He lurched over and – in that fruity baritone – told her 'I' (imagine the Welsh accent being perfectly simulated) 'have fallen in love with you. I am going to write you a poem, a serenade, Dante and Beatrice, Keats and Brawne will pale by contrast, it will make you mine forever – this is how it goes . . .' Larkin, after a breath, wolf-whistled. Even that sounded Welsh. Nearby heads in the Clarendon turned round and looked from him to Monica. It was very funny.

He dominated any conversation by tactical silence: partly because he could no longer hear low-voiced interlocutors like me. At this stage he had difficulty hearing anyone with a voice quieter than klaxon Monica's and he was damned if he was going to crane towards John Sutherland. Or wear his humiliating hearing aids for me. All the time there was that paralysing politeness. Frozen air. Others interpreted it differently. In his funeral eulogy, Kingsley Amis said: 'it was impossible to meet him without being aware in the first few seconds of his impeccable attentive courtesy'. But what, behind that cold still politeness, was he thinking about you? His face betrayed nothing. His letters did: but you would never see those.

I was, frankly, nervous of the man. Not because I feared the Sultanic bowstring or his kicking my arse, as he once threatened Ruddick, for looking in the wrong way at Monica. But I feared he might Svengali me as in company he clearly had Monica. When she was in company with Philip, Monica herself could not – as she told him – 'sparkle'. Or even converse.* The best she could manage was an occasional interruptive bark. As a result, people either took no notice of her or looked at her askance. His force-field, his silent 'cleverness', dwarfed her.

I met him around a dozen times. On one occasion we almost had an argument. I'd described to him how sociology students hid books on far-off shelves, for their own study and to keep fellow students in prophylactic ignorance. English Literature students didn't do this. Different department, different ethos. My point was that the study of literature did indeed civilise. His eyes (I may be imagining this, I've replayed the incident in my head and probably dramatised it) went dark. 'Why', he said coldly, 'do you not stop your criminal sociological pals stealing books.' It wasn't a question but an indictment. Hoping to interest the man, I'd infuriated the librarian. The poet was nowhere in the saloon bar. I said nothing. In his last reference to me in *Letters to Monica* he asks, noting my not turning up: 'I suppose he *does* exist. I've certainly met someone you *introduced* as Sutherland, years ago.'

His final judgement on me was that I was 'a case of arrested development'. By which he meant I should have outgrown Monica and got

---

* See below, pp. 173–174.

a life. She protested bitterly – 'because he still likes me, hay?' In 1967, after I was gone from Leicester and making my professional way at Edinburgh University, Monica wrote of me to Larkin:

> But in the last, the very last, it's Sutherland who's with you, he's the Barnes and Hardy man, the man who knows what's the real thing, the man who can really be really moved by the real thing; I didn't teach him – he came to me – a Barnes and Hardy man & like me because I liked them. He left me a Scott man, as well . . . Sutherland is the nearest to you with jazz* and all.

Reading this, I feel that she saw something very worthwhile in me. It warms me to know that.

I can't claim that that I knew Philip Larkin, although through Monica he had an influence on my life. I'm a Scott man, as Monica grandly calls me, and, as regards my 'nearness' to Larkin, I'll echo what he said about Burns: *Virgilium tantum vidi.* I saw the man, and that was enough. And he me? He didn't give a toss. Monica, I'm grateful to say, did. And I agree with her: he was the most 'real thing' living English poet of my lifetime.

---

* Like Larkin, I had a love of jazz music. Monica told him that I wanted to discuss with him someone called 'Bird' (Charlie Parker, as she well knew) doing a pretty riff on 'shall I call [him] bird or but a wandering sax'. 'Perhaps Sutherland could take over your column', she mischievously speculated when he was on holiday with her in Sark that year. 'It could have "Philip Larkin is away" at the bottom', she added. The only interest Larkin ever showed in me (apart from what I wrote about him in my finals papers) was what I thought about his 'Ban the Bird' Parker piece adding, '[he] thought it was all cock, I expect'.

29

Teetering, 1962

'Darling, I feel frightened'
                    Monica to Philip, 1962

My closeness to Monica in the 1960s was, she made clear, a welcome thing. We drank, coffee and alcohol, and she gave me many hours of her time in which we talked literature and chortled seditiously. But I noticed there was an odd tremulousness about her, an overwound, constantly quivering, quality. Now, having seen her letters to Philip over the period, it makes sense. In the arctic conditions of early 1962, Monica's new flat proved another place to be alone, but colder.

Philip, whose affair with Maeve was now a fixed thing, despite his denials, writes unconvincingly erotic letters to compensate for his absence over 1962, such as:

> I wish I could be with you and we could plunge into bed – I wished it yesterday *very* much. Do you remember putting on your red belt & open-work stockings? I shall always remember that, cataclysmic spiritual experience.

'Spiritual' is a key word in Maeve's lexicon. God is always watching, she believed. Monica and her open-work stockings are now past tense for Philip.

Monica has a mouse watching her in her new flat. 'He grew', she thought, 'both more intelligent and more affectionate the longer I had him.' She sees a lot of Bill, who was probably better for her sanity than Brer Mouse, whom she passed on to the Craiks' six-year-old, animal-loving Roger. She is grateful but a little frightened by Bill's attention to her. He is 'scrupulously correct' but if he offered open affection, 'I should almost have wanted to accept it . . . it frightened me'.

Her letters portray a woman on the edge. Philip more than once protested his relationship with Maeve was over after a year or so. Monica remained suspicious: 'Something you said on holiday made me think that you were feeling a tug in that direction again.' He was. 'I feel pointless as though I am waiting for something,' she says. She had another pregnancy scare and wrote a long, urgent letter on the possibility. It was a false alarm.

Under the strain her reason is precarious. She sleepwalks in her large flat and writes him letters at night she can't recall writing next morning. 'Darling, I feel frightened.' She is a 'broken reed'. Worse still she must spend the vacation, in solitary confinement, in Haydon Bridge. It's been two years but she knows no one in the village. 'Today I am wearing the green-striped narrow jersey dress you know, the one that is too small for me' she tells him. Can he still remember her 'figger'? It's been so long.

That summer of sixty-two, solitary in Haydon Bridge, Monica could not but see that her drinking now verged on dangerous:

> I do seem now, unable to do without it, to keep going, which I don't like, I really have to have my tipple now and *sometimes* I drink a lot, though not as badly as I did just after my parents died.

Now over the bar her income had crept up to £1,660 p.a. Her parents' house had brought her £3,000. She was academic poor (colleagues her senior had fine town houses) with an only child's once-in-a-lifetime windfall.

The relationship with Maeve intermittently makes Philip harsh towards her – unconsciously he wants Monica to ditch him but cannot bring himself to do the deed himself. Consciously he does not want it. She complains: 'You do sometimes say shattering things . . . I can't

stand being shattered'. He has told her they are 'out of sympathy . . .
I can't face it . . . I never know what you are thinking and thinking of
me . . . I accept don't I & *without* private reservation or grudge that
you don't like me enough to marry.' She is bent out of the shape of
the woman she was fifteen years earlier when she first fascinated him
and their relationship was one of equals.

What, above all, has happened to her mind? It flashes, still, in
lectures, in tutorials and in conversation with students with whom
she feels intellectually intimate. But she is a woman whose life has
become an obsessional nightmare about Philip and what she is to
him. She recalls letters long ago from Belfast: 'you simply wouldn't
talk except about bits of nothing'. He had said, not so *very* long ago,
that 'once your Mother died you wd look for a wife – look for one
elsewhere; I really try to think that you can't have meant this.' Can
he, she wonders, really be capable of such 'cool calculation'? The letter
finishes plaintively, 'I wish you could have come I'd have liked to give
you a grouse dinner'.

He came to Leicester that week – not for grouse but Acker Bilk at
De Montfort Hall. He had taken Maeve to hear the same clarinettist
play in Hull. Acker was close enough to Philip's god, Pee Wee Russell,
to fork out for two tickets in two places.

At the end of the term the department, in lieu of promotion, gave
her a better room, opposite ARH's. I helped her move. Philip was
again deceiving her. He told her Maeve had had her 'chap pinched
after 5 years' but Monica had no sympathy, declaring 'I would remind
you and her that she was quite prepared to try and pinch you from
me after twice five years and more'. Which Maeve had, in point of
fact, now succeeded in doing. In the near future Maeve and Philip
would be invited out in Hull and to librarian conferences as a near-as-
dammit married couple. Monica, like his mother, was an obligation,
to be kept out of the way and seen by rota.

A Good Year for John, 1963

'Everybody is nasty to me'
Monica to Philip, 1963

New Year 1963 brought in another terrible winter; there were power cuts and every lead pipe in Leicester froze then burst. It was the January Sylvia Plath gave up. 'She does sound to have been in a state,' Monica commiserated. Life with poets was hard for women and who knew better than she? The winter months of 1963 saw the end of Monica's beloved 'badgers' – a pair of woollen stockings Philip had given her for Christmas in 1959. She put her hand-washed treasures to dry on the line in the garden of her Stoneygate flat. They were nicked. Someone had clambered over the fence. Their loss triggered paranoid delusions, always buzzing like bluebottles around this highly strung woman at this time of her life. She was *disgusted* by the thought of 'horrible fingers' caressing her intimate apparel.

Was it some sex maniac who worked out from other washing on the line that a single woman lived at 1A Cross Road? Would he come back one night and use those very tights to violate and strangle her? Monica later shared her anxieties with me, adding that Philip himself had warned her never to hang out sex-identifiable washing but use the indoors clothes-horse. More likely the 1963 thief was an agile mini-skirted girl, frozen to the bone, who fancied Monica's woollies during the Big Freeze power cuts. One night she heard a strange knock on her door. She cowered and did not dare answer. The next day, from the two 'lesbians' (AKA the 'bags') living above her in the first-floor flat, she learned they were a couple of youths selling firewood.

Philip gives her a pretty bedside lamp for her birthday. She often writes to him alone, in bed. Spring, a warm one, brings relief and raises her spirits. She is doing well with her research students – Wendy Craik is passed by the venerable John Butt at Edinburgh. Monica contemplated flight or suicide at the prospect of the ordeal of the viva there, but was gratified to find that Butt was old-world courtly – a veritable Colonel Brandon. Bill was applying for jobs everywhere, and I was now in my final undergraduate year. Monica kept her distance in my final undergraduate term. We met from time to time over coffee in the student common room and I would walk her back across Victoria Park. We spent an hour looking for a bay tree in gardens alongside the park, I recall, for herbs that, hopefully, would please Philip's palate.

Monica gave me two pieces of advice. One – after she had seen me more 'sloshed' (her word) than usual – was to cut out the booze. I, clinically pre-alcoholic, did not drink for five months. The other advice was to spend twenty minutes before any exam reading a Dr Johnson *Idler* or *Rambler* essay – 'loose sallies of the mind' as he called them. I did this religiously. She instructed Ruddick to keep an eye on me. I went into purdah: working through the hours vacated by my not drinking. I'd worked out that the exit door from Leicester – which Monica had never managed to unlock – was a degree which excelled Leicester. That might, were I lucky, trampoline me out. And the exams went extremely well, thanks in large part to my new sobriety.

Monica marked Shakespeare with ARH, but wanted to get a look at the Moderns paper where I had written about Larkin. 'You can feel bucked to have made the exam and to be answered on by S., who I expect answered v. well,' she told him. I doubt he was bucked.

The test that year was against the West Indies. She exulted at the thought of the annual visit with Philip to Lords, Dexter smiting and Fiery Fred Trueman hurling thunderbolts. She liked the spectacle of male violence. The vexatiously concurrent examiners' meeting provided further exultation. 'Well, you can write to Sutherland,' she told Philip, 'a magnificent 1st (actually he had 7 First-class papers out of 8, the 8th was a B++ – nearly made a grand slam) . . . I had a quick look at his essay on you – it had got 80 per cent. v. on the ball – quoted Dockery.' What sobriety will not get you. It took me another twenty years to fully learn that lesson.

My run of finals papers earned the highest marks ever awarded in the department. Lest my head still seems swollen with that Lilliputian glory I recall boastfully telling a former close schoolfriend, about to do a second degree in philosophy at Cambridge. He smiled and said: 'That would make you, in my field, the best philosopher in – say – Battersea Polytechnic.' My crest fell. But that tinpot success meant a career-long ride in a profession where I could think, write, and read as I liked. Freedom of mind is the highest reward of academic life. And what I wrote in the examination hall was repayment to Monica. She was the one who was moving my hand in those scripts. But I was smart enough to disguise this for examiners not to be able to punish her through me. We were both victorious. It was as much Monica's triumph as mine. One in the eye for the department. They now knew what Monica Jones could do as a teacher. Inspire.

I duly received a short congratulatory letter from Philip, not written but typed – clearly by his secretary. He wrote letters that mattered in his own calligraphic-quality hand. He had a rubber stamp of his signature for autograph hunters, although I escaped that indignity. Monica was right to say I was 'thrilled with [the letter], it just crowned a magnificent week for him. He came around to show it to me – accompanied by Bill, who, since S's success seems to have appointed himself S's manager.'

The letter ('Dear Sutherland', signed 'P. A. Larkin') congratulated me on my 'serene' performance. What he didn't tell me was that he had secretly prevailed on the external examiner, the head of English at Hull (a 'loony' Monica called him), to see what I wrote about him in the Moderns paper. According to Monica, his verdict was 'sensible enough' (i.e. B++?). Monica referred to my essay a couple of times later, reminding him, meaningfully, of my endorsement of 'Larkin's idealism'. What I wrote I can't recall. But, fifty-odd years on, and knowing what I now know, idealistic Larkin seems a harder case to make.

Lords and Sark went well in summer 1963. Sark, now well known (a fourth visit), she experienced this year as 'some loved home of childhood'. The holiday photographs showed how her bathing costume went 'wonderfully with the colour of the landscape'. She had no one in the world to show her pictures to.

She goes on a good-resolution diet (cucumber sandwiches) but has not given up the booze – just replaced G&T with white wine. 'Minibisks' figure emaciatingly. She is reading Helen Gurley Brown's *Sex and the Single Girl* – she is still single but is she still sexy? Is she still a 'girl'? The Sark photographs of herself in a bathing costume give rise to thought. 'I was never so whistled after & spoken to by men when I was 34-23-35 as I am at 38½-28-39 (40 to be honest),' she tells Philip. She wears her 'tight girdle' every day to show off her figure.

He comes for a week to Haydon Bridge, but stays again in the Beaumont Hotel. They walk along Hadrian's Wall and photograph each other. More pictures for her alone to treasure, like Silas Marner counting his gold. She forgives Philip the infidelities she senses him committing, but does not want to be his confessor: '*I don't* ask you to have a bad conscience, I don't mind that so much as the feeling that you get rid of it for a time by talking about it.'

She is re-reading *Jill* for him, which is being reissued. She can't imagine the feeble-minded hero could (as she did) win an Oxford scholarship. On the narrative evidence, young Kemp couldn't pass O-level English. She will come up with ten pages of corrections. Much of the book's Oxford now strikes her as unreal. It's poor work by his standards, she implies. But Philip has a following and it will sell on the strength of *The Less Deceived*. When will the next slim volume come, though? The poetry-reading world is waiting eagerly.

Bill comes to the cottage for a day with his friend David, laden with fresh vegetables and gossip. 'I can hardly talk abt anything but personalities,' she says. She has bought a sponge bag for 7/3d. There is comfort in little things. A Hardyesque thought. At the local church the vicar still dashes from the pulpit to the organ, doing double duty. Alone after church she changes into one of Philip's shirts, which comforts her. But sometimes at Haydon Bridge, she tells him, 'I am so lonely I cd cry'. She had by now learned that Philip, propelled by Maeve, had really come up to Haydon Bridge in September with 'the intention of breaking off with me' and then lost his nerve. Or perhaps he found he didn't want to. Perhaps two women of a very different kind satisfying different needs suited him very well, thank you.

The leaves fall and it is back to Leicester in October, five lectures a week, the first at 9 a.m. on Monday. 'My hand is worn out with lecture writing,' Monica complains. She is burdened with twice as much teaching as other senior colleagues. She visits Philip for a weekend in Hull: 'I wish we were nearer & could be together oftener,' she tells him. As Maeve is, every Monday to Friday forty-eight weeks a year.

'Going a Bit Mad', 1964

'It is a very hard lesson to learn how absolutely little anything to do with me means to you'

Monica to Philip, 1964

New Year 1964, her holidays having been spent alone, finds Monica's nerves in tatters. She feels forty-one and much more. She longs for the 'dead dreamless sleep' she once had. She is racked by anxiety dreams – missing trains principally and Philip being cross with her and 'not listening when I explain the countless hardships wh have beset me'. She wakes, 'clenched all over' feeling like a 'batty Coleridge' after too much opium the night before. Is she going mad? She won't tell anyone but him in case they cart her off to that 'loony bin' in London – the Maudsley (previously Bedlam) as another Bertha Mason. Sensing her distress, ARH drops by and gives her a tiny box of chocolates 'of utterly unknown make'.

Perversely the crowning blow of the year is *The Whitsun Weddings*. This masterwork marked a change in relationship between Philip and Monica as regards his poetry. She had been if not collaborative then creatively companionable in his breakthrough volume, *The Less Deceived*. He had put poems in draft her way, years before they appeared in print. She passed judgement on them. Manifestly her critical opinion mattered to him – even if he did not feel obliged to follow it. They were solidly of a mind as to what good poetry was. And, of course, there was the supreme flourish: 'Monica Jones' on the dedication page. Other than a proposal of marriage it was, in 1955, the most valuable gift in Larkin's power to give.

The contents of *The Whitsun Weddings*, when she received a bound copy on the eve of publication, came as a horrible surprise when she saw a dedication to Maeve. There was a painful back story. Larkin had earlier published a poem – 'Broadcast', in the *Listener* (25 January 1962) – inspired by the other woman. She is pictured listening to Elgar live in Hull's City Hall: he, simultaneously, is listening to the same concert on the radio. 'Broadcast' was, Larkin said, as near as he ever got to an 'outright love poem'. It was inscribed 'To Maeve'. The notion that Monica and, even more hurtfully, others, would not come across the magazine was naïve. There was a row, a humble apology, and, as usual, grudging absolution. But then, two years on, Larkin had gone and published the poem again, with the same public dedication to Maeve Brennan. Monica was given no forewarning. It was a double slap in the face.

'Broadcast' is a fine poem and one Larkin was disinclined to waste by leaving it in the back numbers of a weekly journal. When she got her prepublication copy of *The Whitsun Weddings* Monica opened the volume eagerly and was instantly paralysed. 'I have sat and stared', she told him,

> absolutely incredulous, that you have published Broadcast after all your crocodile tears – expressions of regret at its appearance before. I shouldn't have believed it if I hadn't seen it with my own eyes.

She had shed tears, and forgiven the poem (with difficulty) when it was first printed in the *Listener*. But:

> It's taken its place in the Larkin oeuvre now . . . it seems a bloody incredible thing to do . . . the jacket of the book is horrible . . . I hate and despise it . . . each day I have slept till about 12. I feel and look very pale and poor, can't eat.

His excuse was 'complete forgetfulness'. A transparent fib. 'Broadcast' reprinted proved two things to Monica: Poetry came first and perhaps Maeve did too. Monica? The also-ran. Bill Ruddick brings her the expectedly hurtful gossip:

> the SCR [Senior Common Room] people knew it could not be me because the girl was 'beautiful' that settled it . . . It is a very hard lesson to learn how absolutely little anything to do with me means to you, well useful to get that learnt!*

She calculates she has seen Philip only once in three months. She is going 'a bit mad'.

The concurrent news that he has learned to drive (without telling her) passed the test (ditto) and has bought a car (ditto ditto) seems 'in my gloomier madder moments all part of this long separation, you changing your life, wanting to, & pushing me away with the changes . . . I can't think what you want [a car] for except to take women out'. One woman in particular. Was that wretched vehicle worth the extinction of his brilliant series of classic train poems? ('I Remember, I Remember', 'Sunny Prestatyn', 'The Whitsun Weddings'). His 'gazelle' did a Beeching on one of the richest tracks in his writing. If, as Larkin said, deprivation was for him what daffodils were for Wordsworth, steam (the ranker odour of diesel, even) in his nostrils was what the rotten apple in the desk drawer was for Schiller. Those rubberised automobile wheels betrayed Larkin's poetry. Philip later, as his fame grew, graduated five years on into a before-needed hearse in the shape of an 'enormous 4-litre Vanden Plas Princess, with a Rolls Royce engine'.

Guilt inspired a bombardment of conciliatory letters. 'I have nothing to live for without you,' she responds. *Vogue* is going to use the epochal picture she took of him on the England sign at Coldstream – she recalls they walked to Flodden & saw a hare in the lane, 'we thought it was a dog'. *The Whitsun Weddings* is published on

---

* The allusion is to the poem 'Wild Oats', about Ruth Bowman '[there] was an agreement / That I was too selfish . . . / And easily bored to love. / Well, useful to get that learnt.'

27 February: she swallows her pride and brings herself to congratulate him – it is 'solider' than *The Less Deceived*, she grants. It bears out 'Sutherland's point' about his 'idealism', she says. 'ARH said "glad to see Philip is getting such good reviews".'

Philip gives her his 'mono' gramophone, which is the most expensive gift there is any record of his giving her. However she must buy her own stylus as his is worn down. The *Telegraph* has given him a stereo for his jazz reviews, so he will bring the old machine down in his car. She dreams at night that her mother and father have died in a car crash and in another dream sees them 'clinging to some cliff, waiting for the help I had promised to bring'. She visits Hull, learns more about his continued involvement with Maeve, and falls vomiting sick. 'You didn't turn round to wave to me as you went out of the station . . . I watched your back go out of sight.' That last reads like a tiny Hardy poem.

Had he wanted to, 1964 would have been the point at which Larkin could have separated from Monica forever. He didn't. Why not? Andrew Motion suggests he was trapped in a sexual bipolarity which mattered to him. Larkin needed (or selfishly exploited) the virginal 'heavy petting' (but at the moment no more) Maeve offered, he forever the wooer, she forever his coy mistress. At the opposite pole, he needed the all-the-way bed-relationship with Monica which satisfied (his word) his 'randiness'. Motion's is a convincing explanation at the level of Larkin's gonads, but there was more. Monica – whose mind was as important to him as her body – reassured him, with exactly the same thinking about literature as his, that he was right to define himself as a traditionalist poet. Their joint assertion on the subject would be made public in the field-defining, collaborative *Oxford Book of Twentieth-Century English Verse* ('bloody OxBo', as Larkin called it). Monica was not involved in the writing of his poetry but she helped erect around him the scaffolding which let his poetry happen. That union of critical sensibility, prejudice at its extreme edge, was a main supportive strand of their almost four-decade relationship.

Supervisor and Pub Pal, 1963–1964

'You have things to live for without me. I have nothing to live for without you'

Monica to Philip, 1964

Monica, in the usual swing of the pendulum way, was cheered by spring 1964. Her spirits rose with the nasturtiums. She could even bring herself to make jokes about Philip's love-chariot. The marque – Rover? Too Conradian. Singer? 'from the red gold keep thy finger' (Lucy Ashton's song, Walter Scott). Gazelle? A trifle too James Elroy Flecker, perhaps. She hated the damned machine and the passenger seat where even more damned Maeve sat. But her display of literary wit made the other woman currently in his life look witless and poorly read.

'Terrible' Malcolm Bradbury came to his alma mater to read from his novel in progress. She 'disengaged myself from him as soon as I could'. She knew he had 'done' her as Viola Masefield in his last novel, damn him. Her back has ricked itself – it is probably not physical but 'theatrical'. Her 'spark of life' has been snuffed out. 'My life is dreaming and bed, bed, bed':

1959 was a bad enough year for me, & I do feel damaged by it, but then the ceaseless deaths after it have given me no chance to settle down . . . It has made me old, I look old now when a mere few years ago I looked younger than my age.

In June she had – as she had a few times suspected over the years – a sense, and possible evidence, that she was pregnant: but now, she realised, it must be a 'false pregnancy'. It would be the last of such alarms.

Despite this agonising, never-ending, malaise, Monica set about shaping me as a graduate with career prospects in the same way she had masterminded my undergraduate success. I was granted a state scholarship – a cool £500 p.a., tax free, for three years. But 'Sutherland' she informed Larkin 'is not a scholar'. She continued:

> Sutherland is more our kind of thing [there follows a catalogue of our shared interests] & a happy time we had in his 2nd year, & very good he was, and so I liked him. I enjoyed his second year and he has twice told me that *he* enjoyed it – I don't think I helped him much it was pure identity of interests.

I could certainly, by now, claim some intellectual identity with Monica. I had even subscribed to her non-academic prejudices – authors who were gold (18 carat Thackeray and Scott), others who were 'silly' and to be avoided. And I bought into her visceral contempt for careerist academicism: 'having a field'. She added: 'If Sutherland gets his research grant I think I shall have him to supervise . . . Thackeray . . . ARH says rather contemptuously "well you like Thackeray and you like Sutherland".'

I got the grant and I got Monica with it. Summer 1963 with my degree and money for three more years doing nothing but read were the prelude to happy times for me. And I was a boozer once again. Monica, a year later, recalled how:

> I thoroughly enjoyed the few days at the end of last summer term [1963] after Sutherland got his first & all the work was done, & Sutherland broke training (he hadn't touched a drop all term) &, as it now idyllically seems, we hardly [NB 'we'] drew a sober breath (Larkin's idealism). I was thinking of you all the time, too, & wishing youd've enjoyed the night-after-night. 'We're in the pub, you come too'. It was only about three nights I suppose and

then one night Sutherland and his girl and Bill came here for a cold collation & drink, but it seemed a wonderful endless casting of care aside. No heavy drinking was done, it was just leisurely beers, in June, very nice. And this evening, in April, still light at 8.15, I wish you could come and say 'Come to the pub' that would be best of all.

It was the first of many such evenings over the next year. Monica liked and came to life in pubs: with the right company, the Clarendon was her happy place. For me it was more what water is to fish and air to birds. As Monica intimates, I had evidently resolved never to be sober again after finals, nor was I consistently for twenty years after that.

If summer 1963 was happy for me, I can now see more clearly, as through the wrong end of a telescope, it was happy for Monica as well. For me it was release into a larger world: for her relief from a world smaller than a solitary confinement prison cell. There was a lot of friendly (over)drinking, chat and socialising, all fused as a single experience in my memory.

33

Monica Sparkles, 1963–1965

'I like public houses'
                    Monica to Philip, 1964

'I do like public houses with men, don't I?'
                    Monica to Philip, 1965

The second of the above quotations is truer than the first. I'd gathered an entourage. Monica called them initially 'Sutherland's mad hangers-on', or 'Sutherland's et al'. Then they became her 'boys'. Finally 'my [i.e. Monica's] boys'. We drank customarily in two pubs: the Marquis of Granby when we were lads together – a roughish drinking hole, where Monica rarely joined us; and at the Clarendon – respectable: Monica's Stoneygate local. Larkin himself drank there with her on Sunday lunchtimes when he was in town. She could count on about one weekend a month at this time of her life if she was lucky. Philip's Leicester visits were like throwing a drowning person a lifebelt every half hour, not to save them but keep them from drowning too fast.

Larkin's personality, on those who were genuinely nearest to him, exercised vampiric force: he somehow sucked the life out of you. Monica made the point eloquently:

I do wish you could just *see* me sometimes; I am dull and boring and ignorant with you, I know, but with people less clever and exacting (I don't say that sarcastically; being with others shows me how much cleverer you are than *anybody*, *really*). I can sparkle, be funny, be quick and clever, be a hit, the person who holds the group together. At your weight I'm always hopeless, cut eye in the first round, & I don't mind this a bit, I like you to be what you are, so much better than me & than anyone; but at the next weight down I really think I am able to enter the ring, it's always so with people I know (I'm pretty grim with those I don't know).

He, Philip, did not, she felt, 'get my best self as regards entertaining-ness'. Others 'do find me fun and good company'.

Me and my hangers-on, students all, were less clever than Philip Larkin. We found her, as she describes, fun and good company. Philip, in his library bunker at Hull, kept well away from the students, except as a voyeur. He had a tortoiseshell spy-glass on the windowsill of his office so he could examine any eye-catching women students as they passed by. In his adjoining office cache of porn many of the female subjects were, presumably, student-aged. But the idea of going to the pub and hobnobbing with students would never cross his mind.

His closer female colleagues, apparently, knew about the locked cabinet of porn in Larkin's office. What is it *for* (a naïve question) he was asked by one of his women friends, Jean Hartley, visiting the university. He replied: 'to wank *to*, or *with*, or *at*'. There is something both pathetic and revolting in the scene that remark calls up. The iso-lation is horrifying: Monica yearned for 'a bit of male company' – but it was nothing more than that. Philip told Monica that the thought of her hanging out with students made him uneasy.

She told him, in the crisis of their early 1960s relationship, that she yearned for 'male companionship . . . a bit of male company . . . someone to go to the pub with'. She didn't want sex, just a knock on the door around seven, and a cheery 'coming to the pub?' What Monica found answered her social need was 'the crowd of young people'. Sutherland's mad hangers-on, her boys, offered Eastcheap Tavern camaraderie. She flourished in the warm, nicotine-laden, beer-aromatised, glass-clinking, chatty bonhomie. She couldn't go out and get half-cut by herself in pubs – even hostelries as well run by the public-school-educated Clarendon publican, Giles, who liked to talk about Maseratis he had driven before pulling pints. As a single woman, Miss Jones would have been hit on, or, more horrible, not hit on but laughed at.

She describes a typical night in late 1963:

> When I mean to clear out of College early then comes me Suther-land cranking in . . . then [as evening draws in] comes say Bill & Sutherland saying 'should we have a beer to strengthen us?' and so, of course, I think we should & get home at 8 o'clock instead of the four o'clock I meant. I can't resist a beer, as that wretched Bill knows; he can always detain me by suggesting a beer. Sutherland, of course, is always willing . . . At least Sutherland really *likes* beer – I don't think Bill really does. He just knows I do.

We would duly go, a jolly trio, across Victoria Park. On other occasions I would call unbidden at her house and invite her to join us. She always did. Monica liked us and what we gave her: relaxed, unclever, male company that didn't stop her mouth. Monica made sure Philip knew how chatty her drink-fuelled social life now was.

We accepted Monica as Monica. A studiously good-looking woman, sharp on repartee, who bought her rounds. Monica had told Philip that I was a 'great boozer'. I was, in fact, pre-alcoholic, and so was she.

Monica's heavy solitary drinking dates from a few years after this period. That was the time when she would arrive drunk at an ARH nine o'clock staff meeting with misapplied lipstick. Monica had a good head for liquor at this time in her life. Better than Philip's, as he told her. But by herself, after 1959, the awfullest year of her life, her drinking at home became insidiously more dangerous. In the lonely seventies she would routinely spend Sundays, when not called to the pub, in and out of bed sipping gin and tonic reading the papers or writing to Philip. A few years on, she was waking up alongside bottles she didn't recognise. And, quite often, tearing up what she had unrecognisably written in passion or despair to Philip the night before.

In relaxing company, Monica was a conversationalist and raconteur when drink loosed her tongue. And amusingly indiscreet, with the ever-present tang of malice. Of the many examples I recall, a couple will serve. It was for my ears alone – just the two of us in the pub, me on my fourth pint, with three to come, probably. 'PAWC' (Philip Collins) was the 'leading' Dickensian in the department whom she particularly took against. Meaning to be bonhomous, he vexed her, reminding her of gasbag Major Bagstock in *Dombey and Son*.

She could not abide PAWC's 'tireless forced facetiousness'. He had moved to a large house, commensurate with his leap-frog promotion, three rungs over Monica's head, to a personal chair and new marriage, for which, unlike his previous union, he had great expectations. Duty called Monica to the celebration, but she was disgustedly delighted to see that in the toilet he had hung a Victorian motto plate inscribed 'Thou, God, seest me.' 'Can't imagine the Almighty would be much interested in *him* on the bog,' she said.

Another anecdote featured George Fraser – 'Guzzling George' – who sat opposite her at a dinner party with his legs open and (un-wittingly) flies unconsciously likewise, talking non-stop about his natural home, Literary London, as a Chekhovian fourth sister might talk about Moscow. 'Not much to see' she told me, with a faux sad look on her face. Then the Jones pause (as coldly punctuational as Pinter's): 'Rather too much to hear'.

Monica's venom about colleagues was catching. During my later career I had to beware of it flaring up in myself to get a cheap laugh. And my laughter at her collegial scorn was hypocritical and two-faced. I got instruction from those she mocked. Ronald P. Draper was a Nottinghamshire University graduate and a devoted, later distinguished, Lawrentian. He'd worn Scholl sandals to an official function, Bill, the ever-faithful snitch, told her. 'Life affirming,' she commented. She 'did' Draper as the husband in the 'Ron 'n' Eth' sketch on the radio comedy, *Take It from Here*. She and Philip, around this time, particularly relished such jokes as the prole couple sitting on the sofa and Eth saying (imagine Monica's Brummy accent), 'Oh Ron, I fear I've lost my mystery.' Ron replies, 'Is it just under the cushion, love?' *TIFH* was her and Philip's favourite comedy pro-gramme, listening as a couple simultaneously created an ethereal togetherness. She was the only one of his lovers who had that bond. They were also fans of *The Archers*; the two of them lamented, with the nation, when Grace Archer was burned alive.

Pubs are designed to be unbuttoned talkative places. Monica enjoyed the freedom to be entertainingly malicious. And the three to four years Monica spent in the pub with us were, as best as I can detect from the letters I have now seen, one of the few consistently happy times of her adult life – torn, in her lonely hours, by the inevitable Philip-Maeve problems. They were good times for me as well. I was seeing more of her than Philip was, and ever had seen and drunk with her since the 1940s. Her 'boys', as she referred to them – not just us, but the young men (always) who came after us – filled a vacancy in her life.

Did Monica, as she told Philip, 'sparkle'? It's a word which does not, in biographies of Larkin, attach itself to her. In her boys' company, Monica's face, normally set, became mobile and expressive. She could play practical jokes on us. She had, she told us gravely one evening, interviewed a candidate for a job that afternoon and she noticed that in his nervousness he'd put on different coloured socks. We three young men in her company reflexively looked down at our ankles. 'Ah, yes,' she sighed archly, 'ARH did exactly the same when I told him; we didn't appoint old odd-socks, though his ankles weren't the reason.'

She could tell improper stories which were funnier in the Clarendon than they would be here. When it was her round she would check who was drinking what and, turning to me, say – 'ah yes: and two pints of best bitter for John.' As she told Philip, 'Sutherland really *likes* beer.' She would walk to the bar, after her jest, with the hint of a saucy barmaid swagger of the hips. She had a line in leg-pulling.

I recall the night of the Cooper–Clay (later Muhammad Ali) fight, 18 June 1963. It was listened to on the radio in a quietened Clarendon; national hopes high. Monica was passionate about prize-fighting: men being hurt did something pleasing for her. And she liked listening to fights in pubs, it gave her a sense of being in a crowd, carried away and out of herself. Her fists clenched and worked throughout in response to Harry Carpenter's commentary. When Henry's Hammer, as

Cooper's left hook was fondly called, felled Cassius in the fourth, she shrieked, joyously. Alas, Cooper who, as Ali's trainer Angelo Dundee said, would bleed if you looked at him too hard, was spouting so much precious body fluid that the fight was stopped, welteringly, in the fifth.

I wouldn't have used Monica's word 'sparkled'. It was more that she was, on those occasions and in our company, alive. Whenever I was there, in the Clarendon, with her and Philip and whoever else, she was like a Madame Tussaud's waxwork of herself, her unblinking eyes glued on *him*. She would never have pulled his leg in public or told a story to set the company in a roar.

Who, then, were my 'mad hangers-on' for whom Monica sparkled? Bill Ruddick was the longest-serving of Monica's boys: he was close to her a year before I came on the scene. Bill was a tall, lean, good-looking man, from a working-class coal-mining background. Andrew Motion, as do other biographers and commentators, makes much of Larkin's 'queer disagreeable feeling' about Monica's 'young Leicester admirer', Bill Ruddick. The implication is that he was sexually attracted and Philip was suspicious.

On one occasion Monica reported to Philip that Ruddick had been 'studying' her hips and rear. 'Yesterday,' she preened, 'I looked pretty terrific in scarlet trousers'. She always looked good in trousers, Monica believed, because she had 'the bottom' for them. She also knew, from experience (and what he liked to photograph) that it was one of Philip's foibles. Around this time he told her: 'I should like to stroke your little rabbit brow & large rabbit hindquarters.'

Larkin was, or pretended to be, greatly angered by the other man's trespassing eyes: 'Bill will feel my boot on his bottom if he keeps his eyes on yours.' There is something comic about the bully-boy image and the misapprehension underlying it. Did they really not know that Bill was gay? The evidence stared Monica in the face. 'Sometimes,' Monica told Philip, 'I point out smashing girls to him in the spirit of "look at that lovely pussy there" but all he says is "yes" hardly looking.' She notes his love of ballet, and a succession of mysteriously close, quiet-spoken, out-of-town male friends. Pussy was, perplexingly, of no interest.

Bill's disguise was understandable. Homosexuality was still criminal and ferociously punished. Monica was casually but reiteratively homophobic in her letters and may well have said something to Bill. To Philip she was sarcastic about 'the Lilac establishment'. She describes 'a little mincy bottom-waggling pansy chap in politics'. And East Anglia, she has heard, is all homosexual. 'How Crabbe would spit.' E. M. Forster: 'horrid . . . he exploits all the worst side of nature'.

Bill was good to her and for her – 'I need company to eat properly,' she told Philip. Bill was always available at lunch. She thought he handled his cuttles like a miner's shovel and pick, but withheld comment. When she was in her country home at Haydon Bridge, he would come hundreds of miles by train to bring her nourishingly fresh vegetables. He cared for her. She was not used to it and told Philip he was fuss and botheration. Hopefully 'his desire to see me all the time' would wear off.

For a smart woman, Monica could be very imperceptive. Larkin had worked Bill out. His lover's jealousy was a ploy, as was her hinting sexual interest in Bill. The games they played with each other made correspondence chess look like noughts and crosses. In a letter of April 1964, Philip observed, slyly, there was something 'girlish and eager' about Bill. Monica picked up the hint, saying 'I have quite gone off him'. But she hadn't – love was love wherever it originated and it was in short supply in her life. And Bill was useful to Larkin. Bill gave him licence to play the field. 'Surely,' wrote Maeve Brennan, Philip's current other woman, 'Monica cannot deny you all other contact with female company. She by no means denies herself male company. You have to take her relationship with Bill on trust.' There was nothing to mistrust. He knew.

Most vivacious of my companions, and Monica's boys, was Eric B. Slinn: a man so dandiacal that Huysmans would have been hard put to describe him in full plumage. 'Ah, Slinn,' Monica would sigh as he walked into the Clarendon summer-suited: '*aujourd'hui symphonie en jaune*'. She gave a thumbnail sketch of Slinn decked out in his finery to Philip. She had bumped into Eric coming from the station, she coming from the Cathedral, both in their Sunday best:

he looked a dream in *marron glace* shoes, cream socks, beige trousers, cream shirt, beige tie & a sort of dark apple-green cardigan, like a dark green apple; it mayn't sound good, but looked fine. He had travelled in the cardigan, I could see, because his suitcase is of a rather similar green! Bill can laugh a *lot* at Slinn, but not at his clothes, Bill buys the most awful clothes.

The habitually death-suited Larkin was intrigued. 'Slinn', he mused, 'an odd name':

Clearly I must meet *Slinn*. He sounds quite fascinating – more so than the other two in his own ways. The ability to buy clothes is rare in our walk of life, isn't it? Can you produce him next Sunday?

'The other two' were me and Bill: dull dogs both of us. He'd never evinced the slightest 'must' in meeting us. Eric had, in fact, seen Monica and Philip, without registering who they were. He recalls the first impression of the odd couple they made:

I first saw Monica in the Clarendon in company with a seedy, shifty looking bloke in his late fifties.* I remember it so well because the apparent difference in their ages was so very obvious. To see a striking, blonde, well dressed woman with lovely shapely legs companioned by a what? Her boss – Sugar Daddy – Divorce lawyer – Funeral Director?

The 1964 Slinn–Larkin meeting – in the Clarendon, inevitably – went swimmingly. Eric held court. He told the poet someone should biff Ted Hughes in the guts. Monica and I winced. Larkin's features retained their rhadamanthine impassivity. Later, when a bunch of Slinn's poems were published in *Luciad*, the university magazine, Larkin asked Monica to send them. He actually liked them. Although he never entered into correspondence with any poet he didn't have to or who he felt was his equal, he did tell Monica to send Slinn off to

---

* Larkin, b. 1922, was actually forty-one.

the resident American poetry man, Paris Leary. 'God wants it,' said Philip, mock-solemnly.

My other male mad hanger on was Jim MacNamara. He was second-generation Irish, the best storyteller around, a cradle catholic and the most prolific chain smoker I've ever known. In the right setting, Monica and Philip were up there with him. Monica called him, as no one else did, 'James' – in allusion to Margaret Peel in *Lucky Jim*. She could take that joke in this company. He liked playing the odd joke on her himself. Had she read *Billy Liar*, he asked (he was reading it himself as she came into the Clarendon). No, she replied. 'It is', said Jim, with the air of a cardinal of the old persuasion, 'a book no lady *should* read.' Then he gave it to her.

Jim was the only one of my friends whom I saw seriously engage with Monica about Philip. He was interested in Larkin and the church. Why, for example, did he indulge that faux naïveté in 'Church Going' about the 'holy things' at the altar-end. He clearly knew what a 'pyx' was and had studied his Pevsner. And why was he 'visiting' all these churches and not, despite the poem's title, 'going' to them? Monica, as I recall, nodded in agreement. She had never much, as a churchgoer, entirely liked 'Church Going'. Whenever she met Jim in the pub she would ask him, archly, 'Anything to confess this evening?'

Larkin once called the four of us the Company of Fowlers. It was an allusive nickname. Monica was ornithophobic – violently susceptible to 'bird dread'. A friend recalled that in her schooldays she once refused, on a country walk, to cross a field because there were hens clucking in a far corner. When a bird got into the house she would faint or run. If it were down to her, Monica would have sent the whole feathered tribe the same way as the dodo. The company of fowlers, bird killers, would do it for her. Ornithocide was their business.

By a sadistic culinary twist, Monica loved eating and, particularly, slow-roasting, fowl: like Torquemada dealing with a peculiarly resistant heretic. The only good bird was a dead bird and even better an eaten bird. Her letters are salivatingly rich with chickens (always free range – she and Philip had a row about his defiantly eating battery-laid eggs), partridge and duck. 'Fred', her poulterer, took care of her needs.

'I like cooking more than I like eating,' she said. Particularly her feathered enemies. She could make love to Philip by menu. Her letters to Philip are full of luscious descriptions of food, such as the following, a meal she planned for Philip, in bleak January 1962:

I had a lovely fat pheasant, the best I've had this year & then I had broccoli & *haricots verts* & I just thought last night 'tomorrow I'll make *pommes de terre Dauphinoise*, it's a long time since I've had any of them'. So I did . . . Bow Joe [Beaujolais] too 'for a game bird'.

Philip didn't turn up. She picked at the feast cold over the following days.

It was not our minds that drew Monica into our orbit. We were welcome company. There was, manifestly, an ulterior motive. There was no call for her to write voluminously, as she did, about boozy nights in the Clarendon with ne'er do wells. She was making a point: 'the old bag can still interest the young', she told Philip over and over. And she could sparkle.

Everyone then alive remembers where they were when they heard the news of Kennedy's assassination. It's doubly memorable for me. It was one of three occasions when I caught momentarily a glimpse of Monica's deep vein bigotry, normally a private thing between her and Philip. Monica and I heard the announcement about Dallas in the Clarendon, drinking together. It put a damper on the evening. We walked back the few yards to her home for coffee. It was closing time, Friday night, 22 November 1963. It was dark and Monica was always frightened of fumbling for her key alone in the unlighted porch of the house, one hand grasping the torch she kept in her handbag.

While we walked, I came out with some off-the-*Guardian*-shelf praise of JFK, recalling the close shave of the Cuban Missile Crisis: his civil rights reforms, etc. She cut sharply through my piety. She couldn't be sorry, she said. 'He was an Irishman and he hated England and did everything he could to hurt us.' His father was Hitler's man, she added. I gulped. She wrote much the same to Philip, who also held his tongue being, as he was, still deceiving her (as she had discerned) with Maeve Brennan – as immigrant southern Irish, and Catholic, as her name. 'Mrs K.', Monica added sourly, 'seems to be behaving rather theatrically, isn't she? This refusal to change her blood-spattered suit, not even her stockings one paper said.'

I came across her racism again a couple of years later when she told me that she would pass her verdict on increasingly multicultural Leicester by voting BNP. It was 1965. We were walking in the London Road and townspeople of colour were passing by. She glanced at them by way of explanation. Philip, she told me, was intending to vote the same way at Hull. She didn't go further. I think she was annoyed again at something I had said she considered wishy-washy liberal. I have found no evidence of how she and he actually did vote, if at all.

The third occasion was when she confided to me, jauntily, 'we've appointed a coloured communist' – Dipak Nandy. Her relationship with him would prove complex.* With me, knowing me, I assume she muzzled the casual racism she felt free to let loose with Philip. I should have stood up on each of these occasions and didn't. I was too much in her thrall. And, as she told Philip, I was, by nature, a silent man.

It was a strange and close relationship I had with her over these years. We were important to each other. She routinely told Philip (perhaps to annoy) that I was like him. I wasn't at all like him, but one thing we had in common. We were fascinated by Monica Jones. Why else am I writing this book about Monica Jones?

I did not want to leave Leicester, but circumstance sucked me out. British universities were, in 1964, embarked on a mass recruitment of young academic blood. It was the blip result of the Robbins expansions. Edinburgh, in early 1964, advertised, in one go, five new junior posts in English studies. Any field. No second degree or publication necessary. Monica insisted I apply there and everywhere. She wrote to Philip, 'There is plenty to describe to you, really, a couple of places are interviewing him . . . I think employment stares John in the face.

---

* See below, 'Dipak', pp. 199–205. For my afterthoughts about Monica's racist bigotry see Afterword, pp. 245–250.

I shall be sorry to see him go – next year I shall be without young friends to come and fetch me to the pub and I shall miss them.' After the interview at Edinburgh, the job offer followed me back by night train to Leicester. Bill had got a job at Manchester at exactly the same time. She exulted. Two bull's eyes, two premier universities, two of her boys:

> What a thing – two of our people getting their posts in one term & BOTH MINE. I am bucked, tho' I shall miss my companions, I'd looked forward to having J. for another year.

I most certainly was HERS and I would miss Monica achingly, writing to her from Edinburgh sometimes three or four times a week and coming down, in my first year away, more often from Edinburgh than Philip, closer in mileage, dropped by from Hull. I like to think I had provided some comfort, perhaps changed the way she saw herself, or at least offered some relief from her desperate situation during these years. It is hard to do justice to the ways in which she enriched my life and enabled my career.

34

A Full Look at the Worst, 1964

'my feelings are coming clearer all the time'

Monica, 1964

With her enlarged social life over 1963–64, and the sense that she mattered (at least to her pals in the Clarendon), Monica was seeing things clearer; about herself, her life and her future. After looking herself over she had realised, as she told Philip: 'I am not odd and mad or I can stop being mad, or I can stop being odd & mad, I am a wonderfully attractive woman . . . Each day I get a bit steadier and calmer.'

Clarity did not solve her problems, but it made them liveable with. As Hardy put it – 'if way to the better there be it exacts a full look at the worst'. Maeve was, Monica realised, the 'worst' she must look at. 'She must be very nice for you to love her, much nicer than you've made out to me,' she wrote. Philip had thrown up smokescreens to fool her, but now she sees through them. She suspects he and Maeve make jokes about her. She can hear 'their shrieks of laughter' about her girdle, the holes in her underwear which would once have excited him. Sometimes, she tells him, she too has felt temptation for some-one else but 'you were the only real person for me'. Maeve has 'daily contact: I can't compete with that'.

'I see perfectly what you get from Maeve', she says, 'a feeling of liberation, of exuberant *youth*-like activity, of *normality* . . . of course you want to escape from yourself . . . Life is very unjust. I was just

dealt a bad hand, I think'. The following morning, true to form, she
says yesterday's long, thoughtful analytical letter was 'hysterical' and
'raving':

> I have really examined my feelings today & find I *don't* really feel
> angry or indignant . . . I don't feel much changed towards you . . .
> 'positive love' can make up for 'separation'.

But, henceforth, he must not deceive her: 'Deception builds up a
terrible wall between us.' Let him deceive gullible Maeve. Maeve
knew all about Monica. But Philip did indeed deceive his Hull lover
– hiding, all the while, the 'grosser' Larkin from her; that side of
him was only given free rein in Cross Road and Sark. Maeve was in
love with a man whom she deludedly believed to be teetering on the
brink of ascetic Catholicism – a man who was 'spiritual' not carnal
by nature, monastic by inclination, 'chivalrous' in conduct. Monica
knew and loved the other Larkin.

Monica accepted her half loaf. And, of course, she accepted the
'gross' Larkin – the man who had, as she said in one of her letters, a
touch of the Marquis de Sade about him. She will not, she resolves,
say 'nasty things' about Maeve in future. Nor would she say 'corny'
(i.e. sentimental) things about the other woman and Philip. 'I *must* be
different', she told him. '*You* can manage so much – 2 women on top
of everything else.' Monica also accepted she would never have a place
to call home: 'I do think I shall have to leave the cottage sometime,
it does seem in this short time to have become soaked in unhappy
association.' She notes white hairs on her head.

She must, she resolves, make do with whatever Philip would
find it possible to put her way. Skeletally, what is that? Sark, Lords,
churchy New Year excursions, weekend visits, second in line to Eva
in Loughborough. And, of course, an arterial flow of literary-quality
correspondence. That, for the future, was her Larkin ration and her
letters to him, and his to her, would be her subsidiary contribution
to English Literature. It is now, we can see, a real contribution.
Maeve would surely discover, as Monica told James Booth, that
Philip 'was more interested in himself than in anything else.' More

interested, that is, in the writer in himself. Maeve's younger body and lesser mind would pall on him. Monica's superior mind had longer durability.

Monica could even raise sisterly concern for the woman who, six months earlier, she'd abused for ousting her:

> You told me you had been so obvious with M. that you were now always asked out together – like a married couple – and I ask you as a friend, if this is wise; if you don't mean to marry Maeve, if you don't, then are you wise to give that impression? 'I speak friendly in your ear' . . . If you don't marry Maeve soon then I think you are being indiscreet.

The usual cost was paid. She fell back on her tomato sandwich and raw apple diet and was drinking heavily, while telling him, 'I *will* improve'.

The department was, as ever, a site of humiliation for Monica. ARH – an out and out 'crook' – had gone on a promotion spree. Guzzling George was made a Reader, PAWC got a personal chair, and the promise of a Victorian Studies Centre. Glum Ron was elevated to another Readership to gaze even deeper into D. H. Lawrence's cosmic darkness. She and her one friend Tom Craik were left languishing. Her first reaction was apoplectic and anorexic. She could barely get through a slice of bread and butter. Attending church helped – 'a fairly high one'.

Monica had long accepted her academic standing and that her Oxford promise would never be fulfilled in orthodox ways. The MA gown, now threadbare, that she wore in lectures reminded her it had not always been so. When Helen Gardner, destined to be Professor Dame Gardner, had come to address Leicester's LitSoc she remembered Miss Jones – that clever young 1940s woman with the spectacles. Monica did her level best to avoid meeting the grand woman. Her light, once so bright, was now hidden under a hundredweight of bushel. A lot of that bushel was Philip Larkin. He realised it: 'I have built her in my own image', he said, 'and made her dependent on me, and now I can't abandon her.'* She had built an important part of him, she could have shot back.

On Philip's forty-fourth birthday she sent, to his mother's house, an Orangeman mug to remind him, subversively, of Belfast infidelities. That long summer at Haydon Bridge, a place increasingly uncomfortable to her, she was visited by 'wretched Bill' and the Craiks. She liked their son Roger, an eight-year-old of 'intellectual & naturalistic bias'. Roger recalled, in a memorial he wrote of Monica, his yellow jumper, his wellies, wading in the river and the most delicious fish soup he ever tasted all his life. The Craiks, Monica told Philip, 'don't talk a lot of rubbish'. High praise.

When not feeding others, Monica fell back on her symptomatic 'tomato sandwich fever' and reported to Philip a catalogue of illnesses – some clearly 'theatrical'. Philip told her, unconvincingly, there was another chap after Maeve. She laughed when he mentioned Maeve's 'incredible morality'. A 'flirty trick', she suggested. He visited when it suited him, they took the annual holiday, and their summer 1964 was, despite all, 'successful and delightful'.

Philip gave her to understand that he and Maeve had definitely split up in her parents' house, when her folks were out of town. It had been her decision, he said, and he was sternly requested to leave the house afterwards. 'Maybe', speculated Monica, with grim irony, 'she wanted to have church to go to after she'd done it.' Monica felt momentarily remorseful: that poor woman – alone in her parents' house. 'She isn't used to being alone, as I am, or even you are . . . I hope I have not behaved badly . . . did you say she had dogs?'

'Some guilt oppresses me,' she wrote, now back in Haydon Bridge, 'It does seem that you taking a holiday with me is what has caused this to happen.' Philip could not bring himself to tell the truth. He and Maeve had by no means parted and would be joined as lovers for a further fourteen years. Philip was a master of reserve but no master of concealment. When she learned she was yet again deceived, Monica

---

* Motion dates this as from a letter to Eva, 1 Jan 1961. James Booth, who edited Philip's letters to his mother can't find it. It may be from conversation between Larkin and Motion.

came near to losing her mind. Drunk and furious, she pictured them giggling at her letter of sympathy for cast-off Maeve. She will not come to Hull to see him: 'I have to show I am not a dog.' She phones him, again 'the worse for drink', apologising the next day. Either have a holiday with me or goodbye is her ultimatum. It is 'your presence' she wants, 'not letters and telephone calls'. And 'if all this has to be gone through again, sometime, then I don't think I can bear that'. Every time this happens, it breaks a piece off her.

What was left? Monica looked around in the SCR in 1964 and felt 'separate'. Alone again. 'I wish', she told Philip, 'that I had a pub-companion, I should be much better if I had. John [Sutherland] will be feeling the same thing: he likes pubs.' Too much, as it happened. In the same letter she reminds herself she must send Philip the ten shillings she owed him for food, from when she was last with him in Hull. She is once more living on tomato sandwiches and grapes – 'even tho' I know how to cook.' When Philip first knew her, twenty years ago now, Monica was his Estella. In moods like this, she was on the way to becoming his Miss Havisham.

35

The Old Story, 1965–1966

'*I squeal outside the Guildhall of Life, like a legless beggar*'
Monica to Philip, 1965

Monica, in recoil from the always bubbling Maeve crisis, was becoming seriously worried about her solitary drinking – less controlled than that of Clarendon nights with the boys. Malnutrition makes it acutely worse. She worries that drink keeps her going, but at what cost?

> I am afraid of the hold that the bottle has on me, and I have tried to tell you. It took its hold in 1959, when very often, & for weeks, I could not get a proper meal and, of course, a few drinks kept me going. I don't drink terribly hard but I am near enough alcoholism to be sometimes unable to stop, even sometimes to find a bottle open that I don't remember having opened. I've certainly got no *worse* than I was in 1959, probably have got a bit better, but I don't know if my *will* has got much better, and do see these bad signs, like not remembering opening a bottle . . . at any rate I don't think you & your chosen one will have to help me from a cinema, dead drunk, if only because I do not go to cinemas.

Drink, when it takes over, usually at the end of the day (her morning drinking is still at bay) drives her to erotomania. She tells Philip:

I sit here naked at midnight on the floor before a good fire with
work to do. I have thrown off the dressing gown because the room
is hot. My urgent nipples make me think of you, but I know that
at present you don't care for the like of that. I hope you will again
sometime.

Philip, meanwhile, is on the up. He is doing a *Monitor* TV programme
with his (and her) idol John Betjeman, the talented Patrick Garland
directing. Monica was introduced and was thrilled to be 'going to the
Ritz with Betjers'. Thrilled even more to be seen publicly to exist in
Larkin's world. In retrospect, Larkin's verdict on the programme was
an ejaculatory 'Ogh ogh ogh'. He did not impress himself. He had
watched the programme on a friend's TV (he did not own one), hand
in clutching hand with Maeve. The programme is a glass bucket on
to what he was, physically, in the mid-sixties – still lean, amusingly
self-deprecatory, tired of living, scared of dying, just rolling along and
attached to two women.

As his librarian's life grows more hectically busy it becomes difficult
to fit in trips to Monica – even car-borne. 'I wish you were here,' she
writes:

I have a good clean flat, I could almost shriek with disappoint-
ment. You shd see me, too, looking fine in polo necked busty
blade jersey & Veronica Lake hairdo. How boringly and lifelessly
I write.

There follows another empty Christmas in Haydon Bridge, nothing
to do but a 'vast clear up of the kitchen', church and drink. She quotes,
mournfully, from Tennyson's 'The Spinster's Sweet Arts' about how
the unmarried woman tries to win over the fellow who is no longer
sweet on her with victuals.

Philip could not find time to turn up. In Hull it is the party season
when Philip and Maeve would be in public smilingly together. On-
lookers predicted wedding bells – a peal never to be heard in Larkin's
lifetime.

Monica returns to Leicester from empty Haydon Bridge early and gets some relief from washing floors – an early spring clean. 'If you came here', she told Philip, 'you could take me for a little drive . . . Please try to send me a little letter . . . I suppose I'm trying to press down the manhole cover on my awful feeling about life . . . just writing to you makes me feel less alone'. He is, she notes, strangely remote and unfeeling on the fewer occasions he is with her nowadays.

PAWC's inaugural lecture is entitled 'The Impress of the Future'. Monica anticipates an uncheerful impress for herself. 'I can see the way the department is going. It is profoundly depressing.' She feels ground between millstones. 'Our generation?' She answers the question:

> We were brought up to take 2nd place to the grown-ups & not ex-pect anything for ourselves, anything we *chose*, until we were older & we accepted it because we thought our day wd come, but when we get older it's in a world where the young are the choosers. It's just as well I haven't got any children . . . *You'd* like me better if my life were less shrunken, less dingy, less squalid, if everything around me, and everything I did, didn't cry out 'FAILURE' . . . I'm surprised and disappointed by myself. I expected better of myself.

Churchill has died: the Empire's great full stop. She asks ARH if she can watch on his and Jean's home TV the funeral in St Paul's cathedral where the Battle Hymn was sung after which the body was carried by river from Tower Pier to Waterloo. The Thameside derricks all dipped and hosed imagined tears in mourning. She lives again the wartime forties and Oxford and youth. 'I feel so impressed at being alive at the time of something unique in the world.' The Impress of the Past.

T. S. Eliot (the rattling 'tin can' as they called him) dies. Philip goes to the memorial service in the Abbey without her. She is studying Elizabeth David to find a dish which will tickle his palate and not upset his stomach (a delicate balance nowadays) whenever he should choose to drop by at Leicester. Free-range chicken poached, she thinks, with a sauce of (free-range) egg, cream and lemon.

She re-reads A. A. Milne's *When We Were Very Young* and weeps. At a departmental party the now 'Professor' PAWC compliments her on her dress and asks 'did you get it in England?' knowing full well she has never in her life been abroad. She takes refuge standing by Guzzling George 'who is always glad to see an empty glass so that he can fill his own at the same time'.

There are two young twentyish members of staff, John Ellis and Dipak Nandy, who look likely to replace the old gang of 'my boys' and 'My John'. John Ellis, particularly, is someone

> to whom I can say my mind – he's a very nice intelligent young man with a streak of cynical observation beyond his years. I like him very much & he likes me. I have an immense success with all the *young* men . . . what a strange utterly unexpected middle age I am having. I'd never have expected I'd be a great success with a lot of young men but I can see that they all like me, even are fascinated by me, if that doesn't seem too strong . . . I wish my fascination were more powerful in other directions, only simmering crater dwellers don't seem so enthralled . . . Here I become that character, the good pal to the men. I expect I am what most men want in a woman, but one who's obviously never going to make anything of it.

At the end of spring term she resolves not to go to the cottage – 'I am having a not bad time here . . . I rather shrink from the cottage now, I have had so much unhappiness in it.' Her new 'boys' – particularly Dipak – will be more interesting. She is reading Langford Reed's anthology of nonsense verse, *Sausages and Sundials*. She lives for the postman, she tells Philip.

I came down to stay with Monica a lot over this period and took her on a week-long jaunt to Edinburgh. She continued to chronicle my visits to Philip. 'He's in the sitting room', she told him:

> and I'm in the bedroom, but I have given him lunch and am giving him a proper dinner; so I shall not get to solemn evensong & the choir wearing robes. Lunch was a mixture of kidneys, onions

and peppers, mushrooms, tomatoes, or rice. It is almost post time. Thank you for your train-written letter.

There is a certain swish of the scimitar in this letter. It brushed Philip's neck two days later:

> It seems unjust to the point of absurdity for a decent woman like me to be unwanted by you – with my other advantages, too, like good cooking . . . cooking doesn't really count, of course, but I say cooking after 4 days of John who thinks that my food is the best he has ever eaten and that eating it all the time would be unimaginable bliss.

Monica was, as I now know (but then sensed – it was like a ticking bomb) nearer to complete paranoid derangement than at any time in her life. The indirect cause was the never-ending, festering, Maeve mess. The proximate cause was a break-in at her flat which triggered a period of rape phobia, something common in her life, but more extreme this time than usual. 'Thank goodness I didn't meet the burglar,' she breathlessly told Philip, 'thank goodness too it wasn't in the winter when I should have come home to it in the dark & been terrified in case he was still here.' Her (their) bedroom was turned upside down. She telephoned the police (from a call box) – two uniformed, one plain-clothes turned up 'with finger-print people'.

What was stolen? No jewellery, no money, but 'my brand new nightdress & peignoir'. And, oddly, her sponge bag. It must obviously, she deduced, have been a sex maniac. A fetishist. She shudders at the thought of his 'filthy fingers' on her unviolated intimate clothing. The letter raves on for fifteen sides. He, at the time, is in Belfast, visiting old friends. 'Had you been in England I daresay you'd have come to see me,' she forlornly says. For days after her hands tremble and she dreads going out. The police don't seem to believe her. But are they really police?

> One of the detectives, a gloomy-eyed, hound-faced, silent man is inclined to ogle me when the other isn't looking. They keep com-

ing all sorts of times – how do I know they all *are* police, these plain-clothes men?

Her office had also been broken into – nothing taken, except a copy of Johnson's *Lives of the Poets*. She is certain she was being stalked by a sex maniac (with a perverted interest in Augustan literature?). There are other terrifying phenomena:

> I felt so frightened last Sunday when I'd just staggered to post [you] a letter [the nearest postbox was a hundred yards away, London Road, the only main road in the vicinity, was threequarters of a mile, there and back], & was coming back. A lorry screeched to a stop and the driver asked me if I'd like to come for a ride. Of course, it was easy to say no, but *then* I was shaking, when I was feeling bad. Nobody seems to respect me whatever I do. I dress like a lady, I'm spoken to. I dress dowdily, I'm spoken to.

She can't walk past a building site, she tells Philip, without wolf whistles. Men approach her, with ill intent, in the street.

On May 29/30 she penned a massive screed. It begins with a marginal, hysterical-seeming comment about being molested and approached in the street by Leicester *canaille*. Larkin made no offer to come to Leicester, his one consolation to her being that she'd be glad to have 'John [Ellis] around'. The robbery, Philip thought, was 'a bit petty for a town like Leicester'. (The burglars turned out to be two girls, well known to the police as opportunist thieves).

She gradually recovers her balance of mind. Lords, as always, brightens the horizon: South Africa this year. England are headed by two of the country's most boring batsman: Tom Graveney and Ken Barrington. Not worth the price of the ticket, Larkin fears.

36

Not a Bad Summer, 1965–1966

'This old Bag / she played Shag'
> a nursery poem about herself which Monica invented to be
> sung to the tune of 'This Old Man'

There is short-lived zest in Monica's letters in summer 1965. 'I'm in looks this week', she tells Philip at the zenith of her year, between Lords and Sark. 'You would admire me I feel sure – hair, complexion, seem well behaved, healthy, glowing; I look luscious, get spoken to even by the young men who you'd think wd take no notice of an old bag like me'. She plays music loud on the gramophone he has given her – 'Greensleeves' over and over – 'when I have loved you so long' touches her inexhaustibly. Sometimes, she tells him, she sleeps naked. She has cut back on drink ('dieting') and has reached 'beloved ten stone'. But, just now in Haydon Bridge, she has seen three bats in the corner of her bedroom – are they really there? She breaks off for a needed drink. Should they take their dietary 'Bisks' to Sark? She will remember this year to take their Lapsang. She feels naughty: 'I have been thinking that I wd tell you that I intended to behave *much less well* in future'. She feels in the past she has been 'cheapened and debased'.

To see, even over years' distance, a person, man or woman, writhing in this way, must pain the reader and raise resentment. Is Larkin inflicting this or is he in the same bind as Monica and (in a lesser way) Maeve? Is it a coven of suffering? Did he feel her pain? Was it in some way a stimulus to the writer in Philip Larkin to be the occasion of a loved one's suffering? Or had Monica brought it on herself as love's martyr? It's impossible to read her letters of this period (his, by comparison, are calm and in their usual way stylish) without one's own emotional confusion. I find it hard, at these moments, to entirely exonerate Larkin.

Departmental life goes on. PAWC has married – she was not invited, but fantasises the event. The bride wears the former Mrs Collins's wedding dress for luck (i.e. fertility), a brass band plays Victorian music hall favourites, while the second Mrs Collins carries a bouquet of fennel and columbines and a copy of her husband's inaugural lecture 'suitably inscribed'.

Her paranoia never rests while eating her mind away. A man waiting for a taxi harasses her: 'I'm always being spoken to, honestly – you'll think I make it up.' She hears, or thinks she hears, rapping on her bedroom window, so insistently the glass might break. Then comes an official-sounding rapping on the door – which, through the lock-chain, she partially opens. It is two policemen. The relief is short-lived: 'They had seen a man in my garden trying to get into the house and given chase.' She fears her 'peculiar isolation . . . what I fear now is that these prowlers *are* the *men* friends of the girls who did the robbery'.

One of the pair was the 'plain-clothes policeman *I did not like*':

I am afraid . . . There was another thing that I never told you or the police, it seemed too silly – shortly after my flat was burgled I [and] my room in College had been ransacked . . . in a crime story this would mean I had something wh I didn't know I had & which criminals want . . . and then there was the curious theft of my *Lives of the Poets*.

Sometimes she fears 'there is a real mad man after me – he stole my lace pants off the line, he ransacked my room in College, *he* hangs about & makes me nervous for no reason, *he* tried to get in tonight.' She is writing at 4 a.m.: 'I must sleep.'

She has cut her fringe in a Vidal Sassoon line with a French pleat at the back. 'Like all people who wear glasses I look best with hair swept off the face.' She adds a set of sketches illustrating the point. She remains faithful to Balmain, Vent Vert – strong enough, she jests, to cover any hint of gin. And, when in doubt, buy kippers: when sad, mop floors.

She knows Philip is not being honest about having broken with Maeve – the nice things he says 'are merely to allay my suspicions'. In the department the latest, boyish, member is a new friend: 'John Ellis is my only joy . . . of course, I don't *know* him *very* well yet'. But he is courteous, attentive and witty. On All Souls' Eve she tells Philip she now has a stronger chain on her door. It gives her a sense of security against all the 'utterly mad men' outside who leer at her.

She apologises for the 'absurd outpourings' in her recent letters – but she is still worried about the easiness with which any of her windows could be smashed. She carries a torch with her at all times. 'It is ridiculous for me to live like this . . . I'm breaking up. . . Darling, I'm always thinking of you; tonight I thought you should be here – solid black pants with fishnet tights to the waist . . . I've bought *Larousse Gastronomique*.' A few days later she tells him she has bought him a tea-towel and tells him, in detail, of changes she has made to her body which will entice him and that John [Sutherland] will be coming in a fortnight – it mustn't clash with his visit. A duck stuffed with prunes awaits. He didn't, after all, turn up: 'you probably wdn't have cared for them anyway', she sadly concludes. There were new eruptions of the Maeve problem. Which of them was 'the other woman'? Monica defends herself – she didn't see Maeve as a 'nasty girl . . . I see her in contrast to me a happy girl'. NB 'girl'. The younger rival always has the advantage. Her scent today she wanted Philip (and Maeve, of course) to know was Fleurs de Rocaille.

Over the summer, at Haydon Bridge, Monica read George Eliot, a novelist she detested, intending to get a 'few flings' at that objectionable moralist in the autumn lectures she had been assigned. Eliot, she once told me (over jars in the Clarendon) was a writer who should only be read by Methodists on wet Sunday afternoons.

37

Dipak, 1965–1967

'*I do fancy him quite a bit*'

Monica, to Philip, about Dipak Nandy, 1966

Something out of the ordinary happened in 1965–67. Monica almost
fell for another man – or, perhaps, she didn't really. It may well have
been, to use her word again, 'theatrical'. And, on his side, it may well
have been courtesy warming into intimate friendship. Dipak Nandy
was later founder and first director of the Runnymede Trust; an institution set up in 1968 to confront and correct British racism. One
of his earlier attempts at correction was Monica Jones. Nandy was
appointed an assistant lecturer in the Leicester English department in
1962. It was his first job.

Dipak was twelve years younger than Monica. He had, apparently,
no family connections, no promised future in the UK, no wad of cash
in his pocket. After his arrival from Calcutta he odd-jobbed and slept
rough on Hampstead Heath.* He might have been subjected to racist
abuse and would certainly have witnessed it. Dipak had been well
educated in India at a Catholic school. There remained something
of the Jesuit in his thinking. He was, after hard nights on the heath,

---

* My account is taken from Andrew Waterman's review of *Letters to Monica*,
published in *Able Muse*, 2011. Waterman was a comrade of Nandy's Campaign
for Racial Equality in Leicester. Waterman also gives a lively account of the
Leicester English department in the mid-1960s.

accepted to do English at Leeds, under the wing of Arnold Kettle, a proselytising high-minded communist. Why, though, would Dipak leave India to sleep rough on Hampstead Heath in an England where the placard 'No Coloureds' insulted him every day? To get a degree in English is the given answer, which he did outstandingly. Like Kettle (later a founder of the Open University) he believed that the study of literature could radicalise; his motives were, in everything, political.

I heard Dipak lecture on Swift to my undergraduate class. He explained, with cool disgust, that the fourth book of *Gulliver's Travels* was manifestly satire on British colonialism. The yahoos were Irish 'natives', racially 'other' – Celt bog trotters – a subject people, reduced to sub-humanity by the British oppressor. Was the patrician Dipak Nandy a yahoo? The question hung uneasily in the lecture room. Dipak was ten years ahead of postcolonialism becoming an orthodoxy in English (so-called) Studies. By which time he had left English academic life to reform English society.

University positions at Leicester and Kent, where he moved after three years, were way-stages on his rise to the Runnymede Trust. As a university teacher, which is how I knew him, Dipak had a quality – an 'air' – which was magnetic. Monica's initial response to Nandy was shockingly racist. She did not want to be near the man. She was obliged to teach a course with 'the coloured communist from Leeds', she told Philip, harrumphingly, in October 1962. He is later referred to as 'that lazy Commie black Nandy'.

Gradually, over the months, the epithets modulate. Transitionally he is 'Black Nandy' but by June 1965 he is 'Old Blackers' – a seriously offensive nickname that in her eyes was affectionate. It was an allusion to the cricket radio commentator she and Philip loved, 'Old Johnners', Brian Johnston. Eventually he is 'Nandy', 'Dipak', and Monica's best – nay, only – friend in the department. It was on the face of it as improbable as Billy Budd winning over Claggart. Apropos of her being, at the moment, 'quite a draw to *young* men', Monica tells Philip: 'Nandy took me for a drink on the way home the other evening'. Dipak, it seemed, can be coaxed into the Clarendon for the odd half. He confesses to shame if he drinks too much: an emotion Monica does not share. 'Fancy old Nandy being one for the jug. I thought alcohol was against the religion of some of these coves,' rejoins Philip jovially.

Three days later there is a departmental party. The only person Monica can bear to talk to is 'Nandy' who is 'v. attentive and in-ordinately amused by everything I said'. By now, April, they drop into the Clarendon routinely. At a party at the end of May 'Nandy' glances politely at her décolletage. She claims, to Philip, to be dumbstruck. He tells her 'that he had been knocking me up' this weekend – 'I stared at his face when he said, "I often wanted to knock you up" . . . It seemed innocently to get me to join him in the Clarendon.'

At the time of the second Ali–Liston bout he told her how unusual it was to find a woman interested both in fisticuffs and EngLit. 'I told him that John [Sutherland] wd probably be there tonight but he didn't seem to want John to be there. So you see that I too could be a hit with the married men if I liked . . . I was in my pink trou-sers.' She continued on the theme in her letters to Philip. 'I thought', she says:

> that it would amuse you to think of *me* being fetched to the pub by a married, black Communist. He wouldn't dream of anything more, he has his new-wedded wife but I must say he does *seem to be where I am* quite a lot . . . I do sound a prejudicial old feminist, but you know I am not a bit of that.

Larkin began to take notice, after being introduced one weekend. 'I thought he was a bit eager – too intense for comfort ogh ogh . . . After all you are . . . like a true Oriental woman: see if I'm not right. Then I'll come and push in [his] black face.' Five days later he adds: 'God you have Nandy on the jump: watch it, watch it.' Exactly, one suspects, the response Monica wanted.

Dipak had perfect manners. But unlike me or Bill, he would take courtesy an innocent step further and kiss Monica on the cheek by way of greeting and farewell. The polite pecks were received graciously and reported to Philip. Dipak and his then wife Maggie lived close by and

he habitually walked Monica back across Victoria Park – an ordeal
for her when night fell early. Dropping in at the Clarendon became a
regular event. It was a place where Monica relaxed into her best self.
They did not drink much but conversed wittily. I recall Monica and
Dipak riffing on a colleague called Morris who had been appointed to
a chair. 'Was that a *William* Morris chair?' They pictured what such a
Kelmscotty monstrosity might look like.

By November 1965 – a period in which she was in living terror
from madmen and burglars – Monica told Philip 'what both-
ers me is coming home after dark. I shall force Nandy, who lives
just up the road, to see me to my door . . . Nandy's wife says she
won't go to Canterbury. That's the latest.' 'Nandy tells me that he
is fond of Kipling! It wd take an Indian Marxist – a Red-Indian,
as you might say – wouldn't it? He is a strange mixture.' No less
than she.

At the end of the year Monica suspected 'old Nandy & I are rather
keeping out of each other's way'. But, she told Larkin, '*I do not mind*
the butterfly light hand on my shoulder'. She was amused by his compliment that she had 'subterranean charms'. 'Pretty subterranean by
now', she told Philip, 'tho' for young men in their twenties I seem to
have a fatal attraction . . . of course, time goes on one forgets both Bill
and John are getting on for 28 now, they aren't boys, I do think John
likes me, yes. How well we all behave!' Philip picked up the line of
jest and ran with it a bit: '"subterranean charm" is rather a speciality
of rabbits. I wasn't aware that Bill and John were 28. Are they cases of
arrested development ogh ogh'. 'Because they, like Nandy, like me?'
Monica snapped back.

Nandy, Philip concluded, was 'a nice enough chap . . . anyway, how
you fascinate 'em, east & west, old and young. Darling! How desir-
able you are, & intelligent Vnto ye Bargayne.' At the end of January
1966 she told Philip:

Nandy came to my room on Monday to ask if I were walking
home . . . I think he was going to suggest calling at the Clarendon
but bad luck for him we met his wife in the street . . . not that
he spends all his time with me, not at all . . . American [Lyman]

Andrews [beat poet, now Lecturer in American Studies, aged 28] seems softened by rabbit's fatal attraction too.

The relationship jogged on. By October Dipak was at Canterbury and, dropping by Leicester, called at the flat – knocked her up, as he would say:

> We were so very pleased to see one another; he kissed my face when he arrived; it's just as well he's gone, perhaps for I do fancy him quite a bit . . . perhaps his going away has brought our little mutual attraction more out into the open.

It climaxed when Monica let slip to Philip she might be physically attracted to Dipak. Letters were written and torn up, telegrams flew, accusatory phone calls exchanged, hard things said. Monica collapsed.

She was innocent but her purpose, or one of them, had been clear. She had been trying to provoke a reaction in Philip, and she came halfway to admitting it:

> I tell you about him, as I'm sure you realise, not in order to 'make you jealous' in a cheap way, but on the contrary, so that you need never worry, you can see that I tell you everything – & this is so tiny – there's never any need to wonder what I'm up to. I think you saw this when you wrote abt his visit to the flat; I don't want to *hurt* you & God knows there's nothing in this & I might not have mentioned it if there hadn't been so much pain for me & I daresay a bit for you in the lack of openness about Maeve, tho' it is absurd to compare the two cases. There's never been anything with D. and me but a liking to walk home together – but definitely *liking* it – especially on long summer evenings.

Philip, of course, was spending his own long summer evenings with Maeve.

Dipak turned up a couple of days later and asked her to walk back with him. 'On the usual walk we sauntered along, making it last – I'm being absolutely truthful, we did seem to make it last. But we didn't even stand talking at the parting of the ways . . . it was just a walk home – it is all incredibly little.'

He talked about his 'lovely cottage in Kent. Anyway he did – in a very casual way – ask me to go down & visit him & see the University . . . the cottage has two bedrooms'. She breaks the letter off to wash her hair. And picks up the next morning:

> I've never concealed from you that I wd find it easy to fancy him a bit, you know also that I should never *do* anything abt it even if he did wh he wouldn't & wouldn't want to. He just likes me a bit & his going away has brought it a bit more DISTINCTION . . .
> It is now pouring with rain. Autumn has come.

After Larkin's explosion, her amends, and a few weeks calm, it blew over. Philip apologised rather stiffly: 'I'm sorry I misunderstood you over your Indian colleague. I didn't think it *all* the time, just occasionally out of annoyance I suppose.'

One should not make anything much of the Dipak episode. They were two people finding company, intelligent conversation, charm and wit in each other. Dipak was married; Monica, in her mind, as good as. But both their relationships were currently bumpy. Dipak continued to see Monica on and off. A significant meeting was on 8 February 1968. He came to lunch in Cross Road and told her he had left the Communist Party because 'it seemed to him not for human freedom. He is also leaving Kent and urges me to go and & see it before he does.' The Prague Spring crisis of that year, culminating in Soviet invasion in August, had shaken other party members' faith.

In a letter a couple of days later Monica says Dipak is moving on 'to some new race relations thing'. It was the Runnymede Trust. 'What he really wanted to do', Dipak told her, 'was to finish his 2 books, the Swift and the Conrad.' They would have been books worth reading, but the work Dipak went on to do in British race-relation reform, culminating in the Jenkins Act, was worth much more.

Philip meets Dipak again in the Clarendon and will have noted that Monica 'gave Dipak the kiss on the cheek, beating him to it'.

She has decided she will go to Kent. 'God knows why he wants me to see it.' Philip is 'concerned' at the idea – which, presumably, is what Monica intended. The visit never happens.

38

Alone Again, 1966–1967

'there is nobody I really like now'
Monica to Philip, 1967

Philip Collins had been appointed head of department in October 1966. He circulated a picture of himself in a Victorian bathing dress. 'A revolting sight' Monica told Philip who was meeting up with old friends, including an old lover. 'I feel a bit low when I think of you, now, now, very now', Monica says, 'with Patsy [Strang, now Murphy]'. Patsy is old Belfast history but is Maeve, up there in Hull, really 'off', as he had told her a few weeks ago?

> I won't stand it again if that was just as before, something that you mean to be true for 3 days, or 3 weeks, but that I'm meant to go on believing for ever . . . I thought all this last time, like a fool.

She was indeed being fooled. When she discovered the truth, she raged and then put up with his duplicity, as she always did.

Philip suggests a trip to Edinburgh, where they might call on Sutherland, but calls it off. John Ellis takes her to Stratford, to see Shakespeare – her field. Then, with a company of scholars they visit Lichfield to look at mediaeval manuscripts – John's field. Their minds have met at the same civilised level: an intercourse that hasn't happened with Monica for a long time. Her new boys are giving her higher things than the old Clarendon crew. John Ellis and she went to concerts together ('don't the young men love me?' she asked Philip after a trip with him to Gilbert and Sullivan's *The Mikado*). John was, she and Philip agreed, eminently 'companionable'. But no drinker. He was, Monica ruefully thought, looking back after he'd left Leicester, 'one of the very few people that I've liked at once'. He did not last long as her new boy: 'John Ellis has got the Edinburgh job', Monica told Philip glumly after she returned from the city herself. He would leave in January 1967. Another boy lost. But John, unlike me, stayed loyally in touch with Monica till her last days. J. R. ('Dick') Watson came to fill John's place. He was another boy she liked straight off. The two of them relished raising 'coarse laughs' between themselves at staff meetings. A scholar of Romantic literature and student of hymnody – a mutual interest – Dick would be a staunch friend for twelve years. But Dick was married with children and had other things in the forefront of his life. Monica liked visiting the Watsons. She now had no other senior friend in the department and was in bad odour with them for refusing to have any part in some 'rubbishy thing about Vietnam'. Like Philip, she was resolutely unswung by the sixties.

Christmas 1966 was the usual lonely ordeal and there was no cathedral visit in New Year 1967. Monica was staying instead with Philip in Hull. Tidying up some papers on his desk she found a telltale postcard from an unknown woman with whom he had obviously been unfaithful (to both her and Maeve):

> I was very much . . . more upset (no, not upset, I'm not going to be that again, but changed, hardened) than I showed abt your revelation of yet another affair with yet another girl. Of course I shd not look in your cards – I was not doing so in a prying way.

He evaded male devotees like the plague but would evidently succumb opportunistically to young female admirers at conferences. And, of course, Monica could not be in Hull without the sense of omnipresent Maeve, the resident rather than 'on the side' lover like her.

She returned, emotionally exhausted, to Leicester. Dipak phoned her for a last lunch before leaving. He came to her room, 'he was trying to get a bit of privacy, I *assume*, in order to give the little kiss wh he does on such occasions & wh he knows I'm willing for.' He stays that last evening at Cross Road talking till after eleven:

> I must say there is an atmosphere, perhaps a bit of speaking looks, it's nothing really, by Hull standards, but it is a *bit* to me, so I tell you.

With her two second-generation 'boys', Dipak and John Ellis, gone 'there is *nobody* I really like now'. Dick Watson has not yet endeared himself. When she thinks of Maeve, seeing Philip day in, day out, going to Hull parties with him, her stomach erupts into 'burning bile'.

John Ellis, who had been an undergraduate at Edinburgh, resettled happily there and sent a long letter, 'day-dreaming nostalgically about Leicester wh seems lovely in retrospect'. She had not realised and was pleased to know how important she had been to him. 'I'm not nice to everybody but I am very nice, I think, to those I like. And I liked him. He writes all this to me & nobody else.'

The first generation of Monica's boys had been pub-goers. The second generation (Dipak, John Ellis, Dick Watson) stimulated Monica's mind. She became interested, for the first time in years, about what was happening in the university world and dipped her toe into its 'small world' of conferences, as David Lodge's novel called them. She led the Leicester contingent going to the University Teachers of English conference at York, in April 1967. A bunch of her 'boys' were there (two Johns, Bill, Dick; no Dipak, but his Kent colleagues were keen to ask her about him). Her boys past and present hung out with her. One night she was kept up talking until 4.30 a.m. 'Is there a lock or bolt on your door?' Philip sardonically asked, 'You'll need it among all those men.'

Monica realised, to her surprise, that she was being taken seriously: 'I found some respect for Leicester growing . . . Bill and John S. enjoyed saying "she was my tutor at Leicester".' Dipak had talked her up sky-high at Kent. Philip called by the conference for a day – York

was an easy drive from Hull. He and she were seen together by everyone. Bill reported being asked 'who's the girl, who's the blond with
Larkin?'

Philip was there to hear and despise the windy poet George Barker,
who had been recruited to put some yeast into the doughy scholarly
mix. She and Philip deplored Barker's histrionic 'bardism'. I recall one
thing in his lecture, sitting alongside Monica and Philip. 'The poet',
proclaimed Barker solemnly, 'sees that hole in the sky through which
is – pause – the – heavy stress – the FIRMAMENT''; he then threw
his hand up. 'Yes! Yes!' exclaimed Monica, *sotto voce*, throwing her
head back to 'look high' as if to ascertain that there actually was a hole
in the roof for the rain to get through. Larkin was on the other side
of her, frigidly impassive as ever. Virtually everyone knew who he was
and could work out who Monica must be. She bathed in the respect.
Philip met John Ellis, now a part of the Edinburgh contingent, for
the first time. The young man was a notable success: 'decent chap,
good officer material', he called him. John was cultivated, courteous,
ironic, and an entertaining (and audible) conversationalist. Larkin
liked talking to him.

'Are all conferences full of jealousies and depression?' Monica asked
Philip, who was a regular at SCONUL library conferences (for the
last few years in the company of Maeve). 'This one', Monica wrote,
'seemed to be [so] with the Edinburgh lot, of whom I saw something
with both Johns being there & the chap in whose flat – in whose
bed – I slept last summer. They seemed terribly touchy and jealous
except for John Ellis, that seemingly wonderfully adjusted man.' She
dashed off a last letter from York to Philip:

> Must go, I wanted to see you so much, & with all my boys except
> Dipak there it showed me, not that I needed it, how totally supe-
> rior you are – and not because you're the poet, tho' I'm proud of
> the poet to my heart, but because you're you.

She adds merrily: 'Really the University ought to buy me a dress if I'm
going to go to these things again.'

Three days later, still feeling good, she says: 'you seem to have been quite interested to "see" *my* Conference. I was quite interested to see it myself.' Philip thought the EngLit people 'a gayer & more intelligent lot than librarians'. Unsurprisingly since everyone at York knew his poetry and paid court.

39

Sutherland Shotgunned, 1967

'I think he [Sutherland] is pretty well putting the Leicester era behind him'

Monica to Philip, 1967

In June, I wrote to Monica that I had met someone. 'John Sutherland is getting married!' she wrote, exasperatedly, to Philip:

> I feel sure it must be shotgun, I'm sure at York he didn't know he was getting married; he was talking as tho' all his time in the future was his own, suggesting he visit me again in the summer. I feel sure too it's disastrous . . . I'm sure [it's] a girl who wants 'a wedding' . . . (reception at Prestonfield House, if you don't mind) and these grotty invitation cards with silver lettering that you can't read, *can't* be the girl for John. If I go it'll embarrass me horribly to see him in that sort of situation. Oh dear! I suppose he wants *somebody* to be on the bridegroom's side of the church: & somebody that the bride's Mummy and Daddy will think looks & seems *really quite allright* . . .

Two days later, she wrote to say the wedding was on 27 June – the Lord's weekend. It was no dilemma – she couldn't attend. Philip was unexcited. 'How strange about Sutherland. You wd feel just a little bit like Miss Moffatt in *The C. is Green* for he was your best & favourite pupil, wasn't he. Don't adopt the solution of the play though!'

The allusion is multiply barbed. *The Corn is Green* was a hit play of 1938 by Emlyn Williams. Mid-fiftyish, a spinster, and English, Miss L. C. Moffat comes to the Welsh village, Glansarno, aiming to raise the miners' children to literacy. She discovers what Monica would call a 'star turn' pupil, Morgan Evans, and raises the horny-handed son of labour 'over the wall' to a scholarship to Oxford.

There is a problem – Morgan has impregnated a local girl of dubious character, Bessie. A shotgun marriage and a life in the mines is in prospect. Miss Moffat adopts the child, freeing Morgan to pursue a brilliant career. Larkin realised he had overstepped the mark and wrote to apologise for 'being a bit repressive about Sutherland's & weddings in general. Forget it.'

Monica concluded 'I think he's pretty well putting the Leicester era behind him'. She was right; my marriage was a turning point and I felt a break with Leicester and with Monica. There were, for the record, no shotguns; just two people falling in love and taking the next step. She was also right about it representing a kind of farewell to Leicester – which for me was the frame around Monica Jones.

In early July 1967 Monica had a health breakdown and was taken to hospital. 'The old eyes', she told Philip, 'are still not focussing perfectly'. There were pains in the abdomen. ARH visited, having been alerted by Philip, who wouldn't come himself. The old story: he was frightened of illness – even that afflicting a woman he loved. Reynaud's disease was suspected but the doctors were baffled. Both she and Philip had a practice of defying diagnosis. This was Monica's first age-related hospitalisation. More would come.

On her return from their holiday, at the end of August, the change from Philip's twenty-four-hour company at Sark to twenty-four-hour solitude at Haydon Bridge rendered her 'crippled – only half a person'. She was drinking too much and was showing it when he phoned, as he did every early evening. They both now had telephones – but neither had a TV set. 'You sounded drunk on the telephone,' he wrote, 'It makes me wonder how much you've been drinking knowing how you can outdrink me.'

Alone in Haydon Bridge, she reports: 'It seems that there is a prowler here going about the houses of women living alone.' She draws her curtains and locks her door at dusk. But she hears 'queer noises' very late at night as if nearby windows were being tried. By now he is familiar with her paranoia attacks.

Her letters lose focus: she spends two sides explaining to Philip the virtues of Snowcem (masonry paint), something of a minor domestic obsession with her. She returns glumly to Leicester at the beginning of the year. 'Dick is my friend in the Dept & and I knew he would be & his wife is charming.' But Monica is 'not longing for social life'. She no longer runs open house as she had done for my hangers-on and Dipak. Those 'boys' had been welcome:

because they rather enjoyed the mixture of Bohemianism & scruffy surroundings plus excellent food & plenty to drink, & I count Dipak as one of the boys in that I let him come in. I can tell that he knows what's what no matter how scruffy my surroundings. I know that he knows that I know that I know that he knows what's what (sounds like Thom [Gunn] doesn't it) despite his deplorable associates – I *should* know because he's explained it to me, in case I should tar him with the same brush (tar him, that's rather funny, & it is quite funny to me), told me over and over again tho' there was no need. I cd see that he was a superior type – he's a bit *too* concerned to make me know it, I can see that he is . . . It was almost amusing to see him carefully crumpling the linen napkin I gave him to show me that he *knew* what to do (because you get no bourgeois rubbish like that in his house, not even a paper one).

Monica squeezes in a Christmas visit to Hull. Maeve temporarily makes herself scarce but gives her a present of chocolates, 'an insensitive thing to do'. Monica hits the bottle hard in mingled anger and hurt. 'We won't speak of this again if you don't mind . . . at present I don't want this Christmas to be mentioned either.' Her life in these years is tormented not merely by the imaginary night prowlers around but Leicester 'libery' spies who report on her back to Maeve. 'Bugars' all.

When Maeve learns of Monica's allegations of espionage (groundless) via the library network she (Maeve) loses her temper. A rare thing.

Why would she bother with malicious tittle-tattle? 'I know full well you are not going to marry either of us. Monica must know it too.' He is honest to her (Maeve) but not about her, she tells him. He replies, 'I suppose I am "weak".' A weak excuse.

British universities are being torn apart in 1967–68 by student protest, triggered by the *événements* in Paris. Monica is prevented from going to her office by some 'hairy dwarf' – a demo is underway. The Viet Cong flag has been run up on the College flagstaff. Upheaval has its upside. 'This old bag' is *taken for a student*. Hurrah! Monica admires the Dean, Abraham Wasserstein, a 'tiny little man', a refugee from 1930s Nazi Germany, who stands in front of the library and says to the protesting mob intending 'occupation': 'If you want to get past me you will have to use violence.' The protest melts away. They will leave the violence to Paris and Danny Cohn-Bendit. 'God! Do they deserve decent libraries?' Philip asks.

40

An Ancient Leicester Institution, 1968–1973

'You couldn't help admiring the bravado'
Martin Stannard, a colleague, about Monica
in the early 1970s

Back in Leicester Dick Watson is Monica's 'only joy'. Tell them (the department, that is) to 'stuff it up their academic arseholes', he instructs. It is, Monica tells Philip, 'almost like being with you'. The Maeve situation festers on interminably. 'All the University seems to know', via library staff gossip, 'that you are very more *lié* with Maeve than I think you really are.' She feels as if her life is a 'constant slap in the face'.

In July Philip comes to Haydon Bridge. Monica cannot bring herself to kiss him 'because there may have been what you call "heavy petting" the night before'. He is soiled. In fact Larkin's relationship with Maeve had gone beyond petting. It is, he tells Monica, 'a grindingly painful business'. But it is she who is being ground down. There are fewer letters between the couple in the late sixties and after. The unremembering telephone was taking over. Monica's fingers were increasingly arthritic; she still couldn't type. There was less new to say. Eva's chronic ailments meant more trips by Philip to Leicester via Loughborough.

Monica and Philip examining a book at Haydon Bridge

The outline of Monica's last years can be sketched from those who did know her personally more closely than I did during the years 1968 to 2001. John Ellis remained a loyal companion until, in the 1980s, she no longer opened the door to visitors or answered letters. John had never been inside the Cross Road flat but he was a regular visitor to Knighton Park Road where she moved in 1972. 'The place I think of Monica most is in the kitchen,' he recalls.

In Edinburgh in August 1971 John again put her up in his New Town Edinburgh flat, and entertained her to his own impressive culinary standard when they both attended a Scott conference. Bill was there. I was out of town – out of the country, in fact. John, ever since they first met at York, got on well with Philip. *The Oxford Book of Twentieth-Century English Verse* ('bloody OxBo'), in whose compilation Monica was active, came out in 1973. Larkin was staying with Monica in Leicester but, on the day of the book's launch itself, to avoid the press and photographers, he took off to a SCONUL conference (with Maeve) in Southampton.

John Ellis recalls:

Philip was away on the day of publication, but he suggested that Monica invite me to keep her company at Leicester at that time which I did for a couple of days, discussing the reviews and the book itself with her.

John calls himself a 'bit part player' in Monica's life. He was more.

So too was Peter Keating who came to Leicester in 1968. He offers in his memoir a long pen portrait of Monica – some ninety perceptively sympathetic pages. The magnetism of utter loneliness drew the two of them together. During the four years of their friendship they disclosed nothing of their personal lives to each other. Monica had long experience in that.

Keating had done his doctoral research at Sussex, having decided not to devote himself to jazz – the kind Larkin liked. He was a gifted instrumentalist. His academic field was working-class Victorian Fiction.* He came to Leicester in his early twenties as a probationary assistant lecturer. A 'boy' in Monica's eyes. He was struck by Monica at his first staff meeting. ARH still held such events at crack of dawn. Monica arrived late with a cheerful 'I'm here'. Keating bonded with Monica over morning coffee and grumbles in the common room. They were Victorianists and lovers of the period's off-syllabus minor fiction. He worked on writers like Arthur Morrison. She relished the more roistering 'muscular' school headed by Henry Kingsley. And, pre-eminently for her, the mellowly unroistering Thackeray. Their other bond was jazz – specifically the 'real stuff'. While Louis Armstrong lived, they agreed, there was hope for the world. Keating wondered how this unlikely woman could know so much about the likes of Bechet and King Oliver and things like Wild Bill Davison's trumpet (Peter's instrument) on 'Tishomingo Blues'. Eavesdroppers in the SCR must have been surprised by them scat-singing it.

But who, he wondered, was this 'my Philip' Monica talked about? It couldn't, surely, be 'his' Philip, PAWC, the Victorianist about whom

---

* Keating's magisterial *The Working Classes in Victorian Fiction* was published in 1971. Some of his conversation with Monica was probably inspired by the minor Victorian novelists they both knew.

she was so rude. He noticed her bolt-out-of-the-barn departure from College at the end of the working day and the end of term. Where she went, he had no idea. It was always, he felt, 'as though there was something hidden away inside her'. When, hearing her talk, knowledgeably, about some little-valued Victorian novelist she admired, he suggested she write it up for publication. '"Oh no" she said, slightly shocked as though I was being indelicate. "No, no. I don't do anything like that".' He'd observed that Hardy's poetry, which he liked, was not on the departmental curriculum:

> 'Quite', she said, fluttering her arms about and nodding her head . . . 'They see it as too simple, don't they? It's all too much to the point for this lot here. They think only the difficult is real, when in fact that's the only thing they are capable of teaching.'

Keating, after he had left Leicester, discovered Larkin's poetry. He came to love it – enhanced through the filter of remembered Monica. His essay is a richly extraneous view of her. What defined both their careers, and befriended them, was the shared belief that English Literature mattered.

John Ellis had gone to Edinburgh in 1966 and Peter Keating went there in 1972 (replacing me, as it happened). 'Dick' Watson was around longer, from 1966, before going to Durham in 1978 and he leaves a friendly snapshot of the couple in their doddery fifties:

> I met Philip from time to time . . . at Christmas we would sometimes be invited to make a short call at Monica's flat (a very short call: we had three children, who were eyed suspiciously by Philip); and on one occasion Monica asked if she could bring Philip to our house to watch the film of *The Maltese Falcon* (she had no television set). They arrived one Sunday evening, Philip fiddling madly with his hearing aid, and proceeded to sit in front of the television with huge enjoyment, sharing the dialogue (which they seemed to know by heart), nudging each other at significant moments and chuckling with joy at Humphrey Bogart and Sidney Greenstreet.

Andrew Motion recalled it pleased Larkin, as self-protection, to play the 'old fool' in his later years. It could in part have been pseudo-dodderiness to keep the children at bay.

Monica's last years in post at Leicester are a chronicle of indignity. Martin Stannard, a colleague in the late 1970s delivers a painful vignette:

> Like most English departments in those days, we had our share of drunks and, sadly, by the time I arrived, Monica was one of them. For a 9 a.m. examiners' meeting she arrived half an hour late and already boozed up but somehow gaily acute about the cases in hand. You couldn't help admiring the bravado. But you had to be careful. A young colleague once told her that he was often up in the small hours with his teething baby, whiling the time away by listening to the test match from Australia. Then the telephone calls began, 'Gower's out!' or some similarly breaking news, squawked eagerly down the line like a voice from *The Goon Show*, calls that wrecked his household's sleep until he told her to stop. She had it seems, no sense of others' domestic lives and, intensely isolated, drank all night.

It looks terminal. But it wasn't by any means. I saw Monica occasionally during her last years at Leicester or when she came up to stay with John Ellis at Edinburgh and, on one occasion, she and I holidayed together. We reminisced and cheerfully badmouthed her departmental black beasts. But I had the feeling the fight had gone out of her. Everything had been worn away, leaving only her love for Philip.

41

The Last Hurrah, 1970–1982

'Monica had never had it so good'
Andrew Motion

Martin Stannard's account above portrays, seemingly, the squalid penultimate stage of alcoholism. Monica drank on till her dying days, but the seventies proved one of the three phases of her adult life which were – no other word for it – happy. The first such had been when she and Arthur Collins ran the English department, 1946–47; the second her boozy Clarendon years, with her 'boys', 1963–68; and this, the third, saw Monica Jones enter the world stage, with the flash of news cameras, as, at last, Larkin's official partner. Consort, even. Maeve was relegated to the side before being let go.

The decade began with what must have tasted to Monica like signal revenge. In June 1970 Philip was given an Honorary Doctorate by Leicester. A twenty-five-year-departmentally-dishonoured Monica was by his side in her Oxford MA gown – a memento of what had first bound them together. Would he have been receiving this garland were it not for her, behind him: now alongside him? Others may have doubted but not she. Her part, troubled as it was, had been vital to getting him to where he now was. Monica was also in the business of putting to rest the canard that she did not publish. She merely did it her way. Philip had been commissioned to do *The Oxford Book of Twentieth-Century English Verse*. It was a monumental act of national – English – canonisation (no Yanks, few Celts or Scots) with the freedom to be as idiosyncratic as had been his predecessor, W. B. Yeats, and map out the field he (Philip Larkin) now dominated.

Philip was awarded a two terms' (September 1970–April 1971) fellowship at All Souls (a 'coven of queers', he told Monica) to 'peg away at OxBo' with roaming rights in the Bodley vaults. He was the Phantom of the Library. He was lodged in a house by the river at Iffley – a towpath-walk away. Oxford college life was dying, he thought. But Isis flowed on and he felt important.

His Hull-Loughborough-Leicester routines were broken. In his favourite crustacean image, he came out of 'the frosted, artificially-sealed bivalve behaviour of my life'. Monica's was, I believe, an invisible hand in OxBo, which can be seen as a product of shared, intelligent, thoughtfully hidebound prejudice. Both Philip and Monica believed that poets born before 1914 were better than those born after 1914; and those born after 1914 before 1939 ditto. Platonically, their archetypal OxBo would be half Hardy. There was no 'modern' in the title, merely a chronological marker and, as critics would complain, insufficient modernism in the contents. OUP would not swallow 'The Oxford Book of Hardy' fantasy but the mood of the anthology was as Hardyish as a greenwood tree and imbued with what Larkin called 'the genuine quality of your [Monica's] pessimism'. In totality it was a Larkin–Jones map of twentieth-century poetry. It did not, when published, please everyone but sold like hot cakes. Because it was *right*, Monica would have said.

A crowning moment for Monica, in April 1974, was to attend one of the Queen's parties at Buckingham Palace. A photograph of them outside the gates shows her looking twenty years younger than Philip.

As Motion bluntly puts it: 'Monica had never had it so good' – or so it might have seemed to Maeve. When back from Oxford he was still based at Hull, Maeve was still seeing a lot more of him than Monica, but it was Monica who was now his consort and seen with him in public. They were again at the Palace, appearing in more press photographs, for the award of his CBE in 1975. Then in 1976 they were off together to collect the Shakespeare Prize (and prize money) in Germany, defying the 'general bloodiness of abroad' they both found all too true. 'I have been awarded the Iron Cross, first class, and have to go to Hamburg to receive it,' Larkin wrote, signing himself off 'Marco Polo'.

Seeing more of Philip, and being seen more in public with him, restricted Monica's drinking. Addressing her as his beloved bunny, Larkin laid down rules which she did her best to keep:

Drinking Rabbit's Guide

Only 2 rules

(a) Nothing before 6pm
(b) Always drink *before* something (1) food (2) bed

They were, as the above battle orders make clear, spending evenings and nights in each other's company. Their relationship was fuller.

Photographs confirm Monica dressed by her standards soberly for public occasions with the multiply honoured Dr Larkin, restraining herself to dark clothes, white frills and broad-brimmed hats to shade her increasingly troubled eyes. In June 1974 she accompanied him for an honorary doctorate at St Andrews. She still loved Scotland. He loved doctorates, scooping up a lifetime haul of seven. To the annoyance of undoctored Kingsley. At the 1977 Booker dinner Philip, as chair of judges, she as plus-one, were at the Guildhall front table. She had read more of the long-list than most people at the banquet. When he visited Anthony Powell on their 1976 holiday, Monica was with him – not shown off, but neither hidden like incognita 'Mrs Larkin' in some three-star no-questions-asked hotel in the Scottish glens. Richard Bradford gives a snapshot summary of Monica out of the shadows into the sunlight:

[She] began to assume the role of his official permanent partner. She accompanied him to the Auden memorial service in Oxford [1974]. She sat next to him in church, and he made sure that her name was included beside his on the exclusive list for the lunch and wake at Christ Church . . . More significantly she was with him at the launch party for *High Windows* [1974] held at the Garrick Club, with Betjeman.

Monica at one of Philip's many doctoral awards

Maeve – so long so touchingly close to Philip and so touchingly de-voted – was left in Monica's wake. And, finally, dismissed. The deed was done 'abruptly' by Philip in 1978. 'He felt', he explained, 'that Monica's health would break down before his and when that time came he would want to take care of her.' Philip, Maeve frigidly re-cords, 'had finally determined to end the vacillation of eighteen years and pledge himself to Monica Jones'.

It was a cruel moment to switch pledges. Maeve was forty years old, prostrated by her mother's recent death (she had never left the parental home) with a distraught father to look after. She had undergone major surgery and was suffering acute depression. She was still obliged to be with him in their shared workspace. Why was he able to break up with her when it had so long been unthinkable with Monica? Over their long relationship Maeve had, she confesses, 'eventually yielded to temptation, but only on *very* rare and isolated occasions'. Motion suggests that by surrendering to his lust she vaporised the 'romantic elusiveness' which was the driving force of their 'eighteen-year inti-macy'. Maeve's driving force was simpler. She loved him.

There was an unstated reason for his dumping Maeve. In 1975 Larkin had begun his affair with another library colleague, Betty

Mackereth, three years before breaking with Maeve and while Monica was being seen as his consort on public occasions. Betty was not elusive or showy but 'businesslike' – and funny. She was by nature a behind the scenes fixer who could be trusted not to ask too much: or even be known, as Maeve had been known, as one of Larkin's women. So Larkin 'vacillated' on, but more discreetly and less passionately. He had not been, James Booth deduces, in full sexual vigour for years and the Mackereth affair was quite likely celibate in its later years.

Monica and he were a smiling public couple. Partnership was proclaimed, illustratively, in the papers and at major functions. But she was not living with him. In 1972 she had leased herself a fine flat, overlooking Victoria Park – the part of Leicester she liked best. I visited her there a couple of times to be plied with gin and tonic in glasses the size of goldfish bowls. My drinking at this period was as reckless as hers. She at last could buy big furniture and cook big. The flat at Knighton Park Road was big enough for two. But in the event it meant only loneliness for one.

Larkin himself had been obliged to move, reluctantly, from the bachelor university attic flat he had happily rented for eighteen years. There was no other similar let on offer. As he told his closest woman friend, Judy Egerton: 'I have blindly, deafly and dumbly, said I will buy an utterly undistinguished little modern house in Newland Park.' Little but big enough for two – although at this stage he had no intention that Monica should come under his roof. And he chose something 'undistinguished', although he was now well off, so that it wouldn't look like a marital invitation in bricks.

The seventies were Monica's first and last hurrah. She was acknowledged. Why did Larkin adopt Monica as his public consort in these riding-high years of his mid-life fame? There are plausible answers. They had collaborated and produced a work which was the fruit of both their minds. Larkin had only done that once before: with Kingsley on *Lucky Jim*. Monica's contribution to 'bloody OxBo' was prominently placed as the first and only name (apart from a nod to 'old Thwaite') in the volume's acknowledgements. She could have been on the title page and Larkin told her as much.

The epistolary relationship died away in this decade. There are, in

Anthony Thwaite's *Letters to Monica*, 415 pages of his correspondence from 1946 to 1970. Thereafter 30 pages from 1971 to the last in 1983. Monica's letters are similarly few. They are scraps momentarily necessary when, for one reason or another, they cannot talk. Telephony changed their relationship. They conversed on evenings and weekends at length. His deafness was no barrier on the phone (their drinking occasionally was). He could be confident that nothing spoken into the receiver would survive to embarrass him. The wires brought them closer together than the postage stamp. He needed her but not, after the age of fifty, so eagerly for sex. The phone created a companionate intimacy which they had never enjoyed since their perfect friendship, all those years ago, at Leicester.

The death of his mother was an obstruction removed, as was his casting Maeve away. Betty stayed discreetly unseen. It was useful having Monica as a plus-one at public events as a barrier to prevent anyone else monopolising him, and she could chime in when, as happened a lot, he couldn't hear what was said to him. All in all, the seventies were better years for Monica and gratifying years for the poet and librarian Larkin. But the imminent eighties could not be held off. Larkin readjusted his life for what he 'knew' (superstitiously, but he was right) would be his last decade. He looked age in the face. His great ode to senility, 'The Old Fools', was finished in 1973. Her mind years' gone, Eva died in 1977. Despite a litany of complaint and vituperation to Monica and his close friends, Philip had been a good son, writing weekly, visiting monthly and tender in both demeanour and his letters.

At exactly the same time as his mother died, Larkin finished the composition and publication of his last great poem, 'Aubade'. With that lamentation for himself 'he consciously signalled that his *oeuvre* was complete'. Poetry had given him up. The worst indignities of Old Foolery might, nonetheless, be held at bay. His body was wrecked but he had not lost his mind – despite the alcoholic battering it had received and continued to receive.

Both Larkin and Monica had let themselves decline into terrible physical shape. He could cycle twenty miles in his young manhood, stopping only for churches and pubs, and she could hike the Pennines, or Salisbury Crags in her early forties drinking in the view. Now their bodies were ruined. Alcohol was the culprit. 'We can't give it up,' Monica told me as early as 1964. Neither at that stage could I, but I had twenty years on the two of them.

42

Monica at Sixty, 1982

'A beast'
Martin Amis describing Monica, 1982

Kingsley's son Martin Amis offers a brilliantly harsh caricature of Monica aged sixty. He met her just once apparently though one suspects she was talked about in his family. Philip Martin knew, personally, as his father's sometime best friend and his brother's godfather. In June 1982 Philip ('looking like one of his own self-deprecations') and Monica were coming back from a day's cricket at Lords. Martin saw them, parking his car, looking bemused. He asked them to drop by for drinks. Dinner followed. Martin can date the occasion exactly because Monica corrected him on a detail of the current match against Pakistan and, when writing about the occasion, he consulted his son's *Wisden* almanack.

Monica's eye for cricket was undimmed. Martin was aged thirty-one and in company with his father, mother (now divorced from Kingsley) and stepfather. He first recalled the evening in his mid-life autobiography, *Experience* (2000). In it he calls Monica (still living) Philip's 'virile' girlfriend. Monica, at sixty, was, by now, more dowager than girlfriend. Philip was, in summer 1982, a sick man with three years to live. Amis, freed into greater frankness by the couple's deaths, reviewed *Letters to Monica* in the *Guardian* and gave a 're-experienced' version of the post-Lords evening. It was, he recalled, 'weird'. Worse than that, he looked back on it with 'horror'. He had not realised that

Larkin was 'sexually so miserable'. And as for Monica:

> I have to say she looked like an *urka* [a Russian criminal from the bottom of society]: like a male *urka*. Really butch. And she dominated the evening in a weird way. She was awful. A *beast*. And I thought, that is the love of his life.

In an interview with *Prospect Magazine*, in the same year, he elaborated further. Larkin, Amis recalled, had been 'demurely diffident':

> As for Monica – well, despite her clothes (brown trousers of crushed velvet, wifebeater blouse, plus earrings the size of hula hoops), she resembled an all-in wrestler renowned for an indifference to the norms of fair play. She also dominated the evening, despite the presence of my father, as host.

Why had Larkin stuck with Monica? To Martin the question answered itself. Because 'he simply didn't have the guts to leave her'. In his eyes, Monica 'starved' the poet in Philip Larkin, leaving a pathetic physical husk, all poetry withered out of him.

Another writer met Monica in 1982 and recorded his vivid impression of her in her sixtieth year (she was still universally called Philip's 'girlfriend'). A. N. Wilson and Larkin had first met at All Souls, Oxford, in the Christmas vacation of 1980, and, as Wilson recalls, 'clicked'. Larkin had kept up his connection with the college since working full-time there on 'OxBo'. He liked excursions to Oxford as respite from female entanglements. And the university – particularly his years with Kingsley – had been a rare period of glee in his life.

A version of that 1940s relationship was recreated with thirty-year-old Wilson, who had recently made his name with his first novel. In 1981 Wilson was appointed literary editor of the *Spectator*. Married to a don, and with children, he kept his Oxford home. Larkin was initially warmed towards Wilson by the severity of his journalism. In his new editorial role Wilson elicited some of Larkin's finest 'required writing', as he (Larkin) wittily called his reviews. In Oxford the men drank in college and in pubs. Wilson recalls entering one with the sign 'NO CHILDREN' on the door. The two cheeriest words in the English language, quipped Larkin.

Wilson recalls informative fragments of their conversation – Larkin's belief, for example, that he had not given up poetry: it had given up him, as irreversibly as his hair loss. 'Belief' leads on to the most thought-provoking aspect of their friendship. Wilson had earlier trained at Oxford in an Anglo-Catholic college for the priesthood. He rebounded during instruction into forthright atheism but the Bible, as something literary not doctrinal, remained centrally important to him.

After befriending Wilson, Larkin bought an authorised version of the Bible for £120. He placed the volume in his bedroom and read pages of it while shaving every morning. Scripture was 'balls', but 'beautiful balls', he told Andrew Motion.

His father had laid down atheism as the rule of the house that Philip grew up in. It did not take root. Oxford, in his and Monica's under-graduate years, was still a churchy university. They liked that. One of his best loved poems, 'Church Going', records him in his twenties biking round Northern Ireland to look at these 'serious places'. He and Monica liked to begin the year with visits to England's highest Anglican churches and cathedrals. They attended services together. It meant much to her. And him?

His relationship with Maeve had inspired Larkin to study Cathol-icism and its rituals of marriage when, momentarily, he was steeling himself to ditch Monica but didn't. After his death he left, via Monica (he must surely have requested it), the main bulk of his considerable posthumous poetic revenue to English cathedrals and abbeys.* Angli-canism did very well out of Philip Larkin and Monica Jones.

Wilson first met Monica at the launch party for *Required Writing*, two years after meeting Larkin. He found himself sitting next to her. Attempts at small talk went nowhere. Her appearance was:

to say the least, striking. A wide-brimmed hat, the only headgear in the room, more suited to the consecration of a bishop in a

---

* See below, p. 259.

provincial cathedral town, than to a bohemian London publishing-office, squashed up with caterers' tables and food. Her very full lips were glossy red. Thick specs made it difficult to make out the expression of her eyes. The rig was fancy dress, seemingly. Something between a pantomime dame and *grande dame*. Possibly even a man in drag.

As does Martin Amis, Wilson portrays Monica as a gargoyle on the crumbling edifice of what had once been the country's leading poet. There is, though, an important difference. Amis fixates on the damage he believed Monica had done Philip. Wilson, by contrast, feels the damage Larkin had done Monica:

> Poor Monica. She can't have started out as a monster, when she was an undergraduate at St Hugh's during the Second World War. If she had fallen in love with someone capable of giving her some love back? . . .

Wilson leaves his question hanging. What if she had, in the 1940s, married 'Bish' or 'Arnold'?* She might have been happier. But would she have been more fulfilled than she was as the helpmeet of the man she believed England's greatest living writer? Her answer, one can be sure, would have been a thunderous 'No!'

The evening with the Amises in June 1982 followed one of the last of Philip's and Monica's visits to Lords. Larkin, although now a member (nominated by Harold Pinter), was put off by the rowdiness and racial diversity of modern spectators – a prejudice he voiced foul-mouthedly. Monica was taking early retirement from Leicester on health grounds in the same year that Martin and Andrew Wilson met her. The department had bought her a print of Christ Church College Oxford, with the implication that she had never really taken root in Leicester. I went to the party the department felt obliged to give her – for time served, if nothing else. It was in a colleague's house. Looking for it I drove the wrong way up a one-way street that hadn't

---

* See pp. 30–33, 44, 50–51.

been in Leicester when I was. It seemed vaguely symbolic. What was that poem of Larkin's? 'No Road'? I recall the speeches, Monica fierce-faced and Bill Ruddick close to tears. I felt – like others in the room, I suspect – that I had let Monica down. Bill hadn't.

To commemorate her retiring, Dick Watson, with intuitive grace, arranged with Philip a trip to Weardale – her mother's girlhood home.

> That spring, 1982, she celebrated her sixtieth birthday, when Philip – at her prompting – brought her to Durham [where Watson was now working], and drove her up Weardale, probably for the last time. Tom Craik and I joined them for a birthday dinner. We drank Moselle, her favourite wine, and then claret. We offered to pay our share, but were not allowed to: 'you will go down in history as the men who got a dinner out of Larkin'.

The first wholly misconceived plan was that, once retired, Monica should find a new, more age-convenient, Leicester flat (the lease on Knighton Park Road would soon expire) and spend more time in her cottage in warm months. Academics usually retire with a long-nurtured project which they have sat on, like an unhatched egg but Monica had no such project. Her serious interest in literature had, effectively, finished years before. As had Larkin's in poetry.

A month into her retirement (on 12 October 1982), by herself, she tumbled down the stairs at Haydon Bridge, banging her head badly. 'A menace', Philip had long warned about the stairs, 'I have to come down them like a pregnant giraffe'. She was taken to Hexham General Hospital. 'Umpteen stitches' were sewn. Nothing was seriously damaged and she was discharged to face the winter in her new, large, empty flat.

Having survived that ordeal, in Easter 1983, with Philip in Haydon Bridge, Monica suffered an attack of shingles which near blinded her and caused crippling headaches and 'a great feeling of lowness'. Philip moved her to hospital in Hull, where he could visit. He was on BUPA, she was 'condemned' to 'joyless' NHS hospitals. There was, for the next two years, a litany of complaint about the cursory treatment she received. She had no reason to revise her 1946 contempt of Aneurin Bevan's brave new world of health, all for five bob a week.

With the lease on Knighton Road expiring in June, she was in no shape to house-hunt and had no will to renew. She was, Philip told Judy Egerton, 'not up to living on her own'. She joined Philip under the same roof and 'they nursed each other through two miserable years', as *The Times* obituary records. 'Marriage in all but name,' Motion calls it. There is, Monica and Maeve would have thought, quite a lot in the 'name'. Initially, the expectation was that the cohabitation was for her period of convalescence. But a brief attempt at resettling her in Haydon Bridge left Larkin – himself failing fast – with the realisation, put off for thirty-five years, that they needed each other full-time in mutual collapse, eased by alcohol. As he wittily put it: 'Our walking sticks hang side by side in the hall.' A. N. Wilson has a more poignant recollection; Larkin telling him with 'a strange, revealing smile: "But we both want it, we're so lonely".'

Philip's death was a year-long in happening. Until 1984 he remained gallantly – increasingly pointlessly – in post. He was drinking half a bottle of sherry or more before going to work, drinking bottles of stronger stuff with Monica after work, smoking, over-eating and not sleeping. He could see the mass extinction of humane librarians like himself. Computerisation, robotic-mechanisation and the technocrat were taking over. He turned his face to the wall.

Monica went with him to the award of his honorary D.Litt at Oxford, in June 1984. It was an emotional occasion. Oxford had been their original bond. This ceremony completed the circle. Given his ill health, he should have received the award in absentia. And why was it awarded? Larkin wisecracked: 'if I'm getting it for anything it's for negative thinking'. But for both of them it was consummation. Motion describes it:

When he and Monica arrived for the ceremony itself on 27 June [1984], Larkin had worked himself into a lather. He wore the forty-four-year-old mortarboard he had owned as an undergraduate, but felt that the new suit he had ordered looked like a 'walrus maternity garment'. Throughout the ceremony he looked round anxiously, and swayed 'giddily' as he was introduced in the Sheldonian Theatre.

He was superstitiously convinced he would die at the same age as his father: sixty-three. In the interim he lived a 'triangular existence', the points being home, the library, and the supermarket. With quadrilateral calls at the pub. Monica was housebound, he told Judy Egerton:

> I shd say M. is the worse off of us, going downhill physically, & no one does anything or can suggest anything. It's all *very* worrying. Mentally she is all right: I compared her mind to 'a well-stocked rat-trap,' wch made her laugh, but it's very true. She's not at the end of the line yet, by any mean, but is worse than last year, or even the summer.

She – the heavier drinker, as their friend A. N. Wilson recalls – would, in fact, see seventeen more summers. He would not see one. Wilson, one of the few people they were social with in their last years together, witnessed, painfully, what he saw as evenings which descended into squalid debauch. He describes their final awful months with eloquence in the commemorative TV programme, *Philip Larkin: Love and Death in Hull* (2003). A maestro of gallows humour since adolescence, Philip joked about his imminent end. His rank fear – 'to lie in cold obstruction and to rot' – he kept in reserve for his bedroom-mortuary ode, 'Aubade'. Its publication had fallen like a bomb on his colleagues at Hull a few months before he left them. It exposed a terminally dismal Larkin they had never known. There were, as any examination of his life shows, many Larkins.

Cancer of the oesophagus was diagnosed. It was like having a hedgehog in the throat, Philip said. He loved hedgehogs and certified the fact by writing a touching poem about having accidentally killed one ('The Mower'). Cancer had killed his father. He was hospitalised at Christmas 1984 for tests. Later, when being treated, he asked Maeve to drive Monica to the hospital – oblivious, apparently, or perhaps not, of the embarrassment it would cause both women. Betty, as ever, did her efficient bit behind the scenes.

When Monica and Maeve were together at his bedside on a later hospital visit, in summer 1985, 'the atmosphere bristled with emotional tension which could not have contributed to Philip's well-being'. More so as Philip embraced Maeve tenderly when she left him and Monica to themselves. He was discharged into the home-care of Monica, who, as ever, got a transfusion of energy from Philip's illness. She withheld from him details of the final diagnosis that death was inevitable. He submitted to ignorance – Monica had taken charge.

He died on 2 December. As he had foreseen, it was at the same age as his father: sixty-three. Maeve was informed by a phone call from Monica. But Maeve, not Monica – wholly broken down and unable to attend – was at the funeral, as was Betty Mackereth. Monica, leaning on a friend, made it to the later memorial service at Westminster Abbey. Andrew Motion tells us that Larkin's last recorded words, to a nurse, were 'I am going to the inevitable'. Booth doubts his exit was so theatrical, but it would be a pity not to believe Philip Larkin left the world eloquently.

He had been awarded in his last weeks the Companion of Honour – the highest honour British literary men can achieve. He was too sick to collect it. Monica kept the floods of congratulatory letters but did not answer them. Nor did she apparently answer the many letters of condolence; but she kept that, immaculately handwritten and finely composed, from Kingsley:

There is no point in going into what he meant to me and you. For both of us there will never be another like him in any way. I suppose we must simply be glad he was in both our lives.

It was a gracious amend from the creator of Margaret Peel.

43

Last Years, Final Acts, 1985–2001

*'Monica goes from bad to worse. Having forbidden visitors to
105 Newland Park after the funeral she now goes and burns P's
diaries. He had left instructions to do so but naturally the other
two lit. execs, Thwaite and Motion, were starting to figure out
ways of not doing so. Then they found she'd gone ahead without
consulting them. Partly gloomy self-righteous triumph or however you put it, partly vanity.'*

Kingsley Amis, 1985

Prostrated as she was, Monica could still make important decisions. It
was she who instructed that only one word, in addition to name and
dates, should be put on Philip's headstone. 'Writer'. And that his middle
name or initial be omitted. That was right, she said, '*Writer*, not just a
poet. He lived a *writer's* life'. By which she meant life with her, not with
his Hull colleagues. It was Monica, as senior trustee and executor (and
physical possessor of the literary properties) who ordered the posthumous
shredding and burning of the multitudinous volumes of Philip Larkin's
private journals/diaries. What was in them? According to Motion:

the diaries seem to have been a sexual log book full of masturbatory fantasies, and a repository for his rage against the world –
his grimmest, sexiest, most angry thoughts, the thoughts many of
his poems depended upon, cleaned up and organised in order to
produce achieved works of art.

In other words, disgusting perhaps, but important nonetheless content.

James Booth demurs, following a clue given an interviewer, John Haffenden, in 1981, that they were merely 'a great grumble-book': a diary recording Larkin's dyspeptic chronicle of the day's events. Not thirteen volumes of auto-eroticism. Whatever they contained, the journals (which he began in 1941) would have yielded evidence on the enigma of Larkin. A page or two was furtively glimpsed, in the early 1950s, by Patsy Strang, while he was briefly out of the room. She confirmed what Motion describes, that they were masturbatory record-keeping and fantasy. But it is hard to believe everything in the journals was so trivial.* They were almost grossly libellous of people still living which, arguably, was why Larkin so desperately wanted them destroyed and implored Monica to do it for him.

Monica was the only person who could read in their entirety the journals in the two years she and Larkin were living together. They were lodged in an unlocked cupboard, close to hand from her fa-vourite armchair. In her last and only TV interview her hand reaches casually as if to open it. Not the first time, one may assume. For some time after Larkin's death Monica remained immobilised. The journals were in her possession for weeks before she ordained their destruc-tion. The legal opinion was ambiguous. There were other things, as senior executor and curator, she might have done. She might have deposited the journals in the Bodleian with a cast-iron access and time restriction. She might have charged a trusted mutual friend to winnow the contents for selective publication. At one point in 1976, when he had energy for it, Larkin considered doing this himself in the form of a memoir. Above all she should / could have closely consulted her fellow executors Andrew Motion and Anthony Thwaite. Instead she autocratically commanded destruction. The Thwaites were in Japan, and his letters to her were written in the knowledge she would not reply. Andrew Motion, an executor, not like Monica a trustee and physical owner, was impotent to save the journals.

---

* How many there actually were is unclear. Motion says 'thirty odd A4 volumes', a fact he presumably got from Betty Mackereth. Booth claims thirteen volumes.

The person whom Monica charged with doing the deed was Betty Mackereth. For many years she had been Larkin's 'loaf-haired secretary', and for some years his mistress – something initially unknown to Monica or Maeve. By the time of Philip's death all the cards were on the table. Mackereth admitted that her eye could not but glimpse contents, as they were torn out and fed into the shredder on their way to the sacrificial cremation and, finally, literary ash. 'They were very unhappy. Desperate really,' was her comment. She and Monica also arranged the consignment of Larkin's two-box pornography collection to oblivion. Why did Monica decree this inferno? Arguably to save Larkin from Larkin. As Clive James put it 'The last thing [he] needed was more rope to hang himself with.' And she was doing what he had explicitly told her to do. As early as 1954 he told her 'Journals – diaries – are two edged weapons! I really must arrange for mine to be destroyed when I die.' He gave the same instruction in his 1961 stay in hospital. His will also contained an explicit instruction to do so.

The salient point is Monica chose not to torch her own thousands of letters. The bulk of those letters are so descriptive of her day-to-day existence as to constitute journals. Why did she not shred her papers as well? Because, she resolved, it was her version of their relationship which should survive on the ash-heap of his version. 'I am', she once called herself: 'the sole Arabian bird a Phoenix rising.' Now she was the sole self-generating Phoenix. Monica, as instructed by Philip's will, deposited her 'Letters to Philip' in the Bodleian Library. It was the home Monica wanted for her remains: her Arundel Tomb message to posterity. Her 'Letters to Philip' are what Jeremy Bentham would have called an 'auto-icon': a monument of self.

After Philip's death, attempts were made to get Monica to social functions in Hull as the poet's honorary widow. When she came, she drank – her tolerance for alcohol was shot – and the invitations ceased. Thanks to Larkin's will, the house he left, and her own pension, she was financially comfortable. On the first anniversary of Larkin's death Monica fell and broke her hip after which she became entirely reclusive and non-responsive to letters – but would telephone 'at all hours'. Recipients feared the midnight call. The conservatory she was conned into buying by a sharpster remained plantless and unentered. There were well-meaning attempts, by her physicians and her solicitor, to put her into a nursing home. Friends of Philip's and hers could see she was unhappy (but uncomplaining) and got her back to Newland Park, with twenty-four-hour care. Food was brought and, insidiously, drink. Friends – Virginia Peace (a former academic at Hull, and friend of Philip's), Judy Egerton, Babette Evans (her one woman friend at Leicester in the early days), and Tom Craik visited but gradually gave up on her. She was mute, uncommunicative, and often the worse for drink. She was rich: in the mid-1990s Philip's estate, whose revenues (along with the house and its contents) had been left entirely to her was yielding something under £70,000 a year. Her will disposed of a million pounds, most of it to cathedrals.

Bill, who had given up visiting, took early retirement from Manchester on health grounds in 1990 and died in February 1994. Tom Craik 'represented' her at the memorial services for Bill at Manchester and Leicester. She, after his mother, had been the most important woman in Bill's life. He had been the kindest man in hers. She sent no letter to Tom, but she must surely have felt Bill's early death.

Her last years are described by Andrew Motion, who witnessed them:

> Isolated in Newland Park, ill, virtually unknown to the outside world and a stranger even to the university, she felt her life disintegrate. She had no existence without Larkin. She was a widow without even the consolation of that title . . . Drinking heavily, not bothering to change out of her nightdress and dressing-gown during the day, she surrendered to her sorrow.

Did Monica read this, in 1992, one wonders. She was compos mentis when James Booth visited her seven years later. I think her eyes must have passed over this cameo of her, in proof or published form – she in her nightdress and presumably drink in hand. Numb to whatever further the world could do to her. Motion thanks her in the first sentence of his Acknowledgements page at the head of his biography for having helped him 'more than anyone else . . . She has been unfailingly generous, candid and hospitable. I am deeply in her debt'.

He writes of her as someone still living, but no longer, one presumes, feeling. Motion told investigating journalist, the eminent Rachel Cooke, that when his book was finished 'Monica was enthusiastic'. One wonders whether emotionally she had been able to bring herself to read the book she had helped make.

When Maeve, still capable of pain, discovered from Motion's biography that 'her' Philip (whom she believed 'spiritual') was a user of pornography, her world crumpled. 'When, after his death, I learnt about the pornography collection, I was astounded and upset.' Part of Maeve Brennan was destroyed in the conflagration of that heap of onanistic stimulus which was consigned to oblivion along with Larkin's private journals. Those, probably, would have been even more crumpling. She had been deluded into thinking Philip 'a wonderfully chivalrous, even courtly lover. He concealed the grosser side of his mind from me'. She could, like others, have echoed Kingsley's 'I sometimes wonder if I ever really knew him'. The only person who could be said to have 'really known' Philip was Monica. But did she understand him? No more, perhaps, than he understood himself, or why he caused such damage to the two most important women in his life.

Monica, Maeve and Betty lived through the 1990s backlash following the publication of Andrew Motion's *A Writer's Life* and Anthony Thwaite's *Selected Letters*. Maeve records her personal sense of being buried under a deluge of mud: 'I managed to insulate myself from the torrent of publicity for several weeks,' she writes, but she could not avoid the *Daily Express* review – '"Larkin the secret lover. Hidden affairs of a woman-hating poet" complete with photographs of four of his "conquests", including me':

> Later it was distressing to read captions like: 'The Dreary Laureate of our Provincialism' (*Independent* 18/3/93), 'Hull Life, Low Life' (*Sunday Telegraph* 28/3/93), 'Portrait of a Sumptuous Old Misery' (*Weekend Telegraph* 3/4/93). It was still more painful to see Philip described as 'a foul-mouthed bigot [who] made a small talent go a very long way indeed' (P. Ackroyd, *The Times* 1/4/93).

Maeve, with the help of James Booth, put out a gallant contradiction in the form of *The Philip Larkin I Knew* (2002), withholding its publication, for fear of giving more hurt, until after Monica's death. She, along with Larkin's first love and erstwhile fiancée Ruth, contributed sympathetically to a strangely ambivalent memorial TV programme, *Philip Larkin: Love and Death in Hull*. Monica, two years' dead, features as a 'sparky' girlfriend. Her voice, with Larkin's, is heard shrieking out hideous racist chants on the couple's tape-recorder. They are played by actors drinking sherry over their cornflakes.

This 'heroic' steeping in drink was testified to by A. N. Wilson. Motion's biography and the *Selected Letters* astonished and pained him to breaking point. As he recalled:

> It was genuinely shocking. I began to wonder whether I had ever really known Larkin, or even whether I liked the poetry any more. For some years I did not read him. But many of his lines remained in my head. I had never in my life sat down to learn a Larkin poem by heart, and yet there they were, in my mind.

Wilson offered an amended view of Larkin in the BBC TV programme *Return to Larkinland* in 2015. Larkin, he concluded, was 'the old friend I never liked': a mixed response many have felt.

Monica went into hermit-crab seclusion under the 1993 mudstorm. She made for herself a leftover life – partly living. James Booth wanted to consult Monica on scholarly matters but his letters went unanswered and he took the risk of door-stepping her. The seventy-six-year-old Miss Jones received him in her bedroom and gave him seven interviews. Toast, marmite, biscuits and coffee were offered and taken. The bed was 'strewn with the *Daily Telegraph*, *The Times Literary Supplement*, *About Larkin*, and John Betjeman's poems'. She was under twenty-four-hour nursing care: and reportedly difficult. Only the hair remained strong. Looking back over her life she told Booth, with momentary energy, 'I found it *terribly boring* actually'.

Monica lived on in the house she and Philip had shared until her death, 15 February 2001. His belongings, to the end, were enshrined around her. It was a kind of suttee without flame. Her death certificate records the cause of death as 'old age'. It was a euphemism: smoking, drinking, poor diet and inertia had overcome what was a manifestly stronger constitution than Philip's. John Ellis remembers the funeral on a dry, bitterly cold day. Dick Watson describes her interment:

> Her burial at Cottingham Cemetery was attended by few mourners, because she had been so cut off from the world so long; but she lies, appropriately, just the length of a cricket pitch from the grave of 'Philip Larkin, writer'.

Another cricket pitch away is the grave of Maeve, and on its tombstone: 'What will survive of us is love'. Since the Arundel poem belongs, as a Valentine Day gift, to Monica, the tombstones quarrel spectrally. Invisibly, one likes to fancy, on Monica's stone there is the inscription: 'He lied to me the bugger, but I loved him.' Larkin wavers, like Buridan's ass, between the stones. The service, Booth recalls, was 'very Anglican: lots of mumbling to a brightly encouraging organ'. Monica would have welcomed his levity; the vicar who buried both Monica and Philip might not have done.

CONCLUSION

'We are both of us burnt children'

Monica to Philip, 1955

In the above remark Monica recalls the proverb: 'the burnt child dreads the fire'. Nineteen fifty-five, the year she wrote it, was during the first great crisis in their relationship. Philip had come 'home' from Belfast in 1955, but it soon became clear he had no intention of making any kind of home. Neither he nor Monica wanted the ceremony of marriage, but he could have lived with her. Or, at least, nearer her. That, however, was too fiery an option for Larkin. Instead he installed himself in a job a hundred miles from Leicester which would, effectively, separate them, apart from visits and short holidays, for nearly thirty years. She, on her part, could have left him: but that was too fiery an option for her.

Larkin damaged the lives of two highly able women. It wasn't done malevolently but he did it nonetheless. They conspired in the injury because they believed his literary genius made sacrifice a tribute. And his personality was winning. His 'charm', when turned on, had the word's original meaning of 'magic'. His love and his allowing himself to be loved came at a huge cost. This man – who could not bear thinking of the death of a rabbit without sympathetic agony – made Monica Jones, the woman he nicknamed 'Bunny Rabbit', a very unhappy woman. He knew what he was inflicting. What was it he said in 1958? 'It seems to me I am spoiling yr life in a hideously ingenious way.' True enough, he did. She complained a lot but rarely protested.

Many might think that the human spoilage in the wake of the poems of Larkin's maturity is immaterial. Great literature has many 'invisible women' (as Claire Tomalin calls them) behind great authors. Who really cares about Nelly Ternan in their admiration of *Great Expectations*? Or Frieda von Richthofen's children when she abandoned them to run off with D. H. Lawrence? Literature has its collateral damage. Nonetheless the unhappiness emitted from Monica Jones's letters makes the insider-outsider, like me, resentful and angry.

Biography is a strange combination of power and powerlessness. One feels like an impotent god. I know while reading Monica's letters that she is being two-timed with Maeve, the cottage won't work out, and for God's sake cut back on the booze and find a congenial AA group. Reading her letters, I know her destiny before it happens to her. One aches to intervene: but can't. You are powerless even to warn, like some Shakespearean ghost or soothsayer.

If divinely omnipotent, what, having read Monica's letters, would I change in her life? Dump Larkin and search for happiness elsewhere before you become his limpet? Choose a partner who'll value you for what you are, not what use you are. Write that book on Crabbe and shame ARH? Or, if none of those ways out is taken, in the sixteen years left you after his death write the book only you can write on you and Philip Larkin. Call it 'Burnt Child'. No one can possibly do it better than you. Those, I confess, have been my feelings at times in reading Monica's letters.

But human beings are not chess pieces, to be moved as suits the game of life best. Personally, I think Monica, from quite early on, had worked out Philip Larkin. Intuitively, sometimes consciously (notably in summer 1959), she decided that despite his waywardness he was worth the price loving him exacted. None of the other half-dozen important women in his life saw the Larkin deal as clearly as Monica did. Or bought into it as resolutely.

As this book will have made clear, I am grateful to Monica Jones. All lovers of 'English Poetry of the Twentieth Century' (to use Larkin's and Jones's term) should be more grateful. She was influential. I will end with acclamation of what the Monica I personally knew was.

She was clever, amusing, sharp-witted, attractive in many ways beyond what Philip routinely remarked on, scrupulous, and possessed of high literary-critical sensibility. Carrying the professional label 'lecturer' (which colleagues scorned in someone of her late-life seniority) she was idiosyncratically gifted at the lectern. I was lucky to know her, to have my mind, and sense of what is valuable in my profession, formed by her.

I have been forthright about Monica's failings which have only recently become known to me. They are bruising. Despite the racism and unfair slanders which blemish her letters, my conclusive thought is that I was lucky to cross her path and be taken up by her. I believe that Larkin was luckier by far to have had this woman centrally in his life for forty years. Lovers of his poetry should reserve an appreciative nod for Margaret Monica Beale Jones.

AFTERWORD

The Monica Jones I
Didn't Know, 2021

'*I'm frightened of anything new & when I'm frightened I'm full of hatred*'

Monica*

Reading Monica's letters has been a joy, a privilege and a constant enlightenment – particularly about myself at a crucial period of my life. But at times my response to what I have read has been one of shock and horror. I will describe what most horrifies me splattering the letters. Racism, in a word. What confuses me is that I can see no mitigating reason, no apology, no explanation, no vindication. It is not, as I read it, ironic, it is not self-mocking, or faux attitudinising, it is just there, radiating darkly.

In their lifetimes Philip and Monica kept their views on race very much to themselves. His letters record that he shared them, discreetly, with some of his close male friends. It was Anthony Thwaite's *Selected Letters of Philip Larkin*, along with sections of Motion's biography, which revealed in the early 1990s Philip's ingrained racism. The revelation led to denunciation, educational de-syllabusing and patchy de-canonisation. The disquiet about Larkin and race rumbles on.

James Booth has been almost alone in demanding a closer look at

---

* I'm indebted to Dr Priestman, in conversation, for this self-criticism by Monica.

Larkin's alleged offence weighed in the light of his temperamental irony and playing different parts, some unlike himself, in his correspondence (where virtually all of the recorded racism is). Booth's arguments are thoughtful and should be thought about by all admirers of Larkin's writing. Since reading Booth's biography I have thought about the question a lot – inconclusively. I fear, as I write this, Larkin's statue at Hull railway station may not be standing by the time this book reaches print.

As I observe it in the letters I have seen, Monica's racism is more anti-Semitic than anything in Larkin's writing. It is casually venomous and wholly assured. What made a highly educated woman, one wonders, particularly after the post-war publicity about the camps, feel free to be anti-Semitic? It's baffling and disgusting. There may be, as Booth points out, some clues in the novel 'A New World Symphony' Philip began writing about Monica, set in 1948, before he and Monica were lovers. Augusta Bax (clearly Monica) is shown exasperated by a 'pushy' Jewish refugee, Mrs Klein, whose husband was murdered by the Nazis. Augusta spitefully observes she has some sympathy with them. Monica, one might suspect, said something of the kind in Larkin's hearing. When Oswald Mosley was invited to speak at the Leicester campus in 1961, Monica declined to sign the protest petition. Most of the department and student body did (as did I), and Hitler's man never came. Why would Monica want him to? I knew nothing about her not signing.

It is instructive, though, to look at Booth's scholarly reconstruction of where 'New World Symphony' was going and what Philip's views on Monica's anti-Semitism probably were. As the plot is forecast in his notes:

> Augusta was to quarrel with her mother and Mrs Klein was to develop beyond the anti-Semitic caricatures of the initial description ... Mrs Klein's American relatives, a family of 'Wonderful loving Yanks' were to offer her a lifeline after she had been sacked from her job ... and the novel was to close with a 'hymn to America'.

And Augusta was reborn as an anti-Semite no more. With the implication that the author, Larkin, never had been. James Booth notes, in support of this view, Larkin's close Jewish friends at Oxford, Denis Frankel and Miriam Plaut and his friendship, in Belfast, with Jack Graneek. Booth's view is that 'Larkin was not in the slightest degree anti-Semitic'.

Philip Larkin's recorded racism is typically directed against Britons of colour – immigrants prominently. Nonetheless he could be anti-Semitic. On one regrettable occasion it intrudes into his published verse. 'Posterity' opens

Jake Balokowsky, my biographer,
Has this page microfilmed.

As he exulted to Monica the poem, as it continues, 'gets in Yanks, Yids, wives, Coca Cola, Protest & the Theatre – pretty good list of hates, eh?' Were it not for the second Y-word it would look like Larkin being Larkin. Was he pandering to Monica's by now entrenched prejudice, not voicing his own? Monica's anti-Semitism is overt in letters seen by me. Remarks like Larkin's above suggest it was an understood thing between them conversationally. There is, of course, no such thing as being occasionally racist any more than being occasionally dead. She describes, on 13 November 1960, a dinner party at the Frasers' for 'a young Yid publisher – quite a nice one, within the limits of that description'. A couple of years later she describes hearing socialism talked about favourably in the SCR by 'a horrible little girl philosopher – mincing lisping foreign Jew dwarf – and a girl philosopher – foreign Jew also but bigger and nicer'. Jews, apparently, can be 'nice' or 'quite nice'.

Monica felt secure in her anti-Semitism. Sometimes it slipped out in company. As Andrew Motion records:

Once, at the home of Ann and Anthony Thwaite, she broke into a conversation: 'What can you expect when they're Jews!' Larkin's initial reaction to her was one of empathetic identification.[*]

---

[*] James Booth, *Independent*, 21/8/2014. Booth was told this by Thwaite: neither are entirely sure about whether Philip was empathetic.

Ann knew Monica through her occasionally accompanying Philip socially. 'Tony' was one of Philip's trusted friends. No one in their right mind would presume the Thwaites to be anti-Semites. Larkin, although 'empathetic', holds his tongue. Monica blurts what is going through both their minds. Perhaps she was drunk. Ann Thwaite does not remember the outburst or any like it.

A cross-grain in Monica's racism is her relationship with Dipak Nandy.* What is relevant is that Dipak, a leader in reforming British anti-racism, left not the slightest dent on Monica's inherent racial prejudice. This despite his being, for a couple of years, her closest Leicester friend. Monica, unlike Philip's other 'women', was privy, and clearly contributory, to what Maeve Brennan, when she learned about it posthumously, called Larkin's 'darker side'. Darkest of all is Larkin's ditty:

> *Prison for strikers*
> *Bring back the cat.*
> *Kick out the n*ggers,†*
> *How about that?*

The abhorrent quatrain is first recorded in print in a 1970 letter to Robert Conquest. But Monica and Larkin evidently conceived it years earlier as their response to Harold Wilson's Labour government which came to power in 1964. 'We are the masters now,' George Brown exulted.

Monica calls the verse 'N*ggers' (hereafter, not to slime or over-asterisk the pages, I'll euphemise it as 'the N-song'). On Christmas Day 1966, in a jovial letter sent Monica from his mother's house, Larkin writes:

> Mother gave me a calendar and 2 pieces of soap. I've thought up a second verse for our 'Election Song':‡

---

* See pp. 245–250.
† my asterisk.
‡ NB: *our* 'Election Song'.

Trade with the Empire
Ban the Obscene
Lock up the Commies
God save the Queen!
[chorus]
Commies, Commies Commies, etc

On the whole it's been quite an enjoyable Christmas.

Monica evidently contributed to the song's years' long evolution as well as its origins. In 1967 Monica was evidently singing the N-song to the tune of 'Lillibulero' (itself racially tinged) to 'friends' thought congenial. The friendly congeniality was not always well judged. Tom and Wendy and eleven-year-old Roger visited her at Haydon Bridge in April 1967. She tells Philip she sang the N-song to them. The Craiks were, as she elsewhere laments, '*Guardian* readers'.

She had complained in January 1967 that she now has no one to sing the song to. Whom, then, *had* she been singing it to? Persons unknown. On 24 March 1967, a distant Southampton cousin called on her:

I thought I should have sung [the N-song] for him, he is the perfect audience for it tho' probably not knowing *Lillibulero* & likely not to appreciate the finer points. He certainly shares its sentiments & gave me the usual attack on the Govt bringing in the immigrants & gave me his views on LSE.*

Performance of the song outlasted the Wilson and Callaghan administrations. On 1 October 1968 Monica asks Philip, 'Can you make up another stanza of [the N-song] ending in Powell for Premier?' Both she and he were cheered by Enoch Powell's 'Rivers of Blood' speech. 'Good old Enoch' Larkin called him in one of his late letters. On occasions, Monica says, she sings the N-song to herself 'to relieve

---

* The London School of Economics was in the forefront in the UK student uprisings sweeping Europe and the US.

my feelings'. She and Philip recorded themselves singing it, now immortalised on YouTube in the TV programme *Philip Larkin: Love and Death in Hull*. Hearing it excoriates. She left the recording to the Bodleian (see her will, below).

It raises a nagging question: did the anti-Semitism, racism, and what would now be judged as gutter politics originate with her, or him? Or within both of them, as confluent kindred spirits? It was uniquely Monica, among Larkin's women, who shared this Caligari Cabinet. The innocent Maeve did not even know about his taste for pornography, let alone his racism, until 1990 and seventeen years of intimate relationship. This suggests that Monica's and Philip's joint racism was a secret bond, what the Mafia call, 'our thing'. John Ellis, who knew Monica better than I after 1970 cannot recall her saying anything which could be construed as racist. But guessing they were not of a mind politically he kept off the subject.

If this chapter seems self-righteous, it shouldn't. There were moments, which I have recorded earlier,* when the curtain was momentarily drawn aside to give insight to her prejudice; namely her comment on the assassination of Kennedy, the comment about voting BNP, and her offhand comment about appointing a 'coloured communist' (Nandy). A braver or less overawed man than I would have spoken out. I didn't and feel ashamed I didn't.

This chapter has been an ordeal to write. I have lost part of the Monica Jones I once knew in the place where I was most hopeful I would find her again.

---

* See pp. 182–183.

ANOTHER VIEW, 2021

'I do sound a prejudicial old feminist, but you know I am not a bit of that'

Monica to Philip, 1955

Traditional belief that a male biographer can write authoritatively about a female subject has been shaken in recent years. My explanation for writing, intimately, about Monica Jones is stated in the personal foreword: I am the last living, actively writing person who knew Monica Jones in what were critical years of her life. Nonetheless, I feel a certain uneasiness. I can see Monica clearly but I cannot entirely and always feel with her. A level of understanding is denied me. I have asked women friends what they make of the Monica Jones I describe. One of them, Jane Miller, was born a decade later than Monica but her career has some congruence. Miller studied at Cambridge among a particularly (even for that university) brilliant company of male undergraduates, one of whom she would choose to marry. Like Monica, Miller taught school before moving into higher education. Universities were still a man's world but more open to talent than they had been in Monica Jones's early days. Miller did not, like Monica in 1954, have to protest that 'Professors despise women'.*
But there remained inbuilt inequity.

Miller has read and criticised drafts of this book. She suggested a title to me: 'A Clever Woman: The Unhappy Life of Monica Jones'. Why that subversive sub-title? Because for a woman to be as clever or cleverer than a man was, in Miller's experience, no passport to happiness. Monica was very clever and, for most of her adult life, very unhappy. Miller explains in a letter to me:

---

* See p. 112.

I think some of what I might say about MJ's predicament I wrote
in a book published ages ago called *Seductions*. That we are seduced on all fronts by men, and brought up to believe they're
better at everything and our best move is to emulate them and try
to appeal to them sexually at the same time. It may be impossible.

Seductions: Studies in Reading and Culture was published by Virago in
1990. The book's thesis draws on Gramsci's theory of hegemony: an
oppressive society's ability to make victims buy into, love even, what
oppresses them. Seduction. It is masculinity's great trick; to exploit
and get love in return.

Miller wrote a critique for me with an analysis of Monica which is
authoritative in ways I cannot easily be:

> At one point Monica assures Philip Larkin that she is no feminist,
> and he seems to be relieved to hear it. John Sutherland's book
> presents us with a promising woman's life that has been cramped
> and deformed at least in part by a refusal to see her dilemma as a
> specifically woman's dilemma. The toughness and resilience she's
> constructed for herself leave grievous holes. In asking to be res-
> cued by Larkin she condemns herself to isolation. It says a great
> deal for John Sutherland that he has seen her as an extremely in-
> teresting person in her own right.

Miller leaves hanging the question of whether Monica was ruthlessly
seduced by a man of prepotent charm or whole-heartedly connived
at her victimisation as a kind of suttee. She is for Miller an extremely
interesting, but somewhat repulsive, 'case'.

Miller points to Monica's willed isolation. 'I am alone' she said,
as early as 1960 to Philip, who encouraged, engineered even, that
loneliness. She had a tenured job but no career. Her one recorded
political act – joining the strike against the appointment of Arthur
Humphreys in 1947 – did not help her rise in the profession. Even
less so did her principled disinclination to contribute by publishing
in the shadow world, as she saw it, of literary criticism. She resolved

to share her insights on the real thing by lecturing. For her, printed literary criticism was the menu not the meal. It put her at odds with the way academic studies were moving at large, and left her standing, isolated, on an island of her own making.

What is striking is that after leaving Oxford she had no women friends. She did not want them and resented the other women colleagues appointed (more belatedly than her) into her department. Monica's uneasiness with her own sex made it impossible, as Jane Miller says, for her to see her 'Philip dilemma' as a woman's problem rather than a Monica Jones problem. She was short-sighted in more than one way.

Rosie Boycott was another woman who talked about the book with me. She came into active public life two generations after Monica Jones. Barely out of her teens, and having discarded university after a brief experience of it (men telling her what to think), Boycott joined up with comrades to do battle for women through the seventies. With Marsha Rowe, Rosie Boycott launched the magazine *Spare Rib* in 1972. It would run, influencing female opinion from a vanguard position, for twenty years.

You needed, Boycott says, echoing Miller, to 'look beyond your personal situation to the system'. She moved on from *Spare Rib* to take hold of levers of traditional male power, co-founding a feminist publishing house, Virago, and editing Fleet Street newspapers. Currently Baroness Boycott is a cross-bencher in the House of Lords, whose name she will, I fondly anticipate, succeed in amending.

Boycott has been a force for change. But never alone. 'Sorority', she says, is essential. You need to create 'groundswell' which will give a woman 'confidence'. Without sisterhood 'you blame yourself'. In the sixties and seventies Monica Jones did just that, ever more self-harmingly. Did Boycott know women like Monica Jones? She locates her in another period with a momentarily favourable groundswell for the women's movement. World War Two, she observes, was liberating for many women.

Monica had a good war. She recalled it to me and her surviving letters make clear she, for a few years, had 'confidence' and women friends from Oxford. A short-lived sisterhood. It did not last. As the post-war years rolled on, and the men rolled back to jostle front of stage in academic life, she entered the ranks of what Boycott calls 'incredibly unfulfilled' womanhood.

After ten years of relationship with him, Monica realised she was not the woman in Philip's life or even 'a woman' in his life, but a 'situation'; something to be 'handled'. 'The post-war world', Boycott notes, 'while promising so much, delivered less than zero to women.' That was the larger 'situation'.

Monica Jones was, at twenty-one, as Miller says, 'a woman of promise'. Life had dealt her a good hand. She had a prestigious profession, a fine mind, and, after her parents' death in 1959, money in her purse. How did she become the soured Miss Monica Jones she was at fifty-one? Or, at regrettable moments, the neo-fascist of sixty-one? Was it a failure of nerve? Did she lack the 'courage' which, as Boycott says, was necessary for a woman who decided to step out of line in post-war decades? Or did she fail, as Jane Miller suggests, to 'think' herself into clarity as to what it was, in her lifetime, to be a woman?

As regards this book I owe a large debt to two helpers. Dr Judith Priestman's years of scholarly work on Monica Jones's epistolary remains made it possible for me to know her better than I assumed I already did. Susan Walker undertook deep-digging archival research on my behalf into Monica and her family background which factually underlies the first six chapters of this book.

Monica, Susan Walker pointed out to me, lived with her parents for half, or more, of every year until she was thirty-seven, when they died. She was lucky for most of her adult life if she got more than three or four weeks a year with Philip. My early drafts contained a Larkinesque version of Monica's attitude to her parents, drawing on such remarks as 'my family is so ignorant'.[*] Her mother, as portrayed in letters to Philip, is variously 'terrible' and too docile. Her father comes across as a hard, uneducated, man, patriarchal with 'his' two women, if only as master of the TV controller and dictator of what

---

* See p. 73.

there should be for 'dinner' (never 'supper').

Susan Walker was the first to investigate the trove of bundled, uncatalogued, Monica Jones materials at the Hull History Centre. There are hundreds of letters from Monica's mother from 1941 to 1959 and some from her father. They make clear a mutually loving parental-child relationship. In her letters to him it is clear Monica played along with Philip's phobias about family, home and married life. It created an emotional turbulence in her which, Susan Walker discerns, exploded at her parents' nearly simultaneous deaths, as the 'worst year of my life' and what she later saw as the beginning of her slow descent into alcoholism. As Susan Walker puts it:

I suppose partly due to my own close parents, especially my mother – I wonder at the impact of 'rejecting' them – in her mind if not to their face. It was a betrayal – and must have weighed on her. Also why did she reject the Peart family (as you may recall, one cousin wrote asking her to keep in touch)? That was a deliberate act – one assumes the influence of PL again cutting her off from family – this is an example of what we call today emotional control.

Talking to people who had known her before her final, decades-long collapse, Rachel Cooke formed the contrary image of 'a woman who was clever, eccentric, loud, unusual, flamboyant, opinionated and strong'. Above all 'a woman with a mind of her own'. She was, Cooke said, with a neat turn of phrase, a woman who wore 'outfits', not clothes: she dressed to take the world head-on. A fighter.

In support of 'her' Monica, Cooke cited one of her observations that what Philip was really asking for was a sweet old little dear, who shams yielding wifely stuff and, tough as steel underneath, deceives and manages him for his own good; a women's page person, and he really deserved one.

'Atta girl', comments Cooke: with the hearty implication that Larkin got what he was asking for in Monica Jones – someone 'tough as steel underneath'.

I find Cooke's Monica refreshingly upbeat and a vision of her which chimes in many ways with my recollections in the years I was close to her. The years, I like to think, when Monica Jones was really Monica Jones.

APPENDIX

PHILIP LARKIN'S AND MONICA JONES'S WILLS

Philip's will is ostensibly clear-cut but in the implementation of his literary property it turned out to be a mare's nest. It was drawn up with his Hull solicitor Terence Wheldon on 17 July 1985, five months before Philip's death. His mind was unclouded, although parts of the will suggest rash judgement and hasty revision.

The clearest element in the document is that Monica is principal beneficiary. That her name is misspelled throughout ('Beal') suggests that Philip was dictating not typing and did not carefully look over the document. Monica and Wheldon were appointed trustees, superior in decision making to the three literary executors Monica (again), Anthony Thwaite, and Andrew Motion. The will stipulated that Monica was to inherit 'All my published and unpublished works together with all manuscripts and letters'. After her death what remained was to be divided equally between the Society of Authors and the RSPCA. It is not clear from this whether Monica owned this literary property or merely had a life interest. Larkin's copyright is a vexed topic.

The contentious element in the will was the clause contradicting the previous paragraph: 'I direct that all unpublished writings and diaries and texts and manuscripts in any form whether or not published on the date of my death and in my possession shall be destroyed unread.' He might as well have included a box of Swan Vesta safety matches.

The clause continued with the instruction that all letters 'with the exception of those from said Margaret Monica Beal [sic] Jones, Mr Kingsley Amis, Mr Robert Conquest and the late Barbara Pym which I GIVE to the Bodleian Library Oxford' be destroyed. Copyright of unpublished work was vested in Monica Jones and Terence Wheldon to dispose of, Monica to receive the revenue. 'If at the time of my death', the will continues, 'the said Margaret Monica Beal [sic] Jones is still making her home with me I DEVISE and bequeath to her absolutely my house 105 Newland Park TOGETHER with all my household and personal effects.' The residue of the estate was to be split: 55 per cent Monica, 20 per cent Betty Mackereth. There was nothing left to Maeve, which seems either cruel or motivated by something we do not know about.

Monica was within her legal rights, it would appear from the above, in destroying the journals and pornography. She was following Philip's manifest instruction. But she did not destroy his workbooks nor his letters, despite the instruction to do so. It was a decision, not an oversight, one presumes. Anthony Thwaite, who was in Japan until 1986, could not prevent Monica's burning the journals and pornography, weeks after Philip's death. Nor, without her co-operation could he remotely exercise his executorial duties. Nor, even though he was in London, could Motion. 'I know you don't write letters,' Thwaite wrote forlornly to her, in December 1985, expecting no answer. But he and Motion found the destroy-everything instruction in the will 'puzzling' as they agreed by letter in the weeks following. Destruction involved poetry drafts and working papers of huge scholarly and biographical value.

Thwaite and Motion (it was now agreed Andrew should write the biography and Anthony publish the 'Select Letters') with the passive assent of Monica, presumably, authorised a legal 'Opinion' on the will. The document was delivered on 16 June 1987. It found Philip Larkin's will to be 'inconsistent'. How, for example, could there be collective destruction of papers 'unread'. They would require at least a 'cursory glance' to establish they weren't a later will, codicils or matters of financial or other material significance. Clause 7 of Larkin's will gave the literary executors 'unfettered discretion' but elsewhere denied it with blanket instruction as to total destruction.

The 1987 Opinion came to the conclusion that 'the General Executors can lawfully ignore the instruction to destroy'. This opinion saved the poetry notebooks and working papers, which have proved a rich trove to critics, as well as correspondence Larkin had condemned to be destroyed, which has proved useful to biographers.

Monica's will was drawn up on 24 February 1987, shortly after the consternation among executors about Philip's will. She appoints Terence Wheldon and Tom Craik, her loyallest Leicester colleague, as executors.

Her will donates to the Bodleian 'books gramophone records recorded tapes photographic prints and negatives honours and medals given to me under the will of the late Philip Arthur Larkin, and remaining in my possession at the time of my death'. To Kitty's daughter, Rosemary Parry (Philip's niece) she bequeaths the property of 105 Newland Park after all taxes and legal expenses have been paid. This may have been a request of Larkin's when he was dying.

Monica left to Mary Yarnold, née Stringer, 'a legacy of ten thousand pounds'. Presumably Mary was her principal carer. The rest of her estate, after funeral and other expenses were paid by trustees, she left equally to the 'fabric funds' of St Paul's Cathedral, Durham Cathedral and Hexham Abbey. And an equal portion to the National Trust.

Monica added a codicil to her will on 15 September 1992. The date is significant because it makes clear that Monica was in a good enough state of mind to read Andrew Motion's biography of Philip and Anthony Thwaite's *Selected Letters*. She appointed another, presumably younger, successor to Wheldon as trustee. In all other respects the earlier will was legally confirmed.

The two wills raise a mystery. Larkin left all his literary residue to Monica, she left it to various good causes. Where, then, is the copyright ownership? I'm not a lawyer but I'm curious and the will and codicil seem a clear confirmation of what Monica said, so often in her correspondence with Philip, 'I am alone'.

ACKNOWLEDGEMENTS

My profound debt to Dr Judith Priestman is recorded in the book's foreword and testified to in the dedication. I reiterate it here. In the book's conclusion I record my debt to Susan Walker who did the research spadework on which the first half dozen chapters, following Monica's family and early life, depend. I would have been lost without her and what she ingeniously turned up.

I am grateful for Susan's comment in the book's conclusion and the opinions on Monica Jones of Dame Rosie Boycott and Jane Miller. Jane has read and given advice from the book's first drafts onwards. I have had encouragement and advice from Caroline Slocock whose account of her relationship with Mrs Thatcher (a contemporary of Monica's at Oxford, piquantly), *People Like Us*, has been a model for me in working out how to narrate my relationship with Monica Jones. My old-time friends, Eric and Norma Slinn, supplied much material from the time we were, enjoyably, together in the 1960s.

Polly Samson has been both an encourager and a supplier of practical advice. I am grateful to her and all at Streele Farm – a place where good books come from. Professor James Booth, Philip Larkin's most recent and authoritative biographer, on whom I have relied throughout, gave me generous encouragement and tactfully pointed out errors. Those that remain are mine. I look forward to his review. Andrew Motion's brilliant and trail-blazing biography of Larkin has been both source and model. Anthony Thwaite's editing of Larkin's letters (especially those to Monica) have been my quarry, as for all scholars in this field.

My colleague Mark Ford, one of the few who have written sympathetically about Monica, agreed to take forward the book to press, in the event of my being stricken in the awful pandemic months of its completion. I survive to write this. John Whitbourn read, advised and supplied hard-to-come-by material over the period I was working on the book. The first edition contained errors by me and I am grateful to Ann Thwaite, John Ellis, and Dr Peter Clark for a belated chance to correct them.

I thank Dipak Nandy for looking over and approving what is written about him, (belatedly) for what he taught me half a century ago, and for bringing some pleasure into Monica's generally unhappy life.

I had skilled help get the book accepted into print from my agent, Eleanor Birne, and expert handling at Orion Books from Maddy Price (who drastically reshaped the self-indulgent memoirish text I sent her), Rosie Pearce (project editor), and Anne O'Brien (who copy-edited the text), and Natalie Dawkins who dealt with the tricky business of illustration. I am grateful to all of them. They have done me, and more importantly Monica Jones, great service.

Personally I am most grateful to my wife, Sarah Lee, who has been perceptive, supportive and the most loving of comrades throughout my writing.

NOTES

Based as it largely is on correspondence, the text contains much requiring annotation, most of it date, place and source indication. It has been done by chapter and abbreviated reference. The references themselves take the form of: cue words+source+dates (or page reference with printed sources).

ABBREVIATIONS

'AL 00': *About Larkin* (journal)
'PK p. 000': *Autobiographical Tales* (2013), Peter Keating
'MJ DD/MM/YY': Monica Jones's unpublished letters
'PL DD/MM/YY': Philip Larkin's unpublished letters
'RB 000': *First Boredom, Then Fear* (2005), Richard Bradford
'HM DD/MM/YY': Letters of Monica and her mother archived at Hull
'KL DD/MM/YY': *The Letters of Kingsley Amis* (2000), ed. Zachary Leader
'LM DD/MM/YY', 'LM p. 000': *Letters to Monica* (2010), ed. Anthony Thwaite
'KAL DD/MM/YY', 'KAL p. 000': *The Life of Kingsley Amis* (2006, repr. 2007), Zachary Leader
'PLIK DD/MM/YY', 'PLIK p. 000': *The Philip Larkin I Knew* (2002), Maeve Brennan
'LH DD/MM/YY', 'LH p. 000': *Philip Larkin: Letters Home* (2018), ed. James Booth
'JB 000': *Philip Larkin, Life, Art and Love*, (2014, repr. 2015), James Booth

'SL DD/MM/YY': *Selected Letters of Philip Larkin* (1992), ed. Anthony Thwaite

'AM 000': *A Writer's Life* (1993), Andrew Motion

REFERENCES

Epigraph

No doubt . . . PK p. 155.

Personal Foreword, 2021

I don't want to be . . . MJ 15/7/57; *I've got the boys* . . . MJ 14/6/65; *or worse the slandered Monica* . . . KAL 7/6/86, https://www.theguardian.com/books/2010/oct/23/martin-amis-philip-larkin-letters-monica; www.theatlantic.com/magazine/archive/2011/05/philip-larkin-the-impossible-man/308439/; https://www.ft.com/content/698048c0-338a-11e4-85f1-00144feabdc0; www.independent.co.uk/arts-entertainment/books/features/the-old-devil-and-miss-jones-96263.html; *angled beauty* . . . JB 87; *I love her* . . . JB 442; *rabbit of old Nile* . . . PL 4/11/64; *cared a tenth as much* . . . AM 169.

Chapter 1: Origins, 1850–1922

During winter . . . MJ 22/1/54; *Nor the postcard* . . . MJ 21/7/67; *On leave shortly before* . . . AM 166.

Chapter 2: Llanelli and Kidderminster, 1922–1940

'Halfway', she replied . . . AL 12; *Not just the two big novels* . . . MJ 29/3/55; *100 wpm at least* . . . LM 22/4/64.

Chapter 3: Monica Rises, 1930–1940

I've often felt like a child . . . MJ 12/10/52; *a life chosen by one's self* . . . MJ 6/10/55; *Philip once asked* . . . LM 11/9/52; *provincial middle-class backgrounds* . . . LM p. vii; *I'm slowly digesting it* . . . AL 12; *'poisonous' staff*

meetings . . . MJ 11/1/57; *I couldn't see any others* . . . MJ 1/6/66; *literary Turkish delight* . . . MJ 17/8/49.

Chapter 4: Oxford, 1940–1943

'Cheer up Monica' letter . . . HM 1940; *just say 'bugger'* . . . HM 1940; *the requisitioned colleges* . . . AL 11; *too 'modern' by far for Oxford, AD 1943* . . . AL 12; *proper pre-war quality* . . . MJ 6/10/47; *in woollen clothes* . . . *Jill* (1946, repr. 1998), p. 110.

Chapter 5: First Love, 1941–1943

you will not look my way . . . HM 1943; *even at the time* . . . MJ 7/7/60; *the safety of the word* . . . HM 1940; *but there was birth* . . . HM 1943; *Let me see!* . . . HM 1942; *spoke your name* . . . HM 1942; *my life here for you* . . . HM 1942; *a moment with your own* . . . HM 1943.

Chapter 6: Teaching for England, 1943–1945

we left and were glad to be going . . . HM 1975; *you disdained the tree* . . . HM 1944; *Many as you have taken in your net* . . . HM 1943; *a depressing ugly duckling* . . . MJ 1/7/50; *a skirt apiece in no time* . . . MJ 15/1/54; *with the small hole in!* . . . LM 22/10/54; *end of the village street* . . . AM 364; *much too low at the front* . . . LM p. viii; *never enough bathrooms* . . . HM 1943; *bring myself to clout them* . . . HM 1944; *'Don't call yourself a teacher'* . . . HM 1945.

Chapter 7: Turbulent Leicester, 1946–1947

red tights . . . MJ 11/10/62; *quite mad in some ways* . . . HM 30/1/59; *the crime of youth against you* . . . HM 1947; *They had better look out* . . . HM 1947; *some of his colleagues* . . . HM 30/1/59; *powers above* . . . AL 12; *a woman on your staff again* . . . HM 1947.

Chapter 8: Enter Larkin, 1946–1950

those were the nice hours . . . MJ 3/7/52; *pipe-gnarled face* . . . LM 23/7/50; *his large nose* . . . AL 19; *quite small* . . . AM 165; *his forthcoming novel,*

A Girl in Winter . . . LM 16/2/47.

Chapter 9: Love, Life and Letters, 1946–1950

You are a brilliant letter writer . . . LM 26/10/72; *three-day serial letter* . . . MJ 11/8/47; *that is sufficient* . . . LM 27/6/51; *a bit equivocal* . . . MJ 17/8/49; *Australian rugby team* . . . MJ 6/10/47; *unless Dior designed it* . . . MJ 9/10/49; *'really classy photographs' from him* . . . MJ 17/8/49; *a 1949 Christmas present – perfume* . . . MJ 30/12/49; *totally without consideration* . . . MJ 30/12/49; *the stars lose their glory* . . . MJ 9/10/47.

Chapter 10: 'A Perfect Friendship', 1946–1950

A perfect friendship . . . MJ 23/7/50; *King's High School* . . . PL 13/8/43; *Ruth defied them* . . . JB 84; *instantly frighten me away* . . . SL 18/6/48; *'Heavy petting', as Larkin called it* . . . MJ 5/7/68; *'I'm not a philanderer'* . . . AM 376, PL 16/9/67; *without embarrassment* . . . LKA 2/12/46; *knowing its inspiration* . . . LM 21/11/50; *'Is it natural to like work?'* . . . LM 4/4/48; *a 'rather odd' thing to do* . . . SL 18/6/48; *miserable years of Larkin's life* . . . JB 135; *sooner marry you than anyone else I know* . . . LM 29/1/55.

Chapter 11: Monica Boxed, 1949–1950

'He didn't half keep his life in compartments' . . . KL 17/11/86; *All things to all men indeed!* . . . MJ 8/2/57; *without the aid of props, mask or accent* . . . www.independent.co.uk/arts-entertainment/books-mr-miseryguts-philip-larkins-letters-show-all-the-grim-humour-that-was-a-hallmark-of-his-great-1558190.html; *it was a great grief to me* . . . JB 121; *now aged, woman crumpled* . . . JB 126: *never been 'straightforward'* . . . AL 11; *'but I loved him', she had told Motion* . . . AM 310–311; *the Ministry of Food* . . . AM 143; *both women the same perfume* . . . JB 180; *that kind of thing* . . . AL 12.

Chapter 12: Unhappy Family, 1948–1950

'Mum is at the bottom of all this' . . . LM 16/10/57; *attraction for each other* . . . AM 205; *his underwear* . . . LH 30/9/55; *but to recover* . . . AM 230; *better her cooking was than Monica's* . . . LH 9/12/63; *she hated the idea of*

'getting married' . . . MJ 28/1/55; opening of the new library . . . RB 207; he would marry me . . . PLIK p. 26.

Chapter 13: Happy Family, 1946–1959

not an easy man . . . MJ 7/4/55; 'What did I tell you?' . . . MJ 6/1/55; complaint in her letters to Philip . . . MJ 18/7/55; watch the cricket, she said . . . MJ 12/7/55; 'sc*ld*ng tea' . . . MJ 5/1/54; he was aware she had read . . . MJ 17/8/59; with a drunken fan . . . MJ 4/1/50; 'is so ignorant' . . . MJ 28/5/55; love of Walter Scott . . . MJ 17/8/49; I came to her each week-end . . . MJ 11/12/66; at the oven by her daughter . . . MJ 18/2/68.

Chapter 14: Imperfect Love, 1950

a 'pretty little short story' . . . MJ 4/1/50; Oh, well, well . . . MJ 1/7/50; His 'misengagement' was over . . . LM 23/6/51; I'd rather prefer it not to be me . . . SL 4/5/50; the same as ever it was . . . MJ 19/7/50; 'he had come to me' . . . AM 191; drying stockings . . . LM 1/10/50; 'like gravecloths' . . . AM 196.

Chapter 15: Loved and Left, 1950–1955

comfort in a voluntary exile . . . MJ 3/10/50; Woman's Weekly . . . MJ 1/10/50; 'endless babble' of love . . . MJ 4/10/50; layer upon layer . . . MJ 4/10/50; he reassured her . . . LM 14/10/50; and a talented one . . . MJ 16/10/50.

Chapter 16: Life Sentence Leicester, 1950–1955

commit simultaneously murder and suicide. Exactly . . . MJ 20/10/50; the 1940s and 50s . . . AL 11; at midnight, or 3 a.m. . . . LM 1/9/51.

Chapter 17: Love and the Tuppenny Stamp, 1950–1973

As soon as we came together we parted . . . MJ 22/4/64; 'drab influence' of Leicester . . . AM 199; my Olivetti . . . SL 30/1/84; lipstick on their envelopes . . . MJ 9/10/50; a faint redolence of perfume . . . LM 14/10/50; by the mid-sixties, deafness . . . AM 292; voluminously ... Martin Stannard, New

Walk, spring/summer 2011; *that person when you write* . . . MJ 3/4/55;
Potter House, near Hawkshead . . . MJ 19/4/64; *Does it rouse you? I bet not*
. . . MJ 28/2/66; *hot room* . . . Virginia Woolf, *The Common Reader, Second
Series*, 'Swift's "Journal to Stella"'; *so snug* . . . F. E. Ball (ed.) *The Correspon-
dence of Jonathan Swift*, vol. IV; *with pen and ink* . . . MJ 8/1/64; *it grows
muddy* . . . LM 25/11/50; *My dear rabbit* . . . LM 8/6/56; *both Patsy and
Winifred* . . . RB 123; *self-raising flour* . . . LH 15/6/51.

Chapter 18: Monica Muzzled, 1952

of yourself in full voice . . . LM 11/9/52; *Philip confessed* . . . LM 2/10/55;
things Monica did not know . . . JB 170; *filled in his football coupons* . . .
LM 2/10/55; *inept and ungracious a partner* . . . JB 170; *trusted his contraceptives* . . . LM 23/10/52; *sweet little bunnies* . . . LM 29/11/52; *Monica
wrote* . . . LM 10/2/57; *enjoying rugby football* . . . LM 1/11/51.

Chapter 19: Monica Lampooned, 1955

squirm squirm squirm . . . MJ 12/8/52; *monkey brand catnip* . . . MJ 5/1/54;
Dearest Cabbidge . . . MJ 8/1/54; *when he next comes, she vows* . . .
MJ 12/1/54; *fruit salad this minute* . . . MJ 15/1/54; *pinches and blows* . . .
MJ 21/1/54; *he moans about work* . . . MJ 9/1/54; *a talent greater than my
own* . . . LKA 96; *Kingsley said* . . . KAL 24/9/56; *derisive hatred* . . . LKA
226; *[of our conversation] were you?'* . . . LKA 273; *adhesiveness* . . . Martin
Amis, *Philip Larkin: Poems*, p. xxi; *the 'funniest novel I've ever read'* . . .
LM 14/9/53; *'Margaret Jones' was worse* . . . KAL 8/9/52; *not quite predatory, but still* . . . AM 169; *still on friendly terms* . . . AM 230, MJ 2/7/53;
same at first . . . Martin Amis, op cit; *at the end of her life* . . . AL 12; *Much
love, Mummy* . . . HM 1954.

Chapter 20: Less Deceived, 1955

'Not even a rabbit can like humiliation' . . . MJ 7/4/55; *Chateau Marga-
rine* . . . LM 8/1/55; *'How's horrible work?'* . . . MJ 8/1/54; *going back to
them* . . . LM 28/11/54; *toy to play with* . . . LM 23/11/54; *how much time
they take up* . . . LM 8/4/55; *getting married appals me* . . . MJ 28/1/55;
something to be fixed . . . MJ 19/10/55; *chap who's gone the wrong way* . . .

MJ 14/1/55; *a bit afraid to meet Kingsley* . . . MJ 28/1/54; *of seeing him eat one* . . . MJ 1/2/55; *'you're a real maker'* . . . SL 25/11/55; *the one of this generation* . . . MJ 18/8/55; *such a decision for me* . . . MJ 19/4/55; *to get away from her?'* . . . MJ 19/4/55; *sympathising with his misogamy* . . . JB 201; *the lavatory and vice versa?* . . . LM 6/8/55.

Chapter 21: *I Am Nothing, 1955–1957*

'Professors despise women' . . . MJ 22/1/54; *I don't think you're absurd at all* . . . LM 26/10/55; *slow and stupid* . . . MJ 22/1/54; *convicts' clothes* . . . MJ 2/2/57; *pomposity and foolishness* . . . MJ 2/5/55; *nastier and nastier* . . . MJ 9/10/55; *making love with you* . . . LM 15/12/54; *Blast their eyes!* . . . MJ 9/10/50; *not sure of what you want* . . . MJ 29/4/55; *a working myself up state* . . . MJ 5/5/55; *the progress of our "relationship"* . . . MJ 28/9/55; *than your presence* . . . MJ 22/5/55; *Why aren't you coming tomorrow?* . . . MJ 19/10/55; *'sexually inflaming'* . . . MJ 21/6/55; *You don't read my letters* . . . MJ 7/8/55; *inertia that comes from misery* . . . MJ 27/6/65; *a kind of company* . . . MJ 19/7/64; *something special* . . . LM 12/2/56; *any other poem* . . . JB 220–21; *eternal independence* . . . AM 276; *the appearance of respectability* . . . AM 278.

Chapter 22: *'Ten Years!' 1957*

'I detest to be a figure of pathos' . . . MJ 23/4/55; *we shall know each other?* . . . MJ 11/1/57; *do to a child* . . . MJ 4/1/57; *my linen cupboard gives me* . . . MJ 25/4/55; *he is not his father* . . . MJ 19/4/57; *Lord's will be glorious* . . . MJ 3/6/57; *a rough-house thing* . . . LM 6/7/57; *the sandpaper first* . . . MJ 1/8/57; *and apologises* . . . MJ 8/8/57; *Gracie Allen and Emily Brontë* . . . MJ 4/9/57; *the sack line* . . . MJ 11/9/57; *at all try to stop me* . . . MJ 29/10/57; *he always left ajar* . . . LM 16/10/59.

Chapter 23: *'My Worst Year', 1958–1959*

a hideously ingenious way . . . LM 28/1/58; *homosexual relation, disguised* . . . LM 28/1/58; *only twice* . . . LM 11/10/59; *cremation, 'wh. I hated'* . . . MJ 1/6/66; *cry at her mother's death* . . . MJ 28/7/64; *and couldn't swallow* . . . MJ 1/6/66; *hearing of Monica's loss* . . . LH p. 314; *in her will, she asked*

. . . MJ 8/8/61; *just Collins and me* . . . MJ 14/1/62.

Chapter 24: The Sixties

'*I am alone*' . . . MJ 16/1/60; *the Ringo Starr of verse, he jested* . . . LM 3/3/64; *the unreserved variety with Monica* . . . PLIK 16/9/65; Nothing interests me . . . MJ 16/1/60; *silly bugger ha ha!* . . . MJ 14/08/60; *the mass mouth to swallow* . . . MJ 22/10/60; *it isn't a way I know about* . . . MJ 10/10/62; *not liking most of it* . . . MJ 28/1/60; *her 'figger'* . . . MJ 7/7/60; *duly appointed 'my chap'* . . . MJ 18/8/60; *except being with you* . . . MJ 7/7/60; *the last night at Sark* . . . MJ 9/8/60; *the doors bolted* . . . MJ 6/8/60; *unthinking mayflies that they are* . . . MJ 7/7/60; The Archers . . . MJ 9/8/60; *never dawn on him* . . . AM 296; *though being a writer* . . . MJ 9/8/60; *I do feel ill* . . . MJ 6/9/60; *but I hate it* . . . MJ 18/9/60; *colleagues who look down on her* . . . MJ 7/10/60; *is very low* . . . MJ 29/10/60; *teenage weirdies' clothes* . . . MJ 14/12/60; *invitation was not 'eager'* . . . MJ 22/12/60; *overriding importance to him* . . . LH 18/12/60; *the rest of my life* . . . MJ 28/12/60.

Chapter 25: Lecturer 1960–1961

Oxford University . . . *Jill* (1946, repr. 1998), p.110; *moss-covered* . . . *The Boy Who Loved Books: A Memoir* (2007), p. 173; *in academic life* . . . ibid p. 222; *anti Oswald Mosley* . . . MJ 15/11/62; '*Tom Vole*' . . . PL 9/4/67; *[she] upsets me* . . . MJ 29/10/60; *a few bright ideas* . . . MJ 5/11/55; *attend your lectures!* . . . LM 29/1/57; *unsuspecting student audience* . . . Maureen Paton op cit, 16/7/2003.

Chapter 26: Rooms of Her Own, 1961

'*Shall I ever feel better again*'? . . . MJ 12/2/61; *& a country house* . . . MJ 15/1/61; *My tummy feels awful* . . . MJ 19/1/61; *at his funeral* . . . MJ 23/1/61; *for £2,850* . . . MJ 28/12/60; *looking around Corbridge* . . . MJ 27/2/61; *what really attracts* . . . MJ 5/7/61; *She wished it were 'prettier'* . . . LH 24/9/61; *I find it hopelessly flat* . . . MJ 29/1/61; *dread the vacations* . . . MJ 12/2/61; *a social & moral slum* . . . MJ 13/3/61; *absolutely fed up here* . . . MJ 12/2/61; *He ignored it* . . . MJ 4/1/61; *to send a class away* . . . MJ 14/2/61; *to meet [C.P.] Snow* . . . MJ 9/3/61; *riffling through his* *papers* . . . MJ 11/4/61; *in the event of my death* . . . LM 11/3/61; *even in good health* . . . MJ 11/3/61; *ignited into love* . . . PLIK p. 41; *with gentle affection* . . . PLIK 6/3/61; *you would be yellow* . . . MJ 13/3/61; *that lump in my breast* . . . MJ 21/3/61; *a new pleated skirt* . . . MJ 14/3/61; *as a professional duty* . . . MJ 16/3/61; *dogs I shall never have* . . . MJ 19/5/61; *Her mother had suffered likewise* . . . MJ 8/8/61; *but being with you* . . . MJ 12/8/61; *long nights on the holiday* . . . SL 7/8/61; *Larkin's attentions to Monica* . . . JB 263; *she forlornly tells Philip* . . . MJ 16/8/61; *it seems to emphasise my loneliness almost* . . . MJ 5/8/61; *what I thought of that* . . . MJ 13/10/61; *he cannot come* . . . MJ 22/10/61; *the badness of the finalists' scripts* . . . MJ 18/6/61.

Chapter 27: Finding Monica, 1961–1962

'I could have kissed him' . . . MJ 8/12/61; *William Barnes* . . . LM 5/11/50; *'at your age'* . . . MJ 8/12/61; *my chap* . . . MJ 18/8/60; *Snowcem she needed* . . . MJ 11/9/67; *A bit of a scrounger* . . . PL 28/11/63; *a serviceable scrounger* . . . LM 5/8/64; *or rank (ever)* . . . MJ 13/3/60; *like scrubbing a floor* . . . MJ 11/1/57; *as Philip called them* . . . LM 25/11/50; *a writer like Hardy had* . . . MJ 22/1/55; *never used a dibble?* . . . AM 168; *the almost as good* . . . MJ 27/1/54; *that's really what it is.* MJ 5/6/66; *a bit showy* . . . LM p. viii.

Chapter 28: Me, Monica and Philip, 1961–1967

'Sutherland? . . . I suppose he does exist.' . . . PL 9/4/67; *arranged my audience* . . . MJ 8/11/62; *no hardship* . . . PL 17/2/63; *not willing or not able* . . . LM 18/11/62; *close in his mind* . . . LM p. 310; *can't be heard* . . . MJ 17/11/63; *as Sutherland, years ago* . . . PL 9/4/67; *arrested development* . . . MJ 6/12/65; *'he still likes me, hay?'* . . . MJ 8/12/65; *with jazz and all* . . . MJ 10/4/67; *at the bottom* . . . MJ 27/4/65; *all cock . . . I expect* . . . PL 25/4/65.

Chapter 29: Teetering, 1962

'Darling, I feel frightened' . . . MJ 2/7/62; *cataclysmic spiritual experience* . . . LM 6/6/62; *the longer I had him* . . . MJ 31/5/62; *it frightened me*

... MJ 26/9/62; *waiting for something* ... MJ 26/5/62; *a false alarm* ... MJ 1/7/62; *She is a 'broken reed'* ... MJ 6/7/62; *too small for me* ... MJ 9/7/62; *a grouse dinner* ... MJ 10/10/62; *twice five years and more* ... MJ 9/12/62.

Chapter 30: A Good Year for John, 1963

Everybody is nasty to me ... MJ 6/6/63; *been in a state* ... MJ 17/2/63; *over the fence* ... MJ 26/1/63; *for her birthday* ... MJ 8/5/63; *answered v. well* ... MJ 6/6/63; *v. on the ball – quoted Dockery* ... MJ 25/6/63; *appointed himself S's manager* ... MJ 30/6/63; *in the Moderns Paper* ... MJ 6/6/63; *some loved home of childhood* ... MJ 3/8/63; *the colour of the landscape* ... MJ 14/8/63; *(40 to be honest)* ... MJ 14/8/63; *to show off her figure* ... MJ 11/10/63; *talking about it* ... MJ 19/8/63; *doing double duty* ... MJ 8/9/63; *I am so lonely I cd cry* ... MJ 27/4/64; *she complains* ... MJ 7/10/63; *be together oftener* ... MJ 3/10/63.

Chapter 31: 'Going A Bit Mad', 1964

'It is a very hard lesson to learn' ... MJ 12/2/64; *opium the night before* ... MJ 1/2/64; *an 'outright love poem'* ... JB 266; *can't eat* ... MJ 7/2/64; *complete forgetfulness* ... MJ 10/2/64; *to get that learnt!* ... MJ 12/2/64; *going 'a bit mad'* ... MJ 23/2/64; *to take women out* ... MJ 23/2/64; *Rolls Royce engine* ... SL 8/10/69; *nothing to live for without you* ... MJ 24/2/64; *I had promised to bring* ... MJ 27/3/64; *falls vomiting sick* ... LM 22/4/64; *your back go out of sight* ... MJ 22/4/64.

Chapter 32: Supervisor and Pub Pal, 1963–1964

'I have nothing to live for without you' ... MJ 2/4/64; *with the nasturtiums* ... MJ 11/4/64; *too James Elroy Flecker, perhaps* ... MJ 5/3/64; *as soon as I could* ... MJ 5/3/64; *younger than my age* ... MJ 11/4/64; *false pregnancy* ... MJ 5/6/64; *you like Sutherland* ... MJ 6/6/63; *that would be best of all* ... MJ 22/4/64.

Chapter 33: Monica Sparkles, 1963–1965

'I like public houses' ... MJ 22/4/64; *'I do like public houses with men, don't I?'*

. . . MJ 6/12/65; *with those I don't know* . . . MJ 7/4/67; *good company* . . . MJ 31/8/65; *student-aged* . . . AM 281; *to wank to, or with, or at* . . . AM 222; *coming to the pub?* . . . MJ 22-24/4/64; *the crowd of young people* . . . MJ 22/4/64; *He just knows I do* . . . MJ 6/11/63; *invite her to join us* . . . MJ 5/2/64; *this time in her life* . . . LM 28/8/67; *tireless forced facetiousness* . . . MJ 14/9/62; *under the cushion, love?* . . . MJ 29/4/55; *Bill Ruddick* . . . AM 327, LM 4/10/62; *terrific in scarlet trousers* . . . MJ 5/8/65; *'the bottom' for them* . . . MJ 1/6/66; *large rabbit hindquarters* . . . LM 18/1/62; *eyes on yours* . . . LM 14/8/65; *hardly looking* . . . MJ 14/1/62; *the Lilac establishment* . . . MJ 29/10/60; *pansy chap in politics* . . . MJ 3/12/60; *to eat properly* . . . MJ 21/4/62; *would wear off* . . . MJ 14/9/62; *quite gone off him* . . . MJ 22/4/64; *Bill on trust* . . . PLIK p. 188; *the most awful clothes* . . . MJ 29/6/64; *produce him next Sunday?* . . . PL 1/7/64; *asked Monica to send them* . . . MJ 27/11/65; *God wants it* . . . PL 15/3/66; *Then he gave it to her* . . . MJ 10/10/65; *bird dread* . . . MJ 7/8/63; *clucking in a far corner* . . . AL 12; *I like cooking more than I like eating* . . . MJ 14/8/63; *a game bird* . . . MJ 14/1/62; *Catholic, as her name* . . . LM 28/11/63; *her stockings one paper said* . . . MJ 24/11/63; *I shall miss them* . . . MJ 28/6/64; *having J. for another year* . . . MJ 3/7/64.

Chapter 34: A Full Look at the Worst, 1964

'my feelings are coming clearer all the time' . . . MJ 22/4/64; *steadier and calmer* . . . MJ 27/4/64; *a bad hand, I think* . . . MJ 22/4/64; *gullible Maeve* . . . MJ 4/4/64; *about Maeve in future* . . . MJ 24/4/64; *on top of everything else* . . . MJ 7/6/64; *soaked in unhappy association* . . . MJ 24/4/64; *you are being indiscreet* . . . MJ 7/6/64; *I will improve* . . . MJ 8/6/64; *an out and out 'crook'* . . . MJ 27/4/64; *a hundredweight of bushel* . . . MJ 27/10/63; *I can't abandon her* . . . AM 329; *naturalistic bias* . . . MJ 19/7/64; *tomato sandwich fever* . . . MJ 19/7/64; *A 'flirty trick' she suggested* . . . MJ 3/8/64; *after she'd done it* . . . MJ 13/9/64; *has caused this to happen* . . . MJ 13/9/64; *sympathy for cast-off Maeve* . . . LM p. 340; *I am not a dog* . . . MJ 15/9/64; *he likes pubs* . . . MJ 9/10/64.

Chapter 35: The Old Story, 1965–1966

'I squeal outside the Guildhall of Life, like a legless beggar' . . . MJ 25/11/65;

you will again sometime . . . MJ 19/10/64; *the Ritz with Betjers* . . .
MJ 29/11/64; *Ogh ogh ogh* . . . LM 14/8/65; *and lifelessly I write* . . .
MJ 13/12/64; *feel less alone* . . . MJ 24-26/1/65; *I expected better of myself*
. . . MJ 24/1/65; *something unique in the world* . . . MJ 30/1/65; *egg, cream
and lemon* . . . MJ 3/2/65; *and weeps* . . . MJ 22/2/65; *at the same time* . . .
MJ 25/2/65; *make anything of it* . . . MJ 25/2/65; *so much unhappiness in
it* . . . MJ 2/4/65; *your train-written letter* . . . MJ 25/4/65; *unimaginable
bliss* . . . MJ 27/4/65; *she forlornly says* . . . MJ 20/5/65; *I'm spoken to* . . .
MJ 29/5/65; *John [Ellis] around* . . . MJ 30/5/65; *a town like Leicester* . . .
PL 30/6/65.

Chapter 36: Not a Bad Summer, 1965–1966

an old bag like me . . . MJ 13/8/65; *loved you so long* . . . MJ 31/8/65;
beloved ten stone . . . MJ 22/8/65; *take their Lapsang* . . . MJ 22/8/65;
cheapened and debased . . . MJ 31/8/65; *suitably inscribed* . . . MJ 31/8/65;
you'll think I make it up . . . MJ 27/6/65; *girls who did the robbery* . . . MJ
27/10/65; *he tried to get in tonight* . . . MJ 27/10/65; *sketches illustrating
the point* . . . MJ 24/9/65; *hint of gin* . . . MJ 6/10/65; *to allay my suspicions*
. . . MJ 6/10/65; *I've bought Larousse Gastronomique* . . . MJ 1/11/65;
she sadly concludes . . . MJ 17/11/65; *in contrast to me a happy girl* . . .
MJ 2/4/66.

Chapter 37: Dipak, 1965–1967

'*I do fancy him quite a bit*' . . . MJ 7/10/66; *that lazy Commie black Nandy*
. . . MJ 6/6/63; *way home the other evening* . . . MJ 22/2/65; *some of these
coves* . . . PL 12/3/66; *amused by everything I said* . . . MJ 25/2/65; *join him
in the Clarendon* . . . MJ 31/5/65; *I was in my pink trousers* . . . MJ 31/5/65;
I am not a bit of that . . . MJ 23/6/65; *[his] black face* . . . PL 25/6/65; *watch
it, watch it* . . . PL 30/6/65; *That's the latest* . . . MJ 1/11/65; *a strange mix-
ture* . . . MJ 17/11/65; *out of each other's way* . . . MJ 6/12/65; *hand on my
shoulder* . . . MJ 6/12/65; *How well we all behave!* . . . MJ 6/12/65; *ogh ogh*
. . . PL 8/12/65; *Vnto ye Bargayne* . . . PL 14/12/65; *fatal attraction too* . . .
MJ 31/1/66; *out into the open* . . . MJ 7/10/66; *on long summer evenings* . . .
MJ 15/10/66; *Autumn has come* . . . MJ 15-16/10/66; *annoyance I suppose*
. . . PL 5/10/67; *before he does* . . . MJ 8/2/68; *new race relations thing* . . .

MJ 10/2/68; *wants me to see it* . . . MJ 8/2/68; *what Monica intended* . . .
MJ 8/2/68.

Chapter 38: Alone Again, 1966–1967

'*there is nobody I really like now*' . . . MJ 15/1/67; *like a fool* . . . MJ 12/11/66;
the Mikado . . . MJ 13/3/66; *liked at once* . . . MJ 17/11/68; *the city her-*
self . . . MJ 17/7/66; *at staff meetings* . . . MJ 5/2/67; *in a prying way* . . .
MJ 5/1/67; *so I tell you* . . . MJ 15/1/67; *burning bile* . . . MJ 15/1/67; *&*
nobody else . . . MJ 5/2/67; *among all those men* . . . LM 2/4/67; *he called*
him . . . LM 9/4/67; *going to go to these things again* . . . MJ 7/4/67; *see it*
myself . . . MJ 10/4/67; *than librarians* . . . PL 9/4/67.

Chapter 39: Sutherland Shotgunned, 1967

'*I think he's pretty well putting the Leicester era behind him*' . . . MJ 16/6/67;
really quite allright . . . MJ 12/6/67; *of the play though!* . . . PL 13/6/67;
Forget it . . . MJ 24/6/67; *defying diagnosis* . . . MJ 5/7/67; *only half a per-*
son . . . MJ 24/8/67; *you can outdrink me* . . . LM 27/8/67; *windows were*
being tried . . . MJ 6/9/67; *Snowcem (masonry paint)* . . . MJ 11/9/67; *not*
even a paper one . . . MJ 29/10/67; *be mentioned either* . . . MJ 27/12/67;
'*Bugars' all* . . . MJ 21/1/68; *must know it too* . . . PLIK 14/9/67; *I suppose*
I am weak . . . PLIK 16/9/67; *have to use violence* . . . MJ 8/2/68; *decent*
libraries? . . . PL 26/4/67.

Chapter 40: An Ancient Leicester Institution, 1968–1973

'*We are both of us burnt children*' . . . MJ 26/5/55; *almost like being with*
you . . . MJ 26/4/68; *than I think you really are* . . . MJ 25/4/68; *the night*
before . . . MJ 5/7/68; *a grindingly painful business* . . . PL 28/7/68; *the book*
itself with her . . . AL 11; *something hidden away inside her* . . . PK p. 104;
anything like that . . . PK p. 110; *capable of teaching* . . . PK p. 125; *Sidney*
Greenstreet . . . AL 11; *drank all night* . . . *New Walk*, spring/summer 2011.

Chapter 41: The Last Hurrah, 1970–1982

'*Monica had never had it so good*' . . . AM 471; *peg away at OxBo* . . .
LM 17/1/71; *dying, he thought* . . . LM 5/11/70; *bivalve behaviour of my*

life . . . LM 25/11/50; *thoughtfully hidebound prejudice* . . . LM 5/11/70; *your [Monica's] pessimism* . . . LM 6/10/51; *(1) food (2) bed* . . . HM 15/10/78; *Garrick Club, with Betjeman* . . . RB 238–239; *want to take care of her* . . . PLIK p. 228; *pledge himself to Monica Jones* . . . PLIK p. 89; *rare and isolated occasions* . . . AM 447; *eighteen-year intimacy* . . . PLIK p. 227; *businesslike – and funny* . . . AM 451; *modern house in Newland Park* . . . SL 17/2/74; *great ode to senility* . . . JB 380; *his oeuvre was complete* . . . JB 419.

Chapter 42: Monica at Sixty, 1982

the love of his life . . . https://www.theguardian.com/books/2010/oct/23/ martin-amis-philip-larkin-letters-monica; *Prospect* magazine 1/2/2010; *even a man in drag* . . . *The Oldie* 25/5/2020; *got a dinner out of Larkin* . . . AL 11; *a pregnant giraffe* . . . LM 13/10/82; *'Umpteen stiches' were sewn* . . . SL 21/11/82; *a great feeling of lowness* . . . SL 9/4/83; *'joyless' NHS hospitals* . . . SL 12/4/83; *up to living on her own* . . . SL 31/10/82; *all but name* . . . *Motion calls it* . . . AM 498; *side by side in the hall* . . . SL 21/2/84; *we're so lonely* . . . *The Oldie* 25/5/2020; *not sleeping* . . . PLIK p. 90; *the Sheldonian Theatre* . . . AM 508–9; *even the summer* . . . SL 12/5/85; *would cause both women* . . . PLIK p. 91; *Philip's well-being* . . . PLIK p. 91; *had taken charge* . . . AM 515; *going to the inevitable* . . . AM 521; *in both our lives* . . . HM 1985.

Chapter 43: Last Years, Final Acts, 1985–2001

partly vanity . . . KAL 7/6/86; *He lived a writer's life* . . . AM 524; *achieved works of art* . . . AM 221; *the form of a memoir* . . . AM 460; *Desperate really* . . . AM 522; *hang himself with* . . . www.prospectmagazine. co.uk/magazine/a-life-more-ordinary-inside-philip-larkins-extraordinary-everyday; *destroyed when I die* . . . LM 13/9/54; *as if to open it* . . . www.youtube.com/watch?v=3KQt15rotc4, 'Monica Jones clips'; *she surrendered to her sorrow* . . . AM 523; *enthusiastic* . . . 'In Search of the Real Philip Larkin', *Observer* 26/6/2010; *astounded and upset* . . . PLIK pp. 4-5; *ever really knew him* . . . JB 445; *Philip Larkin, writer* . . . *Independent* 24/2/2001; *including me* . . . PLIK p. 119; *in my mind* . . . *Daily Mail* 20/6/2019; *John Betjeman's poems* . . . AL 12; *but I loved him* . . .

AM 310-11; *brightly encouraging organ* . . . AL 12.

Afterword: The Monica Jones I Didn't Know, 2021

a 'hymn to America' . . . JB 123; *pretty good list of hates, eh?* . . . LM 30/6/68; *bigger and nicer* . . . MJ 26/9/62; *a letter to Robert Conquest* . . . SL 19/6/70; *quite an enjoyable Christmas* . . . PL 25/12/66; *sang the N-song to them* . . . MJ 7/4/67; *gave me his views on LSE* . . . MJ 24/3/67.

Another View, 2021

he really deserved one . . . 'In Search of the Real Philip Larkin', *Observer* 26/5/2010.

INDEX